TALES OF THE RED TRIANGLE

A Social and Pictorial History of Cheltenham YMCA 1855-2005

by
Peter Worsley

Cheltenham YMCA kindly acknowledges the help given by many people with a special vote of thanks to Roger Beacham of Cheltenham Reference Library who painstakingly searched out many valuable documents from within the official archives. Others who made important contributions include Ann Augur, Steve Blake, Keren Bowers, Bernard Bridgman, Derren Brown, Brian Burrows, Chelprint, Ross Cole, Vic Cole, Peter Cruwys, Colin Dymock, Tony Dymock, Jerry Evans, Pat Fazackarley, Lionel Fitz, Don Fraser, Angela Gilbert, Tony Hampson, Michael Hews, Mark Hopkin, Mike Hunt, David James, Jim Jenkinson, Roger Knapp, Mary Leonard, Barry Lloyd, Paul Makepeace, Steve Mattos, Greg Mills, Wilf Pearson, Thelma Pruen, Rachel Roberts, Bill Sargison, David Shoesmith, Don Staight, Anita Syvret, David Wallace, Betty Ward, John Wilcock and Martin Wray .... plus several activity leaders.

Each chapter stands alone but a certain amount of repetition was inevitable in putting all the information into a cohesive historical account. Written over a period of twelve months, it was also necessary to weave and dovetail in new information as it came to light, not always an easy task. However, it is hoped that the final result will do justice to all the many men and women who helped shape Cheltenham YMCA during its first 150 years.

Published on behalf of
Cheltenham YMCA, Vittoria Walk, Cheltenham, GL50 1TP
by Word4Word, 8 King Charles Court, Evesham, Worcestershire, WR11 4RF

© Cheltenham YMCA 2005

All rights reserved. No part of this publication may be reproduced, stored in a retrieval system, or transmitted in any form or by any means, electronic, mechanical, photocopying, recording or otherwise without first having received written permission from the publishers.

Grateful thanks are expressed to the following for their support in the publication of this book: Rickerbys Solicitors, Cheltenham Ladies' College, Dean Close School, Alastair MacKay, The Famous Outfitters, the Isbourne Foundation, Kohler Mira Ltd., This England magazine, the University of Gloucestershire, and Wilkinsons.

ISBN 0-9551677-0-1
(ISBN-13 978-0-9551677-0-6)

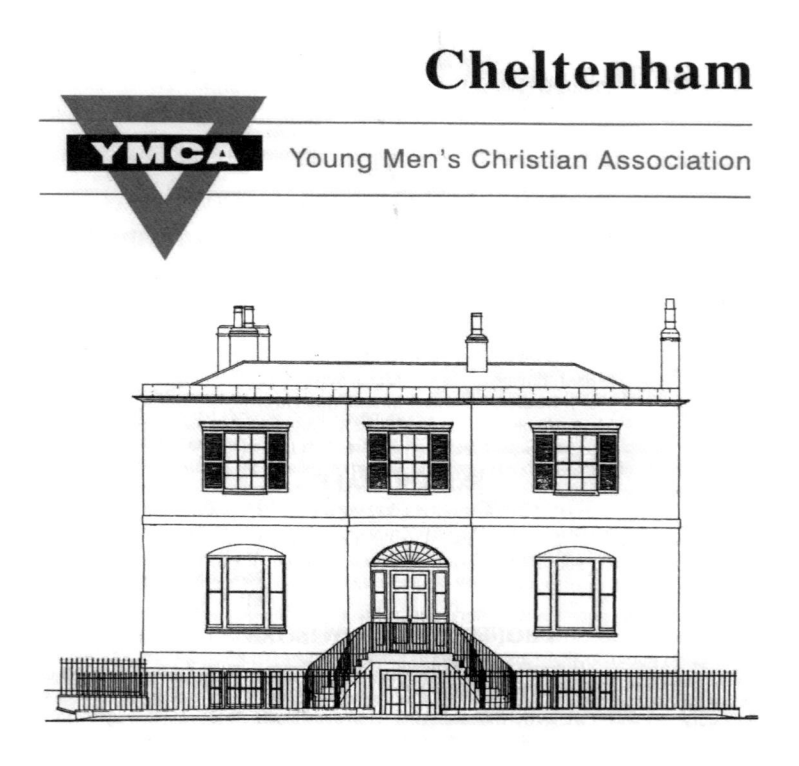

Cheltenham
YMCA Young Men's Christian Association

CONTENTS

Chapters	Page number
Title page	1
Acknowledgements	2
Contents	3
Foreword	4
Introduction	5
International YMCA Timeline	6
Cheltenham YMCA Timeline	7
Chapter 1 YMCA England	8
Chapter 2 The Founding of Cheltenham YMCA	9
Chapter 3 The Story Unfolds 1855-1921	12
Chapter 4 First World War 1914-1918	38
Chapter 5 The Promenade 1921-1939	46
Chapter 6 1938 Annual Report	64
Chapter 7 Second World War 1939-1945	74
Chapter 8 Baker Street YMCA 1940-1967	98
Chapter 9 The Promenade 1945-1956	108
Chapter 10 Centenary Move from the Promenade	114
Chapter 11 Vittoria Walk 1956-2005	118
Chapter 12 YMCA Activities	140
Chapter 13 A President Looks Back	156
Chapter 14 A Vision for the Future	164
Chapter 15 Pictorial Supplement	166
Index	195
Bibliography	200

FOREWORD
by Terry Waite CBE

The Young Men's Christian Association was established more than 160 years ago to promote Christian fellowship between young men away from home in unfamiliar places.

Since then the YMCA (as it is now universally known) movement has spread all over the globe, and is present in more than 120 countries. It offers every conceivable type of person – male and female, young and old – a personable place of refuge, fun and friendship, a place where they can indulge in sporting and social activities, or simply retreat from the clamour of everyday life for a short while. In short, the YMCA is 'home' to millions.

There are still many in the world who do not know what it is like to have a permanent roof over their heads or regular food in their stomachs. Twenty years ago I had the privilege of co-founding Y Care International, the international development and relief agency of the YMCA in the UK and Ireland.

The charity works in partnership with YMCAs across the developing world, funding and supporting grass roots development programmes that help young people lift themselves out of poverty.

I believe that every young person assisted to have a better life, and assisted to contribute to the development of their own community, is a step towards achieving a fairer, more just and more humane world.

A percentage of the sale of this book goes to this deserving cause. I therefore warmly commend it, and the story behind it, to you.

Our forefathers – and not just in Cheltenham – were a dedicated group who did their utmost to point young people in the direction of everything good in the Christian life. It is by attempting to follow their example that we are where we are today.

Terry Waite CBE, Co-founder and President of Y Care International

INTRODUCTION

The purpose of this book is to outline the major events which took place during the first 150 years of Cheltenham YMCA and to place them in an overall historical context. The true historian always makes allowances for time and space and that is how the information should be treated. For social engineers with a political agenda, however, there is a tendency to compare the past unfavourably with the present but linking like with unlike is both invalid and unhelpful, and has no place in this volume. We can learn a great deal about ourselves by studying what our ancestors thought and did, and should marvel at how much they achieved in a century and a half.

All references to present day items or places, e.g. shops and locations, are for 2005 and will inevitably change as time progresses. There was no easy way of avoiding this and in any event the descriptions were historically correct at the time of publication.

Once the research got under way and the evidence began to unfold it became clear just how important Cheltenham YMCA has been in the life of the town. For many years it was the only fitness-related centre available to the general public and when the current sports hall was opened almost 50 years ago it was described as the largest in the south west of England. How times change!

They have also changed socially and spiritually, and it became abundantly clear how the nation's conscience was once seen as an important individual but paradoxically collective affair, rather than a secular corporate responsibility as manifested today. Whereas the emphasis is now on general fund raising it was once firmly and squarely on the shoulders of every individual to do something for his neighbour. This in turn built up a group spirit which was clearly evident during the first two decades after the move to Vittoria Walk when students and apprentices bonded together in a remarkable manner. More recent attention to social housing and short term accommodation has changed this considerably. Indeed, in society generally, short-termism has replaced long term career planning and nobody is any longer guaranteed a job for life. A far cry from the slower but much steadier pace of the past where everyone "knew their station in life" and responded accordingly.

This is a remarkable story, beginning in 1855 with an enthusiastic band of clergymen from all the major denominations, together with an equally enthusiastic band of young male supporters, determined that Cheltenham should have its own YMCA. It went through various teething problems and closed briefly at least three times through lack of funds but was never far from the hearts of local civic and church leaders. It also played a significant local role in two world wars, each of which has a chapter to itself.

Initially, it rented several premises before acquiring Number 31 Cambray Place in 1898. In 1921 it moved to the Promenade amid loud official celebrations and fanfares. Then, in 1956, seeking extra accommodation, it moved to its present location in Vittoria Walk, formerly a Cheltenham Ladies' College boarding house called Farnley Lodge. To this was later added a sports hall, squash courts and a large new accommodation block.

As the 21st Century unfolded there were plans for further redevelopment as Cheltenham YMCA kept pace with modern life and the needs of the local community.

This is how it was. Some of the photographs are not of the highest quality but still paint a fascinating picture. Read on and enjoy the book ……

INTERNATIONAL YMCA TIMELINE

1844 YMCA founded in London by George Williams

1851 YMCA founded in America, addressing physical fitness via gymnasiums and a wide programme of activities.

1852 Great Exhibition in Hyde Park - visitors enthusiastically take home the idea of the YMCA and, aided by the spread of railways, branches spring up across Europe and North America,

1855 First International Conference and formation of YMCA World Movement in Paris

1855 Cheltenham YMCA founded

1861 American Civil War – YMCA work begins with troops

1882 YMCA English National Council formed

1891 Basketball invented by YMCA in America

1894 George Williams is knighted by Queen Victoria. 405 YMCAs now in the British Isles

1895 Volleyball invented by YMCA in America

1900 English YMCA workers serve troops in the Boer War

1908 Scouting for Boys pioneered by Baden-Powell under the auspices of Birkenhead YMCA

1914-1918 The Great War – the British YMCA provides services to soldiers on the front line and a red triangle, signifying "Mind, Body and Spirit", is introduced as the new YMCA symbol

1919 Red Triangle Clubs are established in new purpose-built YMCA huts run by the Women's Auxiliary

1921 The poppy is introduced through the Canadian YMCA as a symbol of remembrance

1932 British Boys for British Farms, and British Boys for British Yachts — two initiatives to place unemployed young men as agricultural workers on farms or seamen in the Merchant Navy

1930s Employment Department finds jobs for 38,000 British ex-servicemen

1939-1945 War sees widespread YMCA huts established as canteens followed by large vans converted into mobile canteens going anywhere and everywhere, wherever the need arose

1944 YMCA Centenary

1946 YMCA reintroduces British Boys for British Farms to rebuild agriculture after the war

1959 Following a government report the British YMCA establishes large numbers of youth clubs

1970 Training for professional youth workers leads to the establishment of George Williams College in Canning Town, London

1975 Saigon falls and the YMCA meets with North Vietnamese to arrange relief work, the only organisation allowed to do so

1978 British YMCA launches Training for Life working with unemployed young people

1983/4 Terry Waite launches Y Care International, a Refugee and International Development Agency

1994 YMCA celebrates its 150th Anniversary

2005 Cheltenham YMCA celebrates its 150th Anniversary on November 23rd

CHELTENHAM YMCA TIMELINE

1855 Inaugural meeting – Old Town Hall, Regent Street (near Regent Arcade west entrance by Ormond Place, facing the Municipal Offices)

1855 – St. Mary's Churchyard building (unidentified, presumably demolished)

1856 – Regent Mansion, 64 Regent Street (now incorporated into Cavendish House)

1863 – Bedford Buildings, Clarence Street/Well Walk (on the Museum side of Library site) since demolished

1864 – 156 High Street (next to the old Grammar School, since demolished – renumbered 253 during the mid-1950s)

1866 – Promenade House, Clarence Parade (also known as Clarence Parade Hall, on the site of former Gloucestershire Echo offices, now Yates's Wine Bar)

1870 – 2 Cambray (now Soho Coffee Shop)

1876 – 396 High Street (renumbered 124 in mid-1950s, now Abbey Bank)

1879 – 7 Clarence Street (renumbered 11 in 1930s, now Bristol & West Building Society)

1881 – 6 North Street over Mr. Pilley's shop (on the site of Boots the Chemist)

1895 – 7 Cambray (now Cambray Dental Practice) opened as a boarding house

1897 – 323 High Street (renumbered 278 during the mid-1950s, now the central section of Furnishing Studios) with 7 Cambray retained as a boarding house

1898 – 31 Cambray (now Carphone Warehouse, coffee shop, hair salon, music company) with 7 Cambray retained as a boarding house

1921 – 16/17/18 Promenade, later renumbered 51/53/55. Also included a longitudinal timber-framed building erected at the rear which served as a gymnasium and an important Services canteen during the war. Known as the Royal Well Hut it was demolished in 1956 and re-erected as St. Thomas' Mission Church on the new Alma Road Estate in Up Hatherley, surviving until all the prefabs in the area had been replaced by modern housing about 20 years later. Number 51 was sold to Pearl Assurance circa 1936, and 53 and 55 to Cheltenham Council in 1956 after which they were converted into extra Municipal Offices, the Council Chamber now standing where the Royal Well Hut was situated.

1956 – Farnley Lodge, 6 Vittoria Walk (formerly a Cheltenham Ladies' College boarding house) to which was added a gym in 1957 which was extended into a sports hall in 1962, and a new accommodation block in 1965

****

Baker Street YMCA – 1940-1967 (now part of Gas Green Baptist Church). Preceded by a brief move to Clare Street Hall (since demolished), the Junior Department moved here when the Royal Well Hut was transformed into the Royal Well Wartime Services Canteen.

Ardwell House, Evesham Road – leased from Church Army for move-on accommodation 1980s

4 Wolseley Terrace – occupied by the YMCA Training Agency, now rented out

33 Rodney Road – occupied by the YMCA Training Agency, since sold.

Balcontan House, Tryes Road – bought for student accommodation, since sold

CHAPTER 1
YMCA ENGLAND

The Young Men's Christian Association – hereafter referred to as the YMCA – began in London on 6th June 1844. The founder was a draper called George Williams (1821-1905), who was knighted by Queen Victoria in 1894 for services to the community generally and London in particular. Nominated by the prime minister, Lord Rosebery, his initial humble reaction was to refuse the honour until it was pointed out that he ought to accept it on behalf of the YMCA.

Before any Scotsman protests that some of the above facts are wrong it should be pointed out that a similar but as yet unnamed young men's Christian movement had sprung up in Scotland slightly earlier and eventually fuelled the Scottish YMCA. It began in Glasgow in 1824 with Paisley not far behind in 1832. Nonetheless, it is widely assumed that the Evangelical fervour and persistence of George Williams is what caused the YMCA to merge all the various elements firstly into a national then an international movement, accelerated by the mid-Victorian growth of railways facilitating easier and quicker travel.

In a lifetime of service George travelled throughout Europe and, along with hundreds of others as the movement grew, made a point of befriending young men and winning them for the Lord whenever he could. This was not achieved simply by word of mouth but by establishing YMCA centres which catered for both domestic and social needs. In many ways it was a natural reaction stemming from an early 19th Century Evangelical revival borne out of a realisation that much of the established Anglican church was not sufficiently Christian and in some areas thoroughly disreputable. Initially the Nonconformists were known as Dissenters but Evangelical fervour soon spread into the Anglican church as well, so much so that the YMCA became synonymous with Christian hospitality and open to all denominations irrespective of colour or creed.

When Williams died in 1905 he was so well thought of that his funeral took place at St. Paul's Cathedral close to where the initial YMCA movement was established among the group of buildings still known today as St. Paul's Churchyard. It was attended by three bishops together with 50 Anglican and 40 Nonconformist clergy. 2,600 tickets were issued and his body was laid to rest in the crypt. Survived by his wife and five sons — three other sons and a daughter having died in infancy and his other daughter at the age of 19 — he was mourned at both national and international level.

His was a long and prolific life culminating in a worldwide movement which has the word "Christian" at its heart. Indeed the YMCA is the country's longest serving Christian charitable body with Cheltenham YMCA amongst the oldest member associations. Down the years it has played a major role in the life of the town and although society has changed dramatically, especially in the last quarter of the 20th Century, it still touches a great many local people. A brief look through the archives and pictures bears testimony to the huge influence it has wielded through 15 action-packed decades.

CHAPTER 2
THE FOUNDING OF CHELTENHAM YMCA

With the founding of any organisation it is important to understand the reasons behind it and Cheltenham YMCA is no exception. What caused a relatively small town in the West Country, albeit situated near the ancient county town of Gloucester, to be in at the forefront of YMCA development in the United Kingdom?

By the 18th Century the established church was in disarray and there was widespread scorn among many for the trimmings and trappings of ecclesiastical life which were seen as being for the well-heeled only. Many livings, both rural and urban, were paid for by rich benefactors and some of the Bishops and Archbishops of the time could not be regarded as remotely spiritual or Christian. One Archbishop of Canterbury even employed several uniformed flunkeys to walk alongside him the few hundred yards to church. In short, the time was set for a spiritual revolution which came in two guises, Establishment and Non-Establishment. The former included the Oxford Movement but there were many offshoots and, as Anthony Trollope observed in his *Barchester Chronicles,* some of the clergy were suffering from an outbreak of Christianity!

The Nonconformist denominations, often referred to as Dissenters, occurred in various forms, not the least of which were the Methodists, effectively established by two Anglican clergy, John and Charles Wesley. John Wesley in particular preached to the common man all over the country and as the lower classes were not generally acceptable to the middle and upper church-going classes, they founded their own chapels. Baptists, Congregationalists, Presbyterians and the like were similarly organised but there was also a revolution from within the Establishment itself. Practising a different liturgy to the High Church it gave rise to a number of reactions with a net result of proliferating churches for both High and Low factions, especially in the growing industrial towns and usually underwritten by wealthy patrons.

Had it not been for the Evangelical revolution then most of the Victorian social reforms would never taken place as early as they did. William Wilberforce and the Slave Trade was one important aspect of parliament but there were many others which attempted to alleviate the lot of the poor.

Compulsory education was another huge step forward and the whole situation is brilliantly explained in a 1930s book called *England Before and After Wesley* by J. Wesley Bready [1]. Sadly, as the country enters a post-Christian era, much of this is now conveniently forgotten and has been swept under the carpet. However, one has only to look at almost 200 YMCAs in the UK alone — not to mention abroad — to realise what an impact was made on contemporary society by this splendid new organisation which spread like wildfire.

Never was this better illustrated than by almost a whole page of close type in the *Cheltenham Examiner* dated November 28th, 1855. This vast broadsheet article ran to about 8,000 words! Entitled "The Young Men's Christian Association" it reported, in very great detail, a meeting which took place at the Town Hall in Regent Street the previous Friday evening, November 23rd, which we can therefore take as the founding date of Cheltenham YMCA. The building, originally Barnett's Riding School, was purchased and converted briefly into the first Salem Chapel before being used for public meetings, travelling shows, and entertainments. The equine connection may have been linked to the rear of the adjoining Plough Hotel which was used for training horses during the first half of the 19th Century. Finally used as a storeroom by nearby Cavendish House, the Old Town Hall was demolished circa 1981 to make way for the Regent Shopping Arcade.

The large audience was described as "…. most respectable" and on the platform the paper noticed R.R. Humphreys Esq., Rev. J. Browne, Rev. C. Evans, Rev. M. Neller, Rev. Dr. Morton Brown, Rev. James Smith, Rev. S. Walker, J. Scougall Esq., C.T. Cooke Esq., R.B. Huddlestone Esq., and the Secretary of the Parent Association, T.H. Tarleton Esq. who was obviously the star turn of the evening. The convenors had tried to attract Lord Shaftesbury but apologised for doing so when they discovered that Mr. Tarleton was available.

Dr. Humphreys took the chair despite protesting his inadequacy, a view which was clearly not shared by his colleagues. He expressed his opinion that a YMCA would be of great benefit to the local community and that it would not adversely affect the churches but rather enhance them. There were clearly some views within the town that a new non-church based organisation might take members away from individual churches but the chairman dismissed these fears as groundless, a statement which was greeted by cheers from the audience. He went on to say: "The Association is composed of men united in the Christianity of the Church." More cheers!

There were further prolonged cheers when Mr. Tarleton rose to his feet to give a fairly lengthy address explaining how he thought a local YMCA would benefit Cheltenham. "Its managing body must be composed of young men, and youth and joyous spirit pervade the whole of its arrangements, which were made to meet specifically the wants and circumstances of young men." More cheers!

Warming to his task the Secretary of the Association went on to make many points of great significance, virtually all of which were greeted with vocal enthusiasm. On the subject of church loyalties he outlined how the YMCA spread across denominational boundaries, believing that in Christianity there was no inclusive or exclusive limit because Christianity enclosed in its affection all who had any sympathy or love for its object

▲ *Where it all began. This picture, taken from the old Plough Hotel in the High Street, shows the area where horses were trained in the yard behind. The Old Town Hall can be seen in the middle with pointed windows. Initially owned by Barnett's Riding School and then briefly by Salem Baptist Church, it was utilised for all kinds of public meetings and it is not difficult to imagine it full of young people crowding in enthusiastically to establish the founding of Cheltenham YMCA on November 23rd, 1855. The mid-19th Century was an exciting time for Christians of all denominations who were determined to put their Lord and Master at the forefront of everything they did. Later used as a store for Cavendish House, the building was subsequently demolished along with surrounding properties, to make way for the Regent Arcade. Regent Street is to the right. In the background on the left is the western end of the present Town Hall, with the Queen's Hotel in the left centre and St. Andrew's Church spire to the right. Once dominated by churches, the Cheltenham skyline has changed radically but it seems that car parking has been a problem for some decades.*

while Churchianity excluded all who did not adopt its particular forms.

The fact that there were supportive ministers present from both the Church of England and Nonconformists obviously made his task easier. One could go further and say it seems most likely that the majority came from the town's strong Evangelical wing which had come under the sway of the dynamic Francis Close, Rector of Cheltenham from 1826-1856. One of the founders of both Cheltenham College and St Paul's Training College he later became Dean of Carlisle and was very highly thought of everywhere he went. He died in 1882, and four years later the Dean Close Memorial School was named after him which has maintained a strong Evangelical tradition ever since.

Mr. Tarleton went on to explain what was happening in London and how 1,500 members had access to sharing their faith with 10,000 others on a daily basis. "It was the first Christian principle of the Association that every Christian had a direct business for Christ in his daily duty, not only at church or chapel but where Christ had placed him in the world." He went on to say how when men were jaded at the end of the day they could enjoy refreshment in Christian company and also use of the library and reading room. His wish was to see a similar organisation in Cheltenham where people desire to be Christ's disciples, associating their efforts together in the extension of his kingdom among young men. "If there were 50 young men in Cheltenham who were desirous to effect this good object, they were first to come together to see how they could combine."

He ended by saying: "Go forth therefore and attend to moral and spiritual things and God will bless your enterprise." He sat down to loud cheering!

The Rev. John Browne rose to propose the first resolution to the effect that the meeting was duly impressed with the value of the Young Men's Christian Association and the great blessing it would prove to the town.

Mr. Scougall rose to second the resolution with a long speech which was also highly acclaimed. Unsurprisingly, when the Chairman put the resolution it was "…. carried by acclamation."

The Rev. Dr. Brown then proposed the second resolution: "That this meeting calls upon the young men of Cheltenham to join the Association and to do what they can to further its objects by mutually co-operating for the conversion of their fellow young men, and to do all it could in co-operating with the society." Mr. Huddlestone briefly seconded the resolution which was also carried by acclamation.

The Rev. Charles Evans then rose to propose the third resolution: "That this meeting views with approval the efforts hitherto made by the society, and trusts that it may continue to be subservient to the advancement of the Gospel of Jesus Christ among the young men." The Rev. James Smith, minister of Cambray Baptist Church, seconded the resolution expressing his "…. deep interest and heartfelt wishes for the prosperity of the institution, observing that much was to be done by earnest and fervent prayer." Coincidentally, the new YMCA was later to occupy three different sets of premises near his new church in Cambray Place.

The resolution was carried unanimously and Col. Hennell then proposed a vote of thanks to the chairman for the efficient manner in which he had conducted the meeting. The Rev. S. Walker seconded the proposition and said, significantly, "…. he was glad the meeting was such as they had expected it to be, and that Church, Methodist and Dissenter had been brought together." He also commented that it was not Mr. Tarleton's doing that a YMCA was to be established in Cheltenham but that of the young men themselves.

It was an historic meeting in many ways. Firstly, because it brought together so many different denominations; secondly because it clearly showed an enthusiasm for Christian outreach; and thirdly, because it firmly established the work of Cheltenham YMCA which is still going strong 150 years later.

[1] *England Before and After Wesley; The Evangelical Revival and Social Reform* by J. Wesley Bready published by Hodder and Stoughton, London, during the 1930s

CHAPTER 3
THE STORY UNFOLDS 1855-1921

It is clear that absolutely no time at all was wasted in the formation of Cheltenham YMCA because in the same issue of the *Cheltenham Examiner* (November 28th 1855) which devoted so much space to the inaugural meeting in the Old Town Hall, there appeared two separate notices! Indeed, one suspects that these notices had been drafted a good deal of time prior to the meeting because the latter was on the previous Friday evening and the paper was published on the following Wednesday.

It seems likely that much activity had been going on behind the scenes, especially when one considers how many different churchmen were present at the meeting. Who was behind it all? One person or many? Presumably the main players were among those on the platform but sadly, we shall probably never know exactly what happened. Whatever the facts, though, Cheltenham owes them a great deal of gratitude for their foresight and enthusiasm.

The first notice was in a prominent position and read as follows:

YOUNG MEN'S
CHRISTIAN ASSOCIATION

The Committee begs to announce that the Meetings for the week will be as follows:

CONVERSATIONAL BIBLE CLASS

THIS (WEDNESDAY) EVENING
At Half-past Eight o'clock. Subject:

"CHRIST AS A MODEL"

Friday Evening at Half-past Eight,   DEVOTIONAL MEETING
Sabbath Evening at Half-past Eight, DEVOTIONAL MEETING

So there we have it! Cheltenham YMCA began with no less than three meetings in its first week of operation in Rooms at St. Mary's Churchyard! Was there a verbal grapevine which spread the word or did people rely on the local newspapers to find out what was going on?

The second notice was next-but-one underneath the first, and read as follows:

YOUNG MEN'S
CHRISTIAN ASSOCIATION

The Committee of the above Society begs to inform their Friends and the Christian Public of Cheltenham that Subscriptions for carrying out the objects of the Association will be thankfully received on their behalf at the following places:-
County of Gloucester Bank, Gloucestershire Banking Company, Tract Depository, Clarence Street; Wight and Bailey, Promenade; Cheltenham and Gloucester Bank, National and Provincial Bank, Mr. New's, High Street; and Davies's Library, Montpellier.

SOCIETY'S ROOMS (pro tem) ST. MARY'S CHURCHYARD

▲ *The mid-19th Century is often, quite unfairly, criticised for its lack of social awareness. In fact the opposite is true and Cheltenham College was the first of the great public schools of the Victorian era. It was overtly Christian and has remained so ever since, having been founded on a tide of spiritual charisma involving, among others, the first two Vice-Presidents, Rev. Francis Close and Rev. J. Browne, both of whom played key roles in the founding of Cheltenham YMCA 15 years later. All subsequent College Principals took an active part within the Association with the famed "muscular Christianity" finding much favour in both camps. Their joint sense of Christian mission was identical in most respects and they therefore worked closely together.*

It was clearly a going concern but subsequent activities, although no doubt plentiful and ongoing, are difficult to find. One suspects they quickly became a part of the Cheltenham fabric but few records have survived to tell us very much more. Clearly the words "pro tem" indicated they were looking for a permanent home and they obviously found one. Exactly where, however, is a matter for conjecture. Some sources say it was a demolished building which was situated on the site of the *Gloucestershire Echo* newspaper offices but this can be discounted because the current buildings pre-date 1855. Another suggestion was that the premises were on the site of the more modern area of Cavendish House which was not very far away, and this seems the more likely. We can be sure, though, that after St Mary's Churchyard the new HQ was somewhere near the town centre so what exactly do the contemporary archives tell us?

The Secretary of the local Association was an honorary position and remained so until 1879 when the first "… paid Secretary or Missionary" was appointed. The mid-Victorian era, whatever faults it may have had in other directions, produced a huge number of Evangelical Christians who believed they had been "Saved to serve", a phrase which echoed down the years until relatively recently when society became obsessed by material possessions. There are thousands who still believe it but the phrase itself has fallen out of general use.

In any event, the first Secretary was Mr. William Creese about whom we know a good deal and who was still around 40 years later when the Association moved to 7 Cambray, later renamed Cambray Place. We also know that the founding father of the YMCA, George Williams from London, paid an annual subscription of 10 guineas, an enormous sum of money in those days and which did a great deal to keep Cheltenham YMCA afloat. Local subscriptions began at 4 shillings, again a substantial amount because it was quickly reduced to 2/6d, or half a crown for those who can still remember this sum or distinctive coin! Presumably 4/- was beyond what local young men could, or would pay.

William Creese was one of the original twelve founder members of the YMCA at 72 St. Paul's Churchyard in London, on June 6th 1844 and remained a close friend of George Williams. He was also the only one to outlive the great man although he did not attend his funeral at St. Paul's

▲ Rev. James Smith was one of many churchmen whose vision changed the face of Cheltenham during the 19th Century. Pastor of Cambray Baptist Church he was responsible for several church buildings including his own large church erected at the same time as he joined forces with others in the Old Town Hall to propose the establishment of a Young Christian Men's Association in 1855. How pleased he would have been, had he lived long enough, to witness Cheltenham YMCA subsequently occupying premises at 2, 7 and 31 Cambray, later called Cambray Place.

Cathedral in 1905, presumably because he was too old. Not only was he the first Cheltenham YMCA Honorary Secretary but, in conjunction with another founder member, Rev. John Christian Symons, he was actually the first secretary of the fledgling national YMCA movement in London! By 1845 Creese, a native of Worcestershire, had moved back west and became a farmer at Teddington just over the Gloucestershire border.

Later describing himself as originally a "stiff young churchman", Creese proved the adage that in Christ there is no denominational distinction because at least three of the other eleven YMCA founders were Congregationalists with Symons being a Wesleyan who died in 1894 during the 45th year of his ministry in Australia. Creese maintained good relationships with George Williams although he occasionally lost patience with him and was sometimes concerned by his health and overwork. His birthday was July 12th and although George Williams often referred to him as "Daddy Creese", he was in fact a little younger than his mentor.

Although no killjoy, Creese lived long enough to see the introduction of new entertainments of which he disapproved. Around the 1890s Gloucester YMCA refused to allow billiards and smoking which resulted in a decline in membership, the same period when strict no smoking rules caused major problems when Cheltenham opened its accommodation at 7 Cambray. Billiards, however, was soon adopted as an important YMCA activity and remained so for several decades.

An articulate and shrewd man, Creese had "a strict faith tempered by an engaging and easily expressed sense of humour". As the oldest son, he inherited his father's 230 acre farm and, employing 12 labourers, enjoyed a modest bachelor life during which he regularly attended National YMCA conferences. He worried about the prospects of nearby Tewkesbury YMCA and one also wonders if he helped and advised Worcester YMCA when they came to the rescue of Cheltenham YMCA in 1874. His farm was home to many Sunday services and Cheltenham can count itself fortunate to have had such a man working up front and later behind the scenes.

****

Less than a fortnight after Cheltenham YMCA came into being the *Cheltenham Examiner* contained the following letter:

Public libraries and the Young Men's Christian Association

To the Editor of the *Cheltenham Examiner*
Sir: - Will you kindly state for the information of a "Working Man" and the public generally, that the Young Men's Christian Association has for one of its chief objects, the very thing which he laments the want of in Cheltenham, i.e. the formation of a Library and Reading Room.

The Reading Room is already open and a subscriber of 2s 6d quarterly, will be entitled to the perusal of the daily papers and periodicals, which will be increased in ratio with the funds.

Already donations in money and books have been received and others promised towards the formation of the library etc., and 'ere long it is hoped that this Association will be found as much a blessing to those who are seeking to cultivate the mind, as it has already proceeded to be to many who are anxious for the cultivation of the heart, and the salvation of the soul.

I am, Sir,
Your obliged and obedient servant,
ONE OF THE ASSOCIATION,

Society's Rooms,
St. Mary's Churchyard,
December 4th, 1855

Thus far we see that the fledgling Association was based near the Parish Church but almost 12 months later, in the *Cheltenham Examiner* of November 19th, 1856, there was a notice which read as follows:

Young Men's Christian Association

"A meeting composed of the members and friends of the above association, including clergymen of different Christian denominations, took place on Thursday evening at Regent Mansion, 64 Regent Street", a building which has since been incorporated into Cavendish House.

The meeting was apparently a very pleasant one, inaugurating the society's new rooms at the above premises. It was chaired by Mr. Downton, deputising for Dr. Cook who was ill. The first speaker was the Rev. C. Evans of St. Mary's Church who delivered an address on "The desirability of Christian union in opposing the errors of false teachers, and strengthening the faith of the wavering." This was followed by "an appropriate address" from the Rev. John Newton of Bethany Chapel after which the Rev. W.F. Handcock of St. Luke's spoke on "The advantages which this and similar institutions offered to inquirers after salvation."

The Rev. W.G. Lewis of Salem Chapel, "in a forcible speech" then referred to "The conduct of the early Christians as an example to the members of the Young Men's Christian Association", the expression "YMCA" having yet to be universally

▲ *Baron de Ferrieres was Liberal MP for Cheltenham from 1880-1885. A keen churchman, in the 1860s he was President of Cheltenham YMCA and was instrumental in acquiring Clare Street Hall for St. Luke's Church to help the poor and needy part of the parish in and around Bath Road.*

accepted as an acronym. "The attendance, chiefly of young men, was very numerous. Bible classes and devotional meetings are held during the week in connection with the association, which also offers to its members the attractions of a reading room and library."

On March 25th, 1857 the *Cheltenham Examiner* further reported:

"The Young Men's Christian Association held their quarterly social meeting at the Regent Mansion on Wednesday evening, under the presidency of E.J. Esdaile Esq., when an interesting conversation took place on the best means of advancing the objects of the association. We were much pleased with the Christian zeal manifested by the speakers, and trust that the association will be the means of effecting much good among the rising generation."

Archive references tells us that the President was Lord John Russell, formerly the MP for Tavistock, Stroud and various places in Ireland, with three different secretaries, Mr. J. Lang (Financial), Mr. Treeby (Correspondence), and Mr. H. Stucke (Members). Cheltenham YMCA was also described as being " … for the improvement of the mental and spiritual condition of young men" and added "Whilst not assuming the dignity of a church, its object is to act as a feeder to all churches." There was quite a move to deliver Christian tracts amongst the town.

****

An excellent summary of the 19th Century facts as we know them is given in the addendum to this chapter, being the verbatim report of Horace Trinley Bush who was to play a significant role within Cheltenham YMCA until his early death at the age of only 56 in 1958, thus making him only 25 years old when he wrote the article!

****

Meanwhile, by May 1863 we learn that the Young Men's Christian's Association now had rooms in Bedford Buildings when a scientific talk by Mr. Notcutt (an unfortunate name whether he was teetotal or not!), was "ably treated and listened to with great attention". These premises were situated between St. George's Place and Well Walk, part of which is now occupied by the Public Library. The President had by now been elevated to Earl Russell with a General Secretary called Mr. Harrison who was one of a band who refused to accept a resolution to close the Association at the previous AGM. It seems that the majority felt: "That the Association has done its work and there is no further need of its existence" but others felt differently and reorganised the Society.

No bones were made about the aim which was "to convert young men". Around 100 attended the Bible class and 24 members had started a Temperance Society. In answer to the question "How is it that your society is not self-supporting" the curt reply was "Ours is a missionary work!" So there! One young man from New Zealand wrote in: "I shall be for ever grateful for the instruction received in your Bible class because through your teaching I owe much of that strength by which God's grace, I have been able to resist wrong-doing." A strong testimony indeed.

In 1864 the Association moved briefly to 156 High Street which was next to the Old Grammar School, since demolished to make way for a parade of shops, including Tesco's.

In January 1866, we learn that the Association had just moved to new rooms at Promenade House in Clarence Parade which was inaugurated with a Friday evening "soiree". The weather was "tempestuous" but the attendance was good. After a "nicely provided tea" the chair was taken by W.O. Bernard with the Rev. Dr. Brown exhorting everyone to pray that the enhanced premises would lead to an increase in membership. In reply, Mr. H.W. Foster spoke of the importance of happiness in Jesus Christ. The premises were indeed "commodious" because they were none other than the former attractive home of the *Gloucestershire Echo* which still stands proudly at the entrance to

▲ *In 1894 Cheltenham YMCA objected to the Council charging for skating on Pittville Lake on a Sunday, a day regarded strictly as the Sabbath. In 1916, the owner of the since demolished Marle Hill House in the background, Mr. J.W. Buckland, paid the subscriptions for many of the local YMCA men away on active service.*

The Old Grammar School was situated where the Tesco parade of shops now stands in the High Street. Next to it on the left, was Number 156, which was home to Cheltenham YMCA between 1864 and 1866. Prior to that it had been housed somewhere within St. Mary's Churchyard, then part of what is now Cavendish House, and then in a building near the Library.

the Promenade just across from Royal Well, now home to Yates's Wine Bar.

Around this time was an outing to Bushley, reached by train to Tewkesbury and then by Shanks's Pony! Members brought their own packet of tea, every one of which was later emptied into a single pot! By 1869 the President was Henry Wilmote with James Page succeeding H. W. Foster as General Secretary and Mr. H. Stucke still in charge of financial matters. YMCA and Literary and Scientific Institute classes included Chemistry, Animal Physiology, Classics and Maths. Clearly the educational side of a young man's development was not being neglected.

In 1870 the YMCA was on the move again, this time to Number 2 Cambray (Place), now the home of the Soho Coffee Company, two doors up from Cambray Baptist Church near the High Street. It seems there had been another dispute as to whether "entertainments" formed a proper part of the local YMCA, although what exactly they were is not related. In any event yet another new Association was formed, inheriting a debt of £50. "Twenty, earnest and energetic Christian men, representing the largest business houses in the town, together with some employers, were enrolled as members with the special promise that they would give at least one hour a week to the prosecution of the work". The clergy and ministers held out every promise of help.

In September 1872 the Rev. J. Aston of St. Luke's Church and a Presbyterian, Rev. J. More, both delivered addresses to the young men present. The premises proved rather unsuitable, however, for the bizarre reason that the landlord, noting the YMCA's new popularity and apparently well-heeled tenants, raised the rent by 50% to an unsustainable level. This actually forced the Association to close again in January 1874 but it was immediately reformed only to discover that no Treasurer could be found. It was therefore wound up – again!

At this point, however, Worcester YMCA came galloping to the rescue and after much fervent prayer, a new Treasurer was elected called Mr. J.C. Cooper. The forceful President at this time was Baron de Ferrieres, Cheltenham Liberal MP from 1880-1885, and the Secretary a Mr. W. Ketley, later succeeded by Mr. T. Fowler.

Several successful open air meetings were held round the town at various locations and in 1876 a new home was found at 396 High Street (renumbered 124 during the mid-1950s). There was a Prayer Meeting on Tuesdays and no fewer than four open air meetings every week at which the Gospel was faithfully preached. Bible Studies took place on Sunday afternoons and Wednesday evenings. An announcement about the new Reading Room and Library was posted in the *Cheltenham Examiner* on October 25th, 1876 giving the opening date as the succeeding Monday, October 30th when the following papers would be available: *The Times, Telegraph, Standard, Daily News, Graphic, Saturday Review, Cheltenham Examiner* (naturally!), *Cheltenham Chronicle, The Christian, Sunday Magazine, Leisure Hour* etc. Terms of admission were 2 shillings per quarter; 3 shillings per half year; or 5 shillings per whole

▲ There is no better way of recreating the past than from old photographs. This picture of the High Street, looking north west the from the junction with Rodney Road, speak volumes about the Victorian pre-motor car age when horse droppings were a permanent hazard and boys were employed to sweep a path across the street for pedestrians. Until it finally acquired its own premises in Cambray just before the turn of the 20th Century, Cheltenham YMCA used many different venues including the Assembly Rooms (bottom left), situated on the site of what is now the High Street branch of Lloyd's Bank.

year. "Application to be made to the Hon. Secretary, Mr. W.A. Dawson, 75 High Street who will supply tickets of admission". The Reading Room was open from 9am to 10pm.

Unfortunately, problems soon occurred and the noise of working machinery above prevented the Reading Room from being functional, and from January to September 1879 the Association found itself homeless before moving briefly into 7 Clarence Street (renumbered during the 1930s, now number 11). A 130 strong petition was sent to Parliament protesting about public houses being open on a Sunday, then another move of premises took place.

The new destination in 1881 was above a shop at Number 6, North Street, which was situated where Boots now stands. It was owned by Mr. Pilley, and playing the harmonium was restricted to certain members only! Obviously someone either misused it or could not play in tune. However, this period proved highly effective in the local Association's work. We learn that open air meetings were quite common, including a visit by Mr. Kirkham from London, Secretary of the Open Air Missions who held forth to a good crowd in St. George's Square. On at least one occasion the open air work had to be moved away from the fountain in the Promenade because the assembled throng was disrupting traffic! We also know that a paid Secretary had by now been employed to do "mission work" for the local Association.

In 1887 the Secretary was Mr. G. Wynn but by 1897 he had been succeeded by Mr. S. Houlton when the President was Rev. E.L. Roxby with premises located at 323 High Street, since renumbered 278 and now the centre section of Furnishing Studios. As explained below, however, 7 Cambray had already been opened as a boarding house, so the High Street was probably a temporary HQ prior to the much-publicised move to 31 Cambray the following year, 1898.

The addendum to this chapter tells of members being trained for the foreign mission field at this time and of a recreation club established in October 1891 to be added to the cricket and football clubs. The inaugural meeting was chaired by the redoubtable Rev. H. A. (Herbert Armitage) James, Principal of Cheltenham College and a popular local figure who had previously been Head of Rossall School in Lancashire. He later turned down the Headship at Clifton, Bristol but in 1895 became Head of Rugby, and in 1909 the

President of St. John's College, Oxford. At Cheltenham, owing to his appearance, he became known as "The Jug" or "The Pot", names which stuck for later College principals. With friends in such high places it is hardly surprising that Cheltenham YMCA was well respected.

James gave a vigorous speech about sport, quoting three 18th Century bishops who had been outstanding athletes, one of whom had been martyred for his faith. He also passionately championed the amateur cause and spoke out against betting in sport which was common in the North of England. As far as he was concerned "Betting is a spirit which prostitutes a noble game" and it should rather be a question of "Play hard, work hard and pray hard."

Other members on the platform that evening were Rev. G.P. Pearce, Rev. Melville Jones, Rev. T.J. Longhurst and Mr. C. Rowbotham. It was the latter who replied to the speech by Rev. James, moving a resolution which was seconded by Melville Jones, to the effect that a Cheltenham YMCA Recreation Club should be formed. James was, unsurprisingly, elected President and one may assume he gave it his full support because it was he who initiated the Cheltenham College Mission in East London which later transferred to the local Whaddon Boys' Club.

In January 1894, another petition was signed, this time protesting that the local Council had allowed, and even charged for, skating on the frozen Pittville Lake on a Sunday. Surprising? Not at all because until the 1960s there was little sport on the Sabbath and even then it created fierce opposition. More than a century ago, skating in a public place on a Sunday, let alone paying for the privilege, would have been tantamount to heresy!

In September 1895 Cheltenham YMCA moved yet again, returning to Cambray (Place) but at Number 7, next but one on the other side of Cambray Church, and now a dentist's surgery. Present were Mr. Creese, the first Hon. Secretary of the Association 40 years previously, Mr. R. Ley Wood (President), Rev. J.A. Owen, Rev. D.W. Pennell, Rev. Lang, Dr. S.T. Pruen, Mr. F. Shirer, Mr. (later Major) T.E. (Thomas Ellerson) Rickerby, Mr. H. Neale, Mr. J. Carpenter and Mr. S. Millard. The rental was described as a modest £38 per annum and it was claimed that no other institution in the town offered young men such splendid accommodation. The religious side of the work would not be overlooked, however with membership reported at 130 but with only eight "associates".

The modern work of Cheltenham YMCA had now been finally established because, following a productive mission to the town led by Mr. Lane earlier the same year, it was decided to appoint a housekeeper to look after the full-time residents, thus the Association now had two paid employees. At a second mission in 1897, Lane's messages were given to crowds in excess of 1,000 people each weeknight and 800 on Sunday afternoon. Notwithstanding churches' full congregations at the time, he must still have been a good preacher.

All was not well at 7 Cambray, though, because there was soon to be an uprising by some of the occupants. On investigation it transpired they had been upset by the strict rules posted in each bedroom and while the matter was quickly resolved, at least one resident was so angry that he had to be escorted off the premises! Other opposition came about because of a ban on smoking which, at the time, was unusual. A compromise was achieved by allowing smoking in the dining hall.

George Williams, the founder of the YMCA movement back in 1844, was no stranger to Cheltenham and, apart from visiting personal friends privately, came to the local YMCA in both April 1884 and May 1898. On the former occasion his aim was presumably to encourage the local Association which was at the time based in North Street and busily engaged in both indoor and outdoor mission. It is also clear that he supported Cheltenham YMCA financially and made a substantial regular contribution in the form of an average annual subscription of around £10, a huge sum. Certainly we know that by today's standards, he was incredibly generous.

On the second occasion he came to the local Association it was as Sir George Williams, to open what was described as a new HQ, this time at Number 31 Cambray (Place) which was slightly up from Number 7 and directly opposite Number 2! It was clearly a publicity coup second only to Royalty because Williams was by now a famous

▶ *This impressive line drawing comes from the 1898 Annual Report when a special effort was made to show off the new premises at 31 Cambray. It was the first permanent YMCA headquarters although a boarding house had been opened opposite at 7 Cambray three years earlier, and the two were now running in tandem.*

The rules of the Association were quite strict and the "Cheltenham Branch of the London Young Men's Christian Association" – the acronym "YMCA" was not yet in regular use although "YM" was occasionally used – has as its object the "Spiritual, Moral, Intellectual and Physical wellbeing of young men, and to provide a Home away from Home."

Rule Number 4 stated that "Any young man shall be eligible for membership who gives evidence of his conversion to God; he shall be proposed by a Member of the Association at any of its Committee Meetings, and elected by such Committee, after satisfactory inquiry as to his suitablility".

Nearly 200 subscribers were listed, with their amount paid. Also published were 80 donors to the Repairs and Purchase Fund of which £21 – a huge sum – was donated by Sir George Williams, founder of the YMCA Movement in 1855. A fellow donor was William Creese, the first Cheltenham Hon. Secretary and one of the original 12 founder members with Williams in London.

international figure with the YMCA movement having spread all over the Western World. The *Cheltenham Examiner* reported that there were now 6,493 YMCAs around the world with a membership of almost half a million. It also reported that Williams gave a donation of 20 guineas – a vast sum of money – which was more than twice the total amount subscribed for the day! As we shall see later, the aforesaid Royalty was not all that far behind and came in the shape of Princess Helena Victoria who visited in 1923 and 1935, and Queen Mary and the Princess Royal who visited in 1942 and 1952 respectively.

What of this third different set of Cambray premises at Number 31 and who paid for it? The building is now divided into two, one half being occupied by the Carphone Warehouse with a slightly extended façade, the other being shared by the Colombian Connection Coffee Rooms, a beauty salon and a music culture development programme. It is believed that the single storey extension at the back was later erected by the YMCA as a games room. Certainly during the early 20th Century it sported the YMCA name no fewer than three times across the front on different levels, possibly the three tenets of the YMCA belief – Mind, Body and Spirit – to be added to the Trinity of Father, Son and Holy Spirit.

The *Examiner* gave a great deal of space to the opening which was timed to coincide with a Regional Conference which many delegates attended. The first session held in the lecture room at 11am, was chaired by Major-General Lewis who outlined the spiritual role of the movement. Time was short, he urged, and many "listless" young men and women could be seen around the town on whom the Church had little or no effect. "The absence of growth was a sign of death" he said, and complimented the local leadership of Mr. Ley Wood.

Sir George Williams was invited to speak on the work of the YMCA generally and he pointed

▶ *By 1906 the artist's drawing had become a reality. The three different inscriptions on the building might well have been deliberate, relating possibly to the traditional Christian belief as God in three persons: Father, Son and Holy Spirit. It may also have been linked to the YMCA concept of Mind, Body and Spirit.*

Although Cheltenham YMCA now frequented two sets of premises in Cambray all was not well under the surface. The boarding house at Number 7 ran into difficulties when residents objected to rules posted in the bedrooms and although this was relaxed and smoking allowed in a designated area, at least one irate inmate had to be escorted off the premises. "Poor Secretary" said the Annual Report.

The problem at Number 31, however, was purely financial. It was the first building owned outright by Cheltenham YMCA but income was not enough to meet increasing expenditure and the amount owing on loans taken out to purchase the property. By 1911 the situation was so acute that the Committee felt it had no option but to recommend temporary closure.

Happily, in 1913 the situation was resolved, partly by a legacy but also by sheer strength of determination and will-power. An appeal to raise £1,000 in a week — a vast sum at the time — was regarded as madness by some but, as the text describes, it was actually exceeded!

out there were no fewer than 72 branches in the Metropolitan area, all doing valuable missionary work. Delegates then spoke and it was learned that Gloucester YMCA, following a special recruiting campaign, had increased its membership from 310 to 600. Bristol had also grown and Bath was holding its own. Calne, meanwhile, said it did not go in for physical exercise because it had plenty of its own on the agricultural front, thus leaving more room for spiritual activities! Although they had formed a cycling club, it was not for leisure but for "Gospel-preaching visits to the villages around".

Mr. Ley Wood spoke about Cheltenham and admitted that it "had for some time been in a hole". However, during the past 12 months, 40 new members had been added and progress was evident in every department. The excellent new premises had been acquired "for the very moderate cost of £450" although there would be considerable improvement expenses on top. Nevertheless, he considered it be a very conducive location and a resident secretary called Mr. Houlton had been appointed. Both the Rooms and the boarding house were being promoted in the best interests of the members.

By the kindness of Baron de Ferrieres, the delegates and a number of Cheltenham friends, were entertained to lunch at the Assembly Rooms, which occupied a nearby site where Lloyd's Bank now stands on the corner of Rodney Road and the High Street. General Lewis was in the chair and was supported by the Mayor, Colonel Rogers; Sir Broke Kay; Sir George Williams; the Rector, Rev. E.L. Roxby; Mr. Hind Smith, the National Travelling Secretary; Mr. Daniell JP from Bristol; Mr. H. Whitwell, Birmingham; Mr. Ley Wood; Rev. H. de Candole; H. Evan Noot; A. Beynon Phillips; J. Glass; Mr. T.E. Rickerby; Mr. J. Sawyer; Mr. G. Wynn and others. The excellent repast was served by Mr. T.A. Cox.

A number of interesting speeches followed including one by the Rector who proposed a toast to "The Churches", and another by Rev. Beynon. Phillips on behalf of the Free Churches of the town. It was made very clear by both that there was absolutely no antagonism between the denominations and that they were all working together for the one Shepherd. Mr. Phillips said how grateful he was for the support from the Established Church which brought applause from the assembled gathering.

The Mayor proposed a toast "Success to Cheltenham YMCA" expressing the opinion that such an organisation had a good effect in reducing crime and in advancing the moral and spiritual well-being of the young men of the town. As head of the governing body, he wished the Association every prosperity (more applause). Mr. G.H. Wynn responded by quoting:

*"I slept and dreamt that life was beauty,
I woke and found that life was duty."*

He believed duty to God could find no better expression than in service to one's fellow men and urged everyone to go forth and win the manhood of England for good and for God (more applause).

Mr. Boorne proposed "The Visitors" and Sir George Williams responded in characteristic style. He remarked that these were fighting days and that the YMCA was engaged in a battle for God against the powers of evil. He hoped every town and village in the district would be captured and that more branches of the Association would be formed (yet more applause).

The new premises were formally opened by the founder at 31 Cambray at 3pm. In addition to the £450 purchase price, £100 had been spent on repairs and renovation and a further £30 on furnishings. Towards the total sum required, promises had already been made of £160 which left £150 still to be met. The premises comprised a lecture room, games rooms, a conversation parlour, a reading room, and accommodation for a resident secretary. This was in addition to boarding accommodation established in the nearby premises at 7 Cambray opened three years earlier. By the time the Association reopened in 1913, after a two year lapse however, it seems that only Number 31 was in use by the YMCA.

Sir George desired "that the rooms should become a school of divinity, where the three Rs – regeneration, repentance and reformation – would be taught." There was no danger of sectarianism within the YMCA and he suggested that if anyone was caught denominational proselytising then they were to be ejected by the scruff of the neck, mentioning his name at the time! Sir George was also delighted to see his old friend, William Creese. The founder was also a funder and, as already mentioned, later donated more than twice the afternoon's subscription to defray expenses.

The afternoon session took place at the Assembly Rooms and the Conference was topped off in the evening by a public meeting at the same venue. Sir George was again prominent as were the Rector and various other local clergy. We can therefore state, without any fear of contradiction, that a rare Christian unity was present between the different major denominations in Cheltenham, which was certainly not the case in many other towns. Cheltenham YMCA clearly meant a great deal to them all and was obviously an important member of an international movement which was still gathering strength.

****

The 1898 President, Major-General H. Lewis, was succeeded a year later by E. Ernest Boorne, and Mr. J. Playle succeeded Mr. H.W. Broom as Treasurer, with Mr. S. Houlton continuing as Secretary. No fewer than 20 Reverends were listed as Vice-Presidents with a further 16 non-clerics making up the numbers. The Committee consisted of 12 non-clerics and was responsible for overseeing the day to day running of the Association which listed some of the advantages as being a Reading Room with incandescent gas; a Library with 400 well-selected volumes; a well-furnished, cosy and homely Parlour; a Recreation Room supplied with bagatelle, chess, draughts, halma (a game played on 256 squares with pieces moved into spaces behind one's opponent, rather like Chinese Chequers), rings, and dominoes; lectures and classes in Greek and Shorthand; a Literary and Debating Society; and Sports including cricket, football, cycling, swimming, and tennis. Members

▲ *This fascinating photograph was taken in the early years of the 20th Century with tramlines clearly visible. On the left is what is now Boots corner and careful study shows the words "YMCA" behind the lamp-post, a throw back to the time when the Cheltenham Association used the premises numbered 6 North Street, above Mr. Pilley's shop. Situated there from 1881 until at least 1895 it was a highly productive time. Although the harmonium was only allowed to be used by certain members – therein must lie a tale – many successful open air evangelistic meetings were held around the town. They were not appreciated by everyone, however, and one gathering was moved from the Promenade fountain to the Clarence Lamp because of traffic congestion. There were even reports of policemen being positioned to prevent objections to loud singing!*

moving to other areas were furnished with letters of introduction, there being more than 6,500 branches throughout the world with seaside homes at Margate, Llandudno, Ryde, Tenby, Ilfracombe, Brighton, Folkestone and Scarborough all on "moderate terms". Eat your heart out Billy Butlin!

Average membership was just over 200 with Sunday evening open-air services well attended in Clarence Street, on one occasion being led jointly by the Rector of Cheltenham, Rev. E.L. Roxby, and the Pastor of Cambray Baptist Chapel, Rev. H.A. Beynon Phillips, both vice-presidents. Other successful services were held at Haresfield and Guiting Power. From October 9-24, 1898, a United General Mission was held round the corner in the Assembly Rooms conducted by Mr. Rowland Edwards of the London Evangelisation Society. Unfortunately, stormy weather prevented higher attendances but much spiritual fruit resulted in many sinners being born again and a revival among many believers.

The Boarding House at 7 Cambray had been well supported with an average of more than 10 occupants but, like the premises at 31 Cambray opposite, was operating at a loss. There was hope that it would soon become self-supporting but there remained an urgent financial need. Nevertheless, under the Matron, Miss Gardner, it had welcomed visitors from as far afield as Australia, Canada, United States, Africa, France, and Armenia. Extracts from the Visitors Book speak volumes: "I came, I saw, I admired"; "Nothing but comfort and happiness here"; "Everything here is delightful – I envy those fellows who make this place their home". It was clearly meeting a need

It was assumed as a matter of course that YMCA men and public school pupils played sport under the true Corinthian ideals of amateurism. In 1891, at a YMCA meeting to start a Recreation Club, Cheltenham College Principal, Rev. H.A. James, spoke out against betting and professionalism. As far as he was concerned everyone should "Play hard, work hard and pray hard." It was a laudable comment which was never questioned in many sports until relatively recently. Both these pictures date from this period. The one above is a rowing match against Shrewsbury School on the River Severn while the cricket pitch below is instantly recognisable, although the backdrop now includes the new Cheltenham College Chapel opened in 1896 and the multi-storey office block occupied originally by Eagle Star and later the Zurich insurance group. Thirlestaine Road is off to the left of the picture behind the spires of the gymnasium.

Cheltenham YMCA mirrored the growth of local public schools and the early principals of both Cheltenham College and Dean Close were active and enthusiastic members of the Association. Vigorous Christian service was the ideal and extremely close links were forged with both students and staff. After the carnage of the First World War both schools made huge donations to a YMCA nationwide appeal for huts to be built in surrounding villages to alleviate endemic social problems.

▲ *The bearded Rev. H.A. James (above centre) was Principal of Cheltenham College from 1889-1895 during which time he played a key role in the establishment of a YMCA sports club in 1891.*

◄ *Rev. William Flecker (seated left) was the first Principal of Dean Close Memorial School and a Vice-President of Cheltenham YMCA.*

Almost 50 people were listed as contributing to the Repairs and Purchase Fund of whom Sir George Williams contributed the vast sum of £21, one sixth of the total raised during the year. Other contributors included Rev. Robert Stuart de Courcy Laffan during his final year as Principal of Cheltenham College before returning to the ministry. His successor was Rev. Reginald Waterfield who soon became a YMCA Vice-President.

The balance sheet for the year showed a total deficit of more than £500.

****

By the turn of the 20th Century the YMCA generally had become thoroughly respectable all over the world and was synonymous with Christian friendship, charity and service. In 1873 the American evangelist D.L. Moody had championed the cause and world conferences were being held all over Europe. 1880 saw the establishment of a boys' work to add to the young men's work and in 1893 a link was established with the Soldiers' Christian Fellowship, thus setting up a valued service to the Regular Armed Forces. Queen Victoria's confirmation of a knighthood on

▲ *Looking north along the Promenade in about 1900. At the time, Cheltenham YMCA occupied premises at 31 Cambray with a boarding house opposite at Number 7. Among the premises previously occupied was what is now Yates's Wine Bar (formerly the Gloucestershire Echo building) which is situated at the far end of this photo just round to the left. After the war was over Dr. Pruen and Major Rickerby, the YMCA President and Treasurer, made it their business to adopt a higher profile and secured a move to 16, 17 and 18 The Promenade (later renumbered 51, 53 and 55). The YMCA could not have been more central and remained there until 1956 when they moved to Vittoria Walk. Cheltenham Borough Council bought their vacated premises, extended their offices and also built a new Council Chamber at the rear.*

George Williams in 1894 coincided with him being made a Freeman of the City of London, where the 13th World Conference was also held.

In 1900 a total of 15 YMCA workers went to serve the British Forces during the Boer War in South Africa and, five years later, Lord Kinnaird was elected YMCA President on the death of Sir George Williams. In 1908, under the auspices of the YMCA, General Baden-Powell introduced a new scheme called "Scouting for Boys" and three years later, King George V set the Royal seal of approval by becoming Patron of the YMCA National Council, succeeded in 1937 by his son, King George VI.

****

The Edwardian period, usually regarded as the time between the death of Queen Victoria in 1901 up until the outbreak of the First World War in 1914 – although King George V acceded to the throne in 1910 – was one of national optimism. For Cheltenham YMCA, however, it was also a troubled time. The Annual Reports of 1906 and 1909 have survived and give us an indication that although there was plenty of activity going on socially, physically and spiritually, all was not well on the financial front.

In 1906 the President was Dr. W. Hutton of Harley House, Cambray and the Secretary was the former Treasurer, Mr. J. Playle of Southville, St. George's Road, although a resident Acting Secretary was listed as C.W. Boyce. Three years later Dr. Hutton was listed as the Chairman with the Hon. Secretary being Mr. E. Jefferies, and the President none other than the Rector of Cheltenham, Rev. F. L'Estrange Fawcett with Mr. Playle now listed on the Committee, alongside Messrs. Rickerby, Pruen and A.N. Cole, more of whom later.

The 50th Annual Report for 1906 was upbeat and began by stating how glad the Committee was to report a successful year of working with the young men of the town and how during the previous half century the local Association had "helped many a 'mother's boy' to live a true and manly Christian life, and join in the work of extending the Kingdom of our Lord Jesus Christ in this and other lands". The financial deficit was a concern but not an embarrassment because the Committee had faith in God that the Christian public would come to the help of the YMCA. They did, but not immediately and the 1909 Annual Report showed liabilities listed at £592 eight shillings and sixpence with assets totalling the same amount, namely 31 Cambray valued at £535 and the furniture and organ at £57 eight shillings and sixpence. No mention was made of 7 Cambray and it would seem these premises were no longer in use. In any event the financial situation deteriorated further and in 1911 the Committee obviously felt it had no alternative but to recommend temporary closure.

This was a big blow because there was still an active work taking place. Sunday Bible Classes started at 3pm with Open Air meetings in Clarence Street every Sunday evening from 8.30-9.30pm, beginning at the start of May and finishing at the end of September. A Churchman (meaning an Anglican minister) and a Nonconformist minister alternated as the main speaker, with a supporting speaker from within the YMCA itself. Mr. W.T. Long was in charge and it was apparently well supported. During the winter months this changed to the Home Circle where the same people kept in touch with an average attendance of 90 people enjoying solos, recitations, and a special item called a Keynote for the week given by one of the members.

Monday was choir practice at 8.30pm; Tuesday had a prayer meeting from 9.15-10pm while Wednesday afternoon (a half day locally and in most other large towns) was devoted mainly to football with the 1906-7 season being the best ever with 16 victories from 20 matches, the other 4 being drawn. This unbeaten record was due in no small measure to the captain, Mr. G. Fisher and the secretary, Mr. H.A. Leak. Medals were awarded to all the team members and a celebration tea held on April 3rd. Cycling also took place on Wednesdays while Thursday evenings included a second set of weekly open-air meetings at the corner of High Street and Henrietta Street. Large crowds attended, two of the members spoke each week and "some bright attractive singing was maintained". As soon as it was over it seems that several members then went swimming under the leadership of the aforesaid football captain, George Fisher.

Earlier on Thursday evenings from 6.30-8.30pm was a new Junior Section run by Mr. W.F. Pyke assisted by Mr. W. White. Any lad from any part of the town was welcome to join in and the Scriptures were brought to life in a lively manner. Certainly there was a good response and high hopes were entertained for future adult membership. Friday night Bible Studies were described as "the most enjoyable and certainly the most instructive meetings held during the week".

Surprisingly, the games room (plural) was described as the Game Room (singular) which was in full swing nightly from 6-30-10.30pm. Games included Cannons (presumably Billiards); Bagatelle (a primitive pinball machine); Rings (presumably gymnastics) along with Horizontal Bars. Chess and Draughts, meanwhile, were found in the Reading Room. The Game Room had been renovated and redecorated and it was hoped that the social side would be developed so that it might "keep young men away from public houses and other undesirable places".

By 1909 the Open Air meetings were still going strong with the wintertime Home Circle now replaced by Evangelistic Meetings at the King's Hall in North Street, which proved helpful to many with the same venue hosting a Christmas Bazaar in an attempt to raise much needed funds. Much to the Committee's regret Mr. Pyke had moved on to Eastbourne and his place in charge of the "lads", on Thursday evenings plus Saturday football, had been taken over by James Chandler with Gordon Cummings as his assistant. In addition, Mr. W. White was now running a fledgling Boy Scouts troop on Tuesday evenings which benefited from a lady supporter donating a piano. They were involved with many activities, including concerts, socials, rambles, outings, football, cricket, and drill. A bonus was Lady Baden-Powell entertaining them at Glendouran during

Without doubt the two most important members of Cheltenham YMCA in its formative years were Dr. Septimus Tristram Pruen, seen above taking tea in his garden at 2 Lansdown Terrace, and Major Thomas Ellerson Rickerby, who founded the firm of solicitors which still bears his name.

Pruen, an eminent paediatric surgeon, was Chairman for a long period before and after the First World War while Rickerby was the diligent Treasurer. Together they devoted a huge amount of time and money to ensuring that Cheltenham YMCA survived during the most arduous of circumstances.

Firstly, they somehow contrived to rescue the Association from financial collapse after it closed down in 1911 and then made a successful appeal for £1,000 inside a week — a vast sum of money in 1913 — which they carried through by personal persuasion.

Secondly, after the war was over they spearheaded a move to new premises in the Promenade when Rickerby personally guaranteed the overdraft, and that after being the recruiting officer for the town and losing his only son during hostilities.

Despite their full-time jobs they ran regular Bible studies for pupils from Cheltenham College at Pruen's premises in Lypiatt Road on Sunday afternoons. In addition, Rickerby was also Chairman of Governors at Dean Close School, and of the Children's Special Service Mission now the Scripture Union, an international Christian organisation with national offices in London.

the autumn, presumably a scout camp in Lanarkshire. The Scouting and YMCA links are well documented with Baden-Powell starting his Boy Scout movement at Birkenhead YMCA in the previous year, 1908, thus making Cheltenham YMCA one of the earliest Scout troops in the country and a testimony to Baden-Powell's change from an active serving Army officer to a more peace-loving role in his later years, trying to build bridges between communities rather than knocking them down.

****

Out of funds, the Association reluctantly shut down in 1911. It was not a situation which had been tolerated lightly and given the high profile of the Vice-Presidents and Committee it was not surprising that a fresh start was quickly made. It had happened before and was about to happen again. The *Gloucestershire Echo* of April 29th, 1913, reported that thanks to a generous bequest of £250 by the late Mr. Leslie Young, augmented by subscriptions from other sources, Cheltenham YMCA had just been resuscitated, and reopened in the same premises at 31 Cambray.

Two meetings were held during the day, one in the afternoon the other during the evening. The afternoon chairman was Rev. A.P. Cox who recalled how as a young man he had been in Exeter Hall, London when it became the centre of the YMCA movement and remembered Rev. Charles Spurgeon, the great Baptist preacher, being present. He believed there were many who felt that if the letters "YMCA" were missing from a town then the town itself was lacking. He hoped the local churches would support the reopening in Cheltenham (applause). The Rev. A. Weaver Evans supported him and suggested the YMCA would not detract from local churches but enhance and help them in training future ministers.

The building had been renovated and redecorated and it was the intention to rent out the lower portion, the rent to be used for general maintenance. How surprised they would have been to know that in another century's time the ground floor would be used for selling mobile phones! £100 was still required to cover the original debt, of which £30 had already been pledged. A new secretary called William C. Turner with previous YMCA experience in Salisbury, Birmingham and Bristol, succeeded Mr. E. Jefferies. Short addresses were also given by Mr. H.A. Dennis of the YMCA National Council who brought greetings from the Egyptian branch in Cairo! Mr. W.A. Boyd, secretary of the Western Division which covered Somerset, Gloucestershire and Wiltshire, also gave a brief address.

The evening meeting was presided over by Dr. S.T. Pruen who was delighted by the large and youthful attendance, showing the need for a "YM" presence in the town. The Rev. Dr. Harvey Jellie also spoke, together with Mr. Dennis and Mr. Boyd. Musical solos were rendered by Mr. Bert Taylor and Mr. Sidney Rayner.

A brief report of the proceedings also appeared in the *Cheltenham Looker-On* dated May 3rd in which a picture of William Turner took pride of place. A social magazine, it dealt only with events deemed worthy of attention by the middle and upper classes, in some respects a forerunner of county magazines.

How to deal with the remaining debt? A small pocket book turned up among the archives which probably belonged to the Treasurer of the time, Major Rickerby. In it was a painstaking series of lists documenting subscriptions for various meeting ranging from a halfpenny up to twopence and against many names was what is presumed to be the home location of the person concerned. Some of the men described as "local" were just that, including Arthur Broom who was killed in action at Gallipoli in 1915, aged just 20. A keen participant in open air meetings, he has no known resting place.

Among others who later perished during the Great War was the name of Gordon Cummings but two others are also of particular interest. Was the entry for Baden-Powell on November 29th, 1909, the same man who started the Boy Scouts? Almost certainly because he was no stranger to Cheltenham and his close association with the YMCA caused him to start his "Scouting for Boys" the previous year. Another name, Flecker, was either the first headmaster of Dean Close School, William Flecker who later became a Vice-

President of the local Association, or possibly his famous son, poet James Elroy Flecker, who sadly died in 1915 from tuberculosis aged only 30.

This pocket book faithfully recorded entries up until 1910 but then was turned back to front and the rest of it consists of newspaper cuttings, initially pre-war, followed by detailed accounts of early YMCA war work. One significant factor is that a big appeal was launched to try and offset the deficit after moving to 31 Cambray. The target was a massive £1,000 to be raised inside a week. Under the guidance of a YMCA expert from London, several prominent people were visited personally, the first of whom, Mr. Unwin of Arle Court, immediately pledged £250 providing the rest of the money could be found by others. Not only was the figure achieved inside seven days but surpassed! To put the amount in perspective it was approximately five times the annual income of Cheltenham YMCA at the time and probably akin to hundreds of thousands of pounds today, possibly as much as a million!

A local newspaper cutting described what happened as almost beyond belief and confided it had been favoured with the names of subscribers but that they were not for general release. That list, however, was published two years later in the 1915 Annual Report on a separate page entitled "Debt Extinction Fund". It included £100 donated by both John Player of tobacco fame and J. McClymont Reid, plus various gifts of £50, two of which were anonymous. Other interesting names included Sir James Horlick, Bart.; London City and Midland Bank; His Worship the Mayor, William Nash Skillicorne; and many other local dignitaries. Testimony was given to the hard work of Secretary, William Turner, and to Messrs. Pruen and Rickerby for promoting the campaign.

It came not a moment too soon because before very long the country was plunged into conflict when Cheltenham YMCA did not shirk its duties. The mortgage arrears had finally been paid off and Cheltenham YMCA found itself free of debt for the first time in 14 years. The original planned extension included a billiards room but every inch of space was now needed for a much more important purpose, that of accommodating soldiers on active service, as explained in the next chapter.

Just prior to the Great War the person temporarily appointed to take charge of 31 Cambray was a young man called Daniel Beak whose leadership qualities obviously shone through because after enlisting on the lowest rank he was awarded the DSO, MC and Bar! Then, to follow this, in 1918 he was awarded the Victoria Cross! His time in charge at the YMCA was relatively brief because he was deputising for his friend, the secretary William Turner who was ill, but the local paper suggested he had been resident for two years. He was gazetted for the VC following action as a Temporary Commander in the Royal Naval Volunteer Reserve at Logeast Wood in France, when he charged several machine gun posts and took a dozen prisoners. He returned to Cheltenham on September 26th, 1919 when he was met at the station by the Mayor, Town Clerk, Rector, and Major Rickerby. Cheltenham YMCA was very proud of its former leader and announced: "Commander Beak came as a guest of the local YMCA where he will stay for an indefinite period".

Born in Southampton in 1891 but a resident of Salisbury, he was very well thought of but was soon on the move again. After joining the Army as a professional soldier in 1920, he rose to the rank of Major General, commanded the 1st Battalion of the South Lancashire Regiment and saw further active service during the Second World War in both France and Malta. He died at Swindon in May 1967.

****

That Cheltenham YMCA had been temporarily back in the doldrums cannot be denied but from now on it quickly shook off its lethargy and got back to business with a vengeance. It was clearly up to the job when the war ended because within three years it had moved to spacious new premises in the Promenade. There must have been wealthy backers, almost certainly found via and among the familiar local family names which kept cropping up. We may also safely assume that great compassion was evident towards the thousands of young men who had survived the wartime atrocities. Sadly, returning to what they thought would

> William Turner was an outstanding Secretary of Cheltenham YMCA who began his service before the First World War in May 1913, and then took on the unenviable task of equipping and converting the premises at 31 Cambray for occupation by visiting servicemen. By all accounts he was extremely successful and was publicly applauded for his efforts. It must have been heart-rending, however, to see around 40 of his members killed during the conflict, approximately one quarter of all who volunteered.
>
> After the war was over, Turner switched his attention to supporting Messrs. Rickerby and Pruen in a high-profile move from Cambray to the Promenade. He was also involved in the national post-war campaign to raise money for YMCA huts for surrounding villages, the provision of wartime "Red Triangle Huts" having been a major triumph across Europe during the war itself. At the time the YMCA was seen as one of the most important organisations in the rebuilding of the nation, with King George V himself commenting publicly on its vital future role.

be a land fit for heroes they were to be initially disappointed and quickly disillusioned. Along with other charitable bodies, Cheltenham YMCA did what it could for these men and their dependants and in 1919 took a huge leap into the unknown. Two years later it was installed on the Promenade in the most central of locations.

****

ADDENDUM TO CHAPTER 3

"OTHER DAYS AT THE YMCA, THE MOVEMENT FROM 1856 TO 1897"

This article appeared in the *Gloucestershire Echo* on December 27th, 1927 and was written by H.T. (Horace Trinley) Bush. At the time a young man of only 25, he later became Mayor of Cheltenham, an Alderman and both Chairman and President of Cheltenham YMCA. Unfortunately, he died aged only 56 in January 1958, thus depriving the local Association of the benefits of his wisdom and old age. Given the introductory paragraph of his piece, this was sad indeed. However, it is such an important archive that it is repeated here almost verbatim but with additional notes added by the author to place the facts in context.

The narrative reads:"Life moves so quickly and holds so many interests nowadays that it is seldom one has the opportunity of giving much attention to matters of even recent history, so it was a particular pleasure to me lately to be able to examine with some care all the existing records of our local branch of the YMCA from its first formation to the end of the last century.

These proved so interesting that I determined to summarise the story of the movement in the town during this period both for the sake of recalling old times to those who took an active part in the work then, and so that those who have more recently become associated with the YMCA may know something of the efforts of their predecessors to win a worthy place for the cause in Cheltenham.

A beginning was made in 1855 and again in 1863. Both of these attempts appear to have failed as the earliest records of a really vigorous organisation is dated 1866 when a committee of twelve, including the Rev. Dr. Brown, Dr. Turnbull, Rev. T. Macpherson, Mr. W. Moody Bell and Mr. John Playle were appointed to draw up a programme of activities at Clarence Parade Hall, (a.k.a. Promenade House) the headquarters then occupied by arrangement with Messrs. Young and Gilling, and now being converted into new premises for the *Gloucestershire Echo*.

▲ On Friday, September 26th 1919, the most decorated member of Cheltenham YMCA, Commander Daniel Beak VC, DSO, MC came to visit his friend, William Turner, the local Association Secretary for whom he had deputised briefly before the war when he was a resident. Seen here at Lansdown Station are believed to be, from left to right, the Mayor (Alderman A.J. Bendall), Daniel Beak, the Town Clerk (Robert Owen Seacome), an unidentified railwayman, and Major Rickerby, the YMCA Treasurer. Beak later joined the Army and rose to the rank of Major-General.

Their labours resulted in Prayer Meetings on Friday evenings and on the first Sunday afternoon in each month, also in a conversational Bible Class which met on Tuesday evenings. The rate of subscription was fixed at four shillings, but soon afterwards was reduced to half-a-crown.

1867 is noteworthy because during that year Mr. Horsley of High Street, was elected to membership and as he still belongs to the YMCA he has the honour of being the 'Father' of the Cheltenham branch. Several ministers in the town were elected as Vice-Presidents, including Dr. Walker and Rev. R.E. Trye of Leckhampton who appears to be the only one still living. Mr. Horace Edwards joined the Association in 1868 and in 1869 Rev. T.W. Jex Blake, Principal of Cheltenham College and subsequently Headmaster of Rugby School and Dean of Wells Cathedral. During this latter year the Association added a summer outing to its attractions, the first one being to Moss Green Shrubberies at Bushley, each member bringing his own packet of tea, all of which would be emptied together into one pot. The economical plan enabled the treasurer, Mr. Albert Beckinsale, to defray the whole of the expenses at a charge of 1s 6d per head.

A change of premises was made in 1870 when three rooms were acquired at 2 Cambray. The move seems to have proved popular because there was an influx of new members, including Dr. Pearce, Mr. S. Batten, Major-General Budd, Mr. Beetham, Mr. W.C. Channon, Mr. H.G. Beard, Mr. J.S. Bartholomew, and Mr. Sexty of Winchcombe. But this prosperity was short lived. The landlord, noting the prosperity of his new tenants, raised the rent by 50% and the Association had to be dissolved, a new one, however, being formed very speedily with Baron de Ferrieres as President.

Unfortunately, dark clouds still overhung the Association and at the end of 1873 nobody could be found to take over the work of the treasurer which Mr. Beckinsale had laid down. All search proving to be in vain it was decided definitely to wind up the Association, this decision being confirmed by the members at their general meeting in January 1874. Six months notice was given to the landlord and preparations made to leave in the following June.

But the branch was not destined to die. The secretary of Worcester YMCA, hearing the work was to be abandoned in Cheltenham, wrote suggesting simultaneous prayer meetings here and in Worcester to ask that young men might be found to uphold the cause. This proposal was welcomed and both meetings were duly held. The cynic may laugh at the suggestion that these prayers had an immediate answer but the fact remains that in June, Mr. J.C. Cooper offered to assume the responsibilities of the Treasurer so the notice was cancelled and the work carried on.

A very successful mission was organised by the YMCA in 1875, open air meetings being held on Monday, Wednesday and Friday evenings, and twice on Sundays. The services were held in different parts of the town and large crowds listened to the addresses and joined in the singing of Sankey's hymns.

Another change of premises took place in 1876, this time a move being made to 396 High Street. The Sunday evening meetings proved very popular here, indeed they became a little too popular because eventually complaints reached the committee about the noise disturbing the neighbours. This was remedied by the appointment of regular stewards to keep the peace and by asking a policeman to stand outside in the passage until the meeting was over!

Various expenses, including the cost of removal, had seriously depleted the exchequer and this question too was successfully tackled by the committee, who interviewed all the parsons in the town, asking them to preach sermons in their churches for the YMCA, the collections being given to reduce the deficit on the balance sheet.

▲ Dr. William Hutton was President of Cheltenham YMCA in 1907.

Early in 1876 it was resolved to appoint for the first time, a paid 'secretary' or 'missionary' but circumstances arose which prevented this being done. Difficulty came about through machinery being set in motion over the rooms of the Association and members complained that the Reading Room had consequently become uninhabitable. This trouble turned out to be very serious and resulted in the Association being homeless from January to September 1879, when a new start was made at 7 Clarence Street.

One of the first activities here was to send a petition to Parliament through the Borough MP, Baron de Ferrieres, praying that all public houses might be closed on Sundays. This was signed by 130 people.

The Association suffered the loss of Mr. C. Williams of Cavendish House from the General Committee in December, 1880, but fortunately his resignation was not prompted by any lack of interest because we find him taking an active part in the general meeting of 1881, after which the Association again moved house, to rooms over Mr. Pilley's shop in North Street. It was resolved that in these new quarters the use of the harmonium be restricted to 'recognised players only'. Doubtless thereby hangs a tale. Mr. Kilminster started a shorthand class in October 1882, and at the end of the same year a watch-night prayer meeting was held, beginning at half-past-ten and finishing at half-past-twelve.

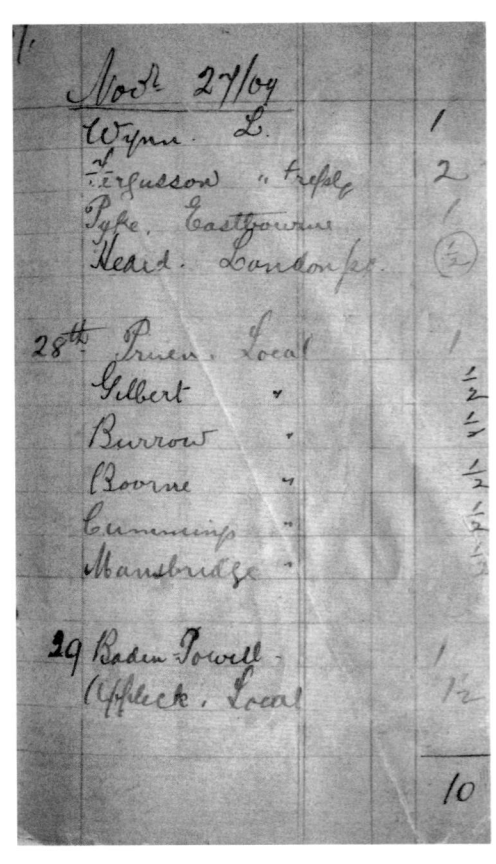

◀ ▶ Two pages from what is presumed to be a pocket book started by Major Rickerby in 1909.
The entry for "Baden-Powell" on November 29th 1909 is almost certainly the founder of the Boy Scout movement which he began the previous year at Birkenhead YMCA. A local Cheltenham YMCA troop started soon afterwards. "B-P" was no stranger to the town and made The Famous outfitters the first official Scout stockist.
Another entry (right) is "Flecker" from Dean Close School but was it father or son? The pocket book, sadly, was soon converted into a First World War diary of local YMCA newspaper cuttings and not all these people survived!

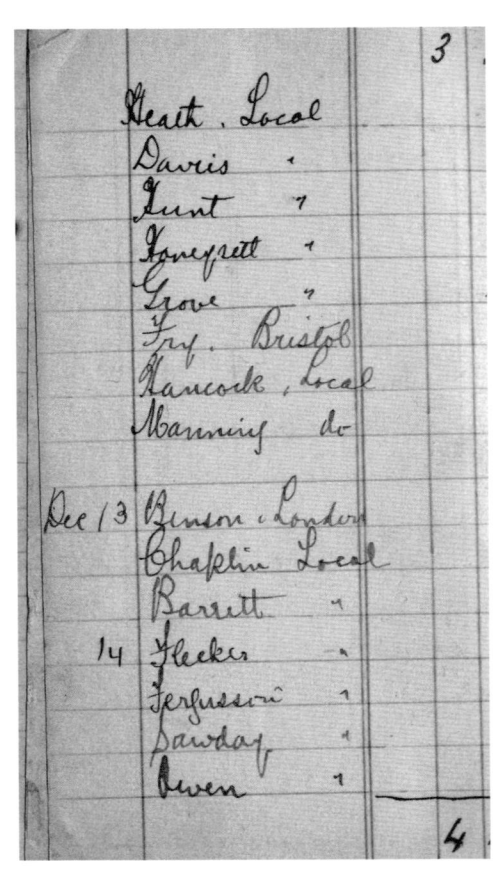

The Secretary's report to the general meeting in 1884 gives an excellent summary of the work of the Association at the time: "The week began with a Prayer Meeting on Sunday morning at 7.30; a Bible Class in the afternoon and another Prayer Meeting in the evening. Tuesday evening was similarly occupied and on Wednesday, the officers met for Bible reading at noon. On Thursday, the members had their Bible Class. During the period under review the Association conducted another open air mission and Mr. J. Marshall worked very hard to make a success of the Book and Tract Department. Dennis Mills was secretary of the Mutual Improvement Class and a special week of prayer for young men brought in 69 new members and associates, bringing the numbers on the books to 200." All this was considered very encouraging by General McKenzie (Chairman) and on the motion of Mr. A. Cummings, seconded by Mr. Slade, the report was unanimously adopted.

One of the Society's red letter days was chronicled in April, 1884, when Mr. George Williams, the honoured pioneer of the movement, came to Cheltenham and met 60 of its members. Altogether, 1884 must be considered as outstanding in the affairs of Cheltenham YMCA, as it welcomed to the work of the organisation such valued supporters as Dr. S.T. Pruen, Mr. E.G. Clare, and Mr. Robert Ley Wood, with Mr. Dennis Mills offering himself for service on the mission field. He was accepted for training at the Grattan Institute, the head of which, Dr. Grattan Guinness, came here in 1886 and conducted a mission on behalf of the Association. Later in the year, Mr. W. Vale, previously of Cheltenham YMCA, was transferred again from Brighton and has since been continuously a member of this branch.

Towards the close of 1888 the rooms of the Association were refurnished, the expense of which it was proposed to defray by asking the Rector, Canon Bell, to deliver a public lecture.

Little worthy of note took place in 1889-90 except that the annual report for the former year recorded that Dr. Pruen was working as a missionary at Riga and Mr. Dennis Mills was in China."

****

In fact Pruen had already spent three years working in Africa because in 1891 he published a book entitled *The Arab and the African; Experiences in Eastern Equatorial Africa During*

▲ *The Cheltenham YMCA Wednesday football team of 1913, many of whom went off to war the following year. A.N. Cole from The Famous outfitters is holding the flag back left. His eldest son Percy is in the flat cap kneeling left. Next to him, with the moustache, is his second son, Reg, who was killed in the war (see page 39), while his youngest son, Jack, is the mascot sitting cross-legged at the front.*

a Residence of Three Years. He returned to England in time to preside at the annual meeting in June, 1891, when he was elected Vice-Chairman and Treasurer, Mr. Robert Ley Wood becoming Chairman and Mr. H.W. Broom, secretary.

Dr. Septimus Tristram Pruen MRD FRCS, to give him his full title, now began to play a key role in the promotion of the local Association and had been Chairman for many years by the time the new Promenade premises were opened in 1921. He was also an active church warden at Christ Church from 1914 to 1929, and, in conjunction with Major Rickerby, continued to be a vital driving cog in the YMCA machinery right until his death, aged 76 following a long illness, in February 1936. He had been awarded the YMCA's highest honour, the Gold Order of the Red Triangle the previous year. The *Echo* recorded his death on February 19th and mentioned his medical missionary time in Africa together with a book he published in 1925 entitled *The Bible, the Poor Man and the Scientist*. Also Vice-Chairman of the Board of Governors at Dean Close, he was a Fellow of the Royal Geographical Society, a member of the National Church Assembly, a member of the Gloucester branch of the British Medical Association, and an avid croquet player. His first wife, Constance Helen Hutchinson died in 1915 by whom he had one son and three daughters. In 1924 he married Evelyn Mary Arbuthnot.

To Pruen and his close friend, Major Rickerby, Cheltenham YMCA owes a huge debt and it seems quite clear that without their dedicated leadership and commitment, the Association would have sunk without trace before the First World War. Instead, as mentioned earlier, they spearheaded a massive publicity campaign which raised more than £1,000 in less than a week. Today's Cheltenham YMCA is their memorial.

****

"In 1890 Miss Beetham presented 50 books to serve as a library, for the use of the local preachers and others who would appreciate the opportunity of using the Association rooms for the preparation of their work. Mr. Edward E. Evans of Stroud wrote to the Committee in 1892 saying that the National Council of the YMCA, at their regional conference at Bridgwater, had appointed him to look after the interest of the work in Cheltenham, and offered any assistance he could.

One of the members made a speech at the general meeting of 1893 deploring the "Laodicean state of the Association"[1] and several suggestions were forthcoming for improvement. Somebody suggested that to be accommodated as they were in North Street was hiding the light of the YMCA under a bushel and somebody else declared that a member of the committee should be present every evening to welcome newcomers. Mr. Slade offered to give a limelight lecture free of charge. This was accepted and it was also agreed to hold conversazione, all items for the programme to be submitted for the approval of the Committee at least a week previously.

January 1894, saw the Association organise another petition, this time to the Mayor and Corporation. It had been cold enough to make Pittville Lake safe for skating which had been permitted on Sunday in return for a fee charged by the Council. A memorial protesting against this was presented to the Street Improvement Committee on behalf of the YMCA by Mr. Ley Wood, Dr. Pruen, Mr. Wynn and Mr. Masters (Secretary). In reply, the Corporation made no very definite promise but resolved in future to endeavour to make 'arrangements that will meet, so far as possible, all objections that can rightly be made.'

Mr. George Williams was knighted by the Queen in 1894 and received the congratulations of branches of the YMCA all over the country, the Cheltenham committee reminding him that without his generous contribution of 10 guineas a year, it would have been difficult for them to carry on.

In September, the open air service at the fountain in the Promenade had to be removed to the Clarence Lamp near Cavendish House, the authorities holding that meetings by the fountain resulted in damage being done by the public, apart from obstruction of the traffic. The annual meeting in December elected Mr. W.H. Broom as treasurer in place of Dr. Pruen, who was made a vice-president and invited to give a series of addresses on "Prophecy" on Sunday evenings, and to introduce also a few words "suitable for the unsaved".

Mr. W.R. Lane held a mission for the Association early in 1895 and September witnessed another change of home. The committee had decided to follow the thorny path of the boarding housekeeper and with this in view took over 7 Cambray. Miss Stanley of Chipping Campden was appointed honorary lady superintendent and the opening of the new premises was celebrated by a house warming party, at which the President, Mr. Ley Wood, described the difficulty the Association had in finding a house suitable for the work they proposed to carry on. They had almost decided after three months search, to consent to the building of a suitable place, when by good fortune they heard of these very suitable quarters in Cambray. The members would here enjoy all the advantages of a club, while the religious side of the work would be by no means neglected. As evidence of the value attached to this, he mentioned they had 130 full members with eight associates.

Amongst those present at this opening night were Mr. Creese, the first secretary Cheltenham YMCA ever had; Mr. G.H. Wynn, another former secretary; Mr. C. Masters, then acting in that capacity; Mr. F. Shirer; Dr. Pruen; Mr. T.E. Rickerby; and Rev. J. Glass, curate of the Parish Church and now Vicar of Leyton.

Great hopes were entertained for the success of the hostel and an advertisement of its attractions was placed in the *Echo* for a week. To the surprise of the committee, this did not have the expected good result owing, it was found, to the rule that no smoking was permitted. So a new rule was made allowing smoking in the dining room only and before very long the house was full again.

It is interesting to note that the Association enjoyed the active co-operation of three well-known clerics, the Rector, Rev. E.L. Roxby; Rev. H.S. de Candole, Vicar of St. James', now Dean of Bristol; and Rev. C. de Carteret, curate of the Parish Church, now Bishop of Jamaica.

Some of the boarders had to be taken to task in August and were reported by Miss Stanley to the committee. Three of them were summoned to appear 'on the carpet' and explain their grievances, which they appear to have been very willing to do. All that was really wrong was the posting of the rules of the Association in the bed-

Cricket was an extremely important game right up until the last 25 years of the 20th Century when, in the face of an ever increasing pace of life, its time consuming and labour intensive nature caused it to fade from the school curriculum. Its social value remains unchanged but fewer people now play the game.

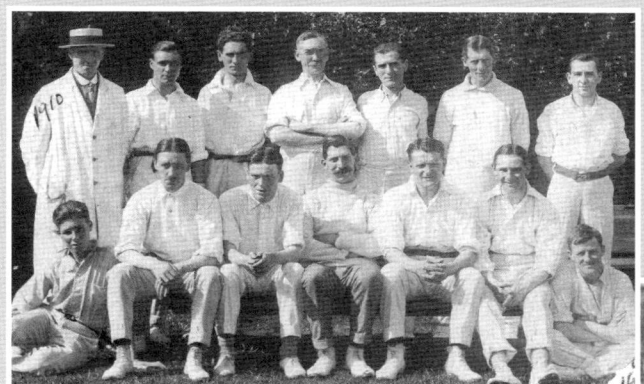

Cheltenham YMCA ran several cricket teams both before and after the First World War. Although the picture above is captioned "1910" and that on the right "1921" it seems the captions may have been altered in error. It is highly unlikely that everyone survived the war and one wonders how many players are in both photographs?

rooms. This ruffled the dignity of the young gentlemen and one of them was so irate that the Secretary was instructed to see him off the premises. Poor secretary! How many and varied are his duties, even to being Sergeant-at-Arms. But this trouble was soon smoothed over and the offending rules displayed in a more suitable position.

Mr. Lane conducted another mission for the YMCA early in 1897 with exceptionally good results. Over 1,000 people attended every evening and there were 800 men at the gathering on Sunday afternoon. 60 persons gave in their names as having been saved or received blessing. This success prompted the committee to depute its evangelistic work to a special sub-committee with Mr. A.N. Cole as secretary.

Later in the year the branch, 'so far unbent' to use the words of one of the local newspapers, 'as to indulge in the mild frivolity of a conversazione and concert at Bennington Hall, where the general happiness which breathed throughout the gathering, which included a large number of the fair sex, amply proved that there is no truth in the libel that the members of the excellent Association in question are noted for long faces and a seriousness above their years.' Bennington Hall, now converted into flats, was situated on St. Margaret's Road between Bennington Street and Oxford Passage, opposite what was once the Black and White Coach Station which, in pre-motorway days, was second only to Victoria Coach Station in London for midday interchanges involving buses from all over the country. The premises were strongly connected with early children's Sunday school work in Cheltenham and the Bennington Trust was still in operation in 2005 giving grants to local churches for children's Christian work.

And so, brought within 30 years of the present year of grace, we take leave of the YMCA as it was known to the 19th Century and pay tribute to those who fought the battles of the red triangle in days gone by and maintained the cause through many discouragements. Some of these men, no longer young in years but green in spirit, are active in the movement today. The Association may count itself fortunate still to command their interest and the benefit of their long experience in going forward to the tasks of the future."

****

The final sentence could be said of H.T. Bush himself, who crammed a great deal into a relatively short life and to whom Cheltenham YMCA owes a great debt of gratitude.

[1] This is a Biblical reference in Revelation, Chapter 3 verses 14-22, where the church in Laodicea, Asia Minor, is referred to as being "lukewarm".

CHAPTER 4
FIRST WORLD WAR 1914-1918

Nobody thought it would actually happen but when it did nobody thought it would last more than a few weeks. However, as the weeks turned into months and the months turned into years, so the emerging catastrophe took a massive and progressive toll on the whole of Europe. The YMCA, by now an international organisation, moved quickly and it is helpful to give a brief overview before turning to Cheltenham itself.

The red triangle was adopted as the official logo and YMCA Red Triangle huts sprang up all over the place. Headed YMCA notepaper was used by servicemen to write home and YMCA helpers did what they could in the face of appalling casualties. When the war was over King George V spoke of how well placed the YMCA was to help those in need and even more huts were established in outlying districts, including villages around Cheltenham.

A 1918 National YMCA hut week appeal brought in local donations of staggering proportions. Cheltenham College topped the list with £900 which was four times the annual income of Cheltenham YMCA! Dean Close School chipped in with £500, and F. Treherne Thomas and Mrs. Thomas jointly donated a further £500, with John Player giving the same amount. Arnold Webb gave £250 with nine others giving £100 each. As described in the previous chapter, some of these people had already forked out huge sums to rescue Cheltenham YMCA from debt just before the war. Many smaller donations were made which just shows the effect that the YMCA had on the national psyche at the time. Offerings for the Cheltenham War Memorial which was erected in the early-1920s, were meagre by comparison. The letters "YMCA" really meant something!

During the actual conflict, thousands of YMCA service centres were set up all over Europe, Russia and the Middle East. Princess Helena Victoria, a granddaughter of Queen Victoria, allied herself closely with the YMCA and recruited 50,000 ladies to the ranks of YMCA war workers. A series of "Red Triangle Clubs" were established in the many huts at home and abroad where servicemen could expect to find "billiards, tea and a warm welcome"! Read on ….

****

It all began with high hopes but the 1915 Cheltenham YMCA Annual Report, entitled "Growth", gave news of what was to come. Of the initial local membership of 140, no fewer than 78 had joined the Army with the remainder described as too old, too young, or ineligible for other reasons. The local Association certainly rallied to the

▶ *The Red Triangle was adopted as the new YMCA logo during the First World War, or Great War as it was referred to at the time. It was a stroke of genius to adopt a symbol so simple and colourful and it has been recognised all round the world ever since.*

A series of timber-framed buildings, known as Red Triangle huts, were established right across the war zone where servicemen could be sure of a warm welcome. In addition to refreshments, they could apparently expect to find a billiard table! The YMCA also provided large tents on training grounds such as Salisbury Plain, where many Cheltenham volunteers worked tirelessly.

▸ *This sad page from the 1916 Cheltenham YMCA Annual Report was the precursor to more deaths. Reg Cole was part of the family firm which still own The Famous outfitters in the High Street, Arthur Broom was an active participant in YMCA open air meetings, while Charles Wigley, a member of the Royal Army Medical Corps, was shot by a sniper at night.*

cause with members being encouraged to train in Swedish drill in order to bring them up to the necessary standard prior to enlisting. When one considers that the Cheltenham recruiting officer was none other than the YMCA Treasurer, Major Rickerby, this is hardly surprising. Among them was his own son, more of whom later.

Those left behind busied themselves in making the rooms and facilities available and welcoming for visiting soldiers. Several volunteered for stints of two to three weeks and five others, Messrs. W.P. Walker, E.M. Kearsey, F.W. King, R.C. Keen and W.J.D. Kelland pledged themselves to working until the end of the war, whenever that might come, in the YMCA huts and tents on Salisbury Plain and across the South of England. How could they have known the war would not end until 1918?

Bible Classes and Prayer Meetings were held regularly but the deaths were reported of Mr. W.T. Lee, "a well-known Christian controversialist" — a phrase which did not mean the same as it does today — and a cheerful and genial member called Cecil Pugh. The brief text for 1915 ended with some lines found in the Prayer Book of a young soldier already killed in the war:

"Just as I am, young, strong and free,
To be the best that I can be.
For truth and righteousness, and Thee,
Lord of my life, I come!"

It was an ironic epitaph which, sadly, was to be repeated many more times before hostilities ended. A tragic and costly waste of life for everyone.

****

In their book *Leaving All That was Dear, Cheltenham and the Great War*, Joseph Devereux & Graham Sacker listed four men who were specifically connected with Cheltenham YMCA but died on active service abroad:

Members of the Cheltenham Y.M.C.A. who have fallen in action.

"They counted not their lives dear unto themselves."

Lance-Corpl. C. J. WIGLEY, R.A.M.C.
Killed in action on May 15th, 1915. His Captain wrote: "I do not think any of us was so well prepared for death. He has set us a splendid example."

Private REGINALD COLE, 1/5 Gloucester Regt. (T.F.)
Killed in action on May 12th, 1915. His Captain's tribute to him was: "He was a brave lad and always did his duty splendidly."

Private ARTHUR BROOM, 9th Worcester Regt.
Killed in action at the Dardanelles. An earnest Y.M.C.A. Open-air Worker. "He loved to tell to all around What a dear Saviour he had found."

Private Arthur Broom was killed in action at Gallipoli in 1915, aged 20. A member of the Worcestershire Regiment, he also came from Worcester but enlisted in Cheltenham and gave the YMCA as his address where he took part in open air meetings. He has no known resting place.

Private Gilbert John Clissold was born in Cheltenham and worked at The Famous outfitters before going to work for the YMCA in the military training area on Salisbury Plain. He subsequently joined the Duke of Edinburgh's Wiltshire Regiment and was killed during the German offensive at Somme Crossings in 1918, aged 22. He is buried in St. Souplet British Cemetery.

Lance Corporal Joseph (Jack) Hounslow was a member of the Cheltenham YMCA football team pictured in the *Gloucestershire Graphic* on January 31st 1914. He enlisted in the Gloucestershire Regiment and was killed in action at Bihecourt in April 1917, aged 28. He is buried in Vadencourt British Cemetery.

Lance Corporal Charles John Wigley came from Edgbaston in Birmingham but gave his address as

Cheltenham YMCA where he was a resident when he enlisted in the Royal Army Medical Corps attached to the Royal Warwickshire Regiment. He was killed near Ypres in Belgium in May 1915, aged 23, and is buried in the Berkshire Cemetery Extension.

These four men were known to be intimately connected with Cheltenham YMCA but the 1918 Annual Report gave a Roll of Honour with more than 120 members who had enlisted by the end of 1917, of whom 14 were underlined as having lost their lives. Closer research, however, revealed a very different story because more than 30 had been killed by the end of the war, some of whom in the confusion, had either been overlooked or news of the dreaded black-lined telegram sent to the nearest relatives had not filtered through to the local YMCA authorities. Alternatively, they were listed as "missing" but presumed still alive which was quite understandable given slow communications and the fact that men simply vanished off the face of the earth. The Thiepval Memorial near Albert in France lists more than 70,000 men from the Battle of the Somme alone with no known grave!

It is now known that in addition to the four men above, nearly 30 more YMCA members also paid the ultimate personal sacrifice although positive identification of some was impossible because several local people listed had the same name. It also seems likely that many more had tentative connections with the YMCA. Further details may be found in Devereux and Sacker's huge volume mentioned above and in the Bibliography:

When searching for archives to research this book, an extraordinary document turned up in the form of a tiny pocket book which dated from 1909 and seemed to have been initially filled with details of subscriptions mentioned in Chapter 3. It probably belonged to the Treasurer, Major Rickerby which would explain why, when war broke out, that most of it was subsequently filled with newspaper cuttings from which we learn a great deal.

One of the executive committee, Mr. A.(Abraham) N. Cole who acquired the family firm of The Famous outfitters on the High Street, volunteered for "active service" and was one of several YMCA helpers who found themselves on Salisbury Plain. He sent an interesting early letter back to Cheltenham, part of which is reproduced here:

"I thought you would like some impressions of my work here. The YMCA has a tent 160 feet long

---

CHELTENHAM YMCA ROLL OF HONOUR 1914-1918

Morris Avers	Jack Hounslow
Arthur Baldwin	William Hunt
William Bowles	Harold Jacobs
Bert Brazener	Harold Keech
Arthur Broom	Edward Keen
Frank Brown (2 Frank Browns killed from Cheltenham!)	Teddy Lewis
	William Maidment
Gilbert Clissold	Harry Mead
Reg Cole	John Rickerby MC
Charlie Cook	Arthur Smith ? (4 Arthur Smiths killed)
Gordon Cummings	Ernest Smith ? (2 Ernest Smiths killed!)
Arthur Giles	Will Smith ? (5 William Smiths killed!)
Percy Godwin	Sid Thomas ?
Percy Gosling	Cyril Wentworth
Ernest Griffin	Albert White
Alick (Alec) Harris ?	John Wigley
Charles Harwood	George Williams

There must have been many others associated with Cheltenham YMCA during the Great War and although they are anonymous this book pays tribute to them all, whatever their experience or fate.

▶ *All deaths were tragic but this one was particularly poignant. Captain John Harold Ellerson Rickerby was awarded the Military Cross in 1916 for quick thinking in action at Aubers Ridge. An officer in the 2/5 Gloucesters, he was also awarded the Italian Silver Medal for Valour but was killed in the area of Holnon Wood during the German spring offensive of 1918. He was the only child of Major Thomas Ellerson Rickerby, the YMCA Treasurer and recruiting officer for Cheltenham. Despite his grievous loss, Rickerby senior renewed his efforts on behalf of the YMCA and was a key player in the move to the Promenade in 1921.*

which accommodates 2,000 men at a time. We get crowded out from 9am to 9pm with an incessant stream of soldiers, all Canadians. The work is very hard for the four workers because we get an aggregate attendance of 10,000 men. Another 1,000 have come in from Nova Scotia this morning. I arrived at four on Monday and to welcome me I had three biplanes circling the Plain at immense speed.

The difficulty we have is with the money. It is all Canadian and Yankee paper money and I hear their pay is twice that of Kitchener's force. However, one soon gets used to nickels and dimes and dollars and quarters and one, two, five, 10, and 20 dollar bills.

The men are a very fine type. The officers and junior ranks all mingle together when not on parade. Their marching is not as rigid as the English battalions but they never seem to tire.

We have a small kitchen and sleeping bunks and I slept all alone in the big tent last night when the Plain was swept by a tremendous storm. They have some very fine singers and speakers among the men. We distribute 500 active Service Testaments every day, inscribed with the name of the man and his battalion.

I must close. The men are forming queues outside shouting 'What time do you open?' We close for one hour at dinner and tea and we need it too.

We are short of literature but I dare not appeal for it as we have no means of getting it to camp."

****

Another report was sent by Mr. Cole from a different camp but this time by the sea. Unfortunately, he was not allowed to divulge exactly where because of censorship but he wrote about reveille at 5am followed by men marching into the sea in their hundreds for a bathe. The noise and bustle went on until 10pm when after going out for scones and pop for supper his group were challenged with "Halt! Who goes there?" The loud reply was "YMCA!"

One of Cheltenham's oldest shops, The Famous, was acquired by Abraham Cole in 1896. A keen YMCA committee man he allowed its use as a recruitment centre during the First World War.

Several of the Cole family went off to war and this picture, taken at a training camp in Epping Forest, shows Percy Cole standing on the far left. Front left is Ernest Zebedee, who worked loyally at The Famous for more than 50 years!

▲ *This splendid YMCA hut stood at Lansdown Station just to the left of the main entrance. It met the needs of servicemen passing through and occupied the same site as a later Second World War hut.*

resulting in "Right!" Then it was into tent and bed with singing from a thousand tents (but no lights), lasting for more than an hour.

Mr. Cole, who later went to assist the Naval Brigade camped at Crystal Palace, then appealed for funds to be sent to help his YMCA work, which the *Echo* gladly agreed to forward. The YMCA Secretary, William Turner, followed this up with his own letter stating that a YMCA worker had been with every batch of recruits leaving the town so far.

Several more reports came from various camps including one from Mr. Cole stating that six YMCA tents had blown down during a gale at different locations on Salisbury Plain but they were not discouraged and the work of erecting huts and pitching tents would continue as long as there was a need. Back home, various people donated money for YMCA huts and several volunteers left to help, new ones being encouraged to report either to the YMCA at 31 Cambray or to 351 High Street. Although no further details of the latter were given, research quickly established it was home to none other than The Famous outfitters, which is still there today, but now renumbered 208. The connection was obvious because A.N. Cole was founder of

▶ *A.N. Cole acquired The Famous outfitters as a family firm in 1896 and did outstanding work as a YMCA volunteer, especially on Salisbury Plain.*

the family firm which clearly approved of what he was doing and were more than happy to encourage others to join him. Several more Coles were involved but sadly, one of them, Reg Cole, was killed in action.

There was clearly no religious discrimination because a groups of Jews stayed at Cheltenham YMCA and their community later donated money for YMCA huts in recognition of help given to Jewish soldiers by YMCA chaplains. This was at a

42

time when Cheltenham College had a separate Jewish house led by D.L. Lipson a YMCA supporter and future mayor, whose Jewish boys wore yellow tassels on their mortar boards instead of the red of the rest of College.

Another item mentioned a fine "pavilion" supplied by the YMCA for the use of the 3/5 Gloucester Regiment camp at nearby Cranham, and there was also mention of a YMCA sponsored camp at Sneedhams Green near Gloucester. Mr. W.J. Charlton, a member of Cheltenham YMCA but from the North of England, volunteered for work with the Expeditionary Force in France in 1914 and spoke of rising at 4am in order to prepare food and drinks for the troops by 5am, then working non-stop until midnight! Family Services were well-respected by all, and every rank of serviceman was catered for. Particular mention was made of the bravery of troops from the front line.

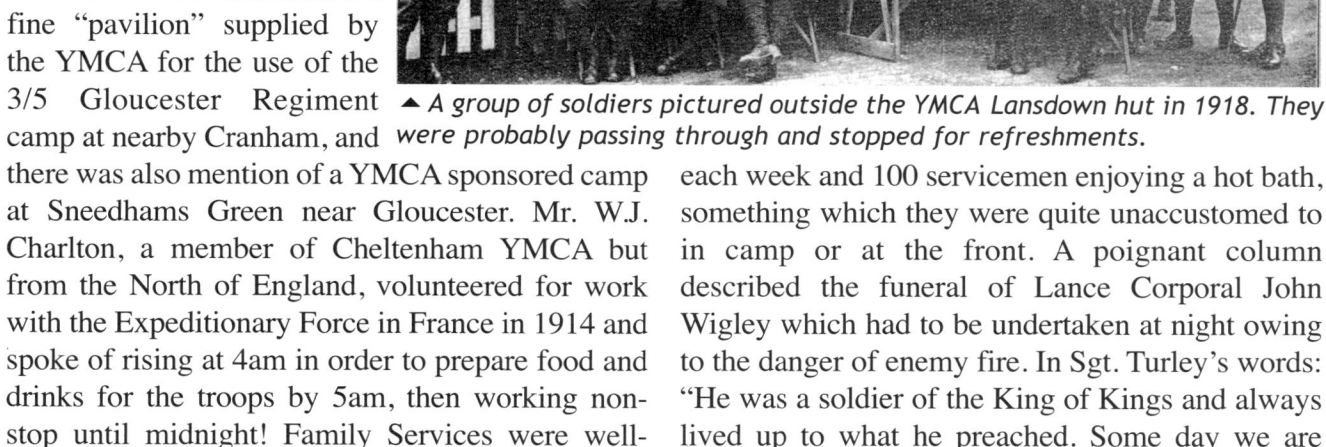

****

Another newspaper cutting explained how Cheltenham YMCA was helping instruct potential recruits in physical training. A harriers club had been formed for regular runs and a faithful band met regularly for prayer. Mr. E. Colwell of Bethesda Brotherhood (presumably from Bethesda Methodist Church) and Mr. H.W. Gill of Kiddieland on the High Street both volunteered for service in the YMCA work camps, ending up with the Royal Engineers at Crowborough in Sussex. Meanwhile, Alfred Purnell was helping Mr. Cole on Salisbury Plain. A letter to the *Echo* from Lt.-Col. H.E. Pritchard, Commanding Officer of the 10th Gloucestershire Regiment, dated November 21st 1914, spoke enthusiastically of the YMCA contribution to his men who were in camp at Codford on the southern edge of Salisbury Plain.

The *Echo* published regular features under the heading "Local War Notes" and the YMCA figured frequently. Its local Cambray HQ was always crowded with an average of 1,000 letters written

▲ *A group of soldiers pictured outside the YMCA Lansdown hut in 1918. They were probably passing through and stopped for refreshments.*

each week and 100 servicemen enjoying a hot bath, something which they were quite unaccustomed to in camp or at the front. A poignant column described the funeral of Lance Corporal John Wigley which had to be undertaken at night owing to the danger of enemy fire. In Sgt. Turley's words: "He was a soldier of the King of Kings and always lived up to what he preached. Some day we are going to build a permanent memorial over his grave so that it can easily be found, should any of his relatives ever make the visit."

Another snippet mentioned the King visiting a YMCA hut and of 10 shillings being donated by a soldier's mother who had been impressed by her son's description of the work being done by the YMCA at his camp.

A vivid description of the Gallipoli Landings made grim reading but the reality was much worse than could be conveyed in a letter. Private Arthur Broom was killed there and a later Cheltenham resident, Captain Richard Willis won the VC there but by the end of the war was the only officer left alive in his battalion. A memorial plaque was unveiled to him at Cheltenham Cemetery in September 2002.

Good news arrived with the announcement that Temporary Commander D. (Daniel) M.W. Beak had been awarded the DSO to go along with his MC and Bar! He was later gazetted for gallantry at Logeast Wood in France, when he charged several machine gun posts and took a dozen prisoners. A former leader at Cheltenham YMCA he was awarded the Victoria Cross for this action and after the war was over, returned to 31 Cambray before enlisting in the Army and rising to the rank of Major General (see Chapter 3).

◀ *An example of the red triangle headed notepaper provided by the YMCA for the use of Armed Services during the war.*

While the war was still unfolding the leaders at Cheltenham YMCA were determined not to let it interfere with their normal activities and a series of Christian Evidence lectures was reported. Other physical activities continued as well as lantern slide evenings. There would have been no shortage of encouragement because of the 41 Vice-Presidents, no fewer than 25 were ordained men, including the Principal of Cheltenham College, Canon Reginald Waterfield, and the Headmaster of Dean Close School, Rev Dr. William Flecker, both of whom saw former pupils cut down in their hundreds. The YMCA President was the Rector of Cheltenham.

The 1916 Annual Report made mention of Mr. J.W. Buckland who lived at Marle Hill, a large Georgian house overlooking Pittville Lake but since demolished, who paid the subscriptions for some of the Cheltenham YMCA men on active service. A room was also placed at the disposal of Rev. T. Cave Moyle, Chaplain to the Forces who held an "At Home" every Tuesday evening which was well attended. In addition, it was publicly stated that the doors were always open to men in uniform whether billeted in the town or simply passing through. A special tribute was paid to the Secretary, William Turner, who succeeded in making Cheltenham YMCA "a home of very high standard".

Mention was also made of the Red Cross affording healing and refuge but that every soldier now recognised the new YMCA Red Triangle as meaning "… the warmest of welcomes and a bright atmosphere of Christian comradeship". The 1916 Report ended with: "Side by side with the appalling unveiling of the human heart seen in German frightfulness has been another unveiling, the opening of heart of brother to brother, which has been followed, as it frequently is, by the opening of heart of sinner to Saviour, so that many who before passed Him by without a thought, have now learnt to love the One they once neglected and to say from the bottom of a full heart – 'I will sing of the Lord because He hath dealt so lovingly with me'."

****

The 1917 Annual Report began by saying that more than 140 local YMCA members were in camps or at the front, two of whom had won the Military Cross and two the Military Medal. Some generous lady friends had also helped to pay the subscriptions for members in absentia.

Thousands of sheets of YMCA headed notepaper were being supplied weekly and special mention was made of a new suite of rooms for boys aged 13-15, a pioneering venture which was well received with 80 young members immediately signing up.

William Turner was not only the hard-working secretary but also Superintendent of the YMCA huts in the area and had overseen the erection of a new hut at the Midland Station at Lansdown which was opened by Earl Beauchamp. Run by Mrs. Becher and a band of ladies the hut established new records each month for the number of soldiers served. Thousands were fed and watered and able to enjoy rest both day and night, the canteen being open 24 hours a day. 40 feet by 15 feet it had a separate kitchen and was located to the left of the main Queen's Road entrance, by the slope leading down to what is the main car park today, the same location as a second but different Lansdown hut which gave splendid service to troops during the Second World War (see Chapter 7).

****

Throughout hostilities, Cheltenham YMCA remained in the capable hands of Dr. Pruen as

▲ *Cheltenham YMCA ran normal activities for those below conscription age and this cricket team seen in summer 1918 shows from left: (standing) Moss, Allen, William Turner (Sec. in uniform), Butler, Stevens: (sitting) Payne, Shelley, Adams, Bloodworth, Satchel: (in front) Hill, Yeend.*

Chairman, Major Rickerby as Treasurer, and William Turner as General Secretary. The Committee of 12 were right behind them as was the long list of Vice-Presidents. By 1918 it was clear that a generation of young men had been wiped out and so the work of encouraging boys had grown apace. Mr. C.F. Argyll-Saxby filled a vital role in this department and mention was made of youngsters being involved in football, cricket, chess, a debating society, rallies, Bible classes, and both Sunday afternoon and evening meetings.

The death was reported of the oldest committee member, Mr. G.H. Wynn and mention was made for the first time of a need for larger premises, something to which Messrs. Pruen and Rickerby swiftly turned their minds and pockets. Indeed, by the time the 1919 Annual Report was published, it was announced that new premises had been acquired in the centre of the town at Numbers 16, 17 and 18 on the Promenade. It was impossible to get any more central than that!

Euphoria was obviously tinged with great sadness but the words of King George V were seized on. In his Victory Message to Parliament he said: "We have to create a better Britain". Cheltenham was going to do its bit and the YMCA was one of its foremost organisations. "Given the necessary funds, the possibilities are almost infinite" shouted the bottom of page 3! The number of members and helpers had been expanded and given the incredible response to fund raising immediately pre-war, the committee was of the opinion that a bright future lay ahead. An account of the opening of the new premises may be found in the next chapter.

****

With 25% of members who had gone to war now dead – a figure mirrored across the whole of Cheltenham – and with many more seriously wounded, Cheltenham YMCA was at the crossroads. It was, however, at great pains to point out that it was not a religion, merely an interdenominational Christian organisation which sought to serve others. "Not only have we made ourselves responsible for the work of this town but by the erection of huts in the surrounding villages, we are endeavouring to arrange that every soldier as he returns to town or country will find that he can obtain clean recreation, good fellowship, and if he prefers it, a quiet reading room near his own home. Will anyone who receives this Report think how best he can help in this work for which everyone is equally responsible?"

The 1919 Report ended: "During the past year we have been able to give meals and recreation to thousands of soldiers, and makeshift sleeping accommodation to hundreds. We desire most warmly to thank all our helpers, especially those many ladies who, amidst the inconveniences of unfinished accommodation and appliances and the awkwardness of building and improvements still in progress, have given us such willing, unwearied and cheerful assistance."

****

There is no doubt about it. During the Great War, Cheltenham YMCA was a beacon of Christianity in every sense of the word.

CHAPTER 5
THE PROMENADE 1921-1939

The First World War of 1914-18, or Great War as it was known at the time, was a truly shocking affair. Untold damage was done to all the nations involved and, almost at a stroke, a whole generation of young men was wiped out. Those surviving were at best traumatised and at worst so severely injured or maimed as to have no real quality of life remaining. The YMCA took a lead nationally and did much to alleviate the problems, followed up at local levels all around the country. Cheltenham was no exception to the rule.

In a relatively short space of time, the local Association went from being moribund in 1911 to being enthusiastically alive by the end of hostilities in 1918. Chairman Dr. Pruen, Treasurer Major Rickerby, and Secretary William Turner were busy beavering away behind the scenes and were undoubtedly the influential power behind the throne. From the proverbial ashes of the immediate pre-war period came a post-war phoenix which, to mix a metaphor, shone out like a beacon.

Cheltenham YMCA actually acquired their Promenade premises in 1919 when they purchased what at the time were numbers 16, 17 and 18, later renumbered 51, 53 and 55. It was a bold and imaginative move from the previous premises in Cambray and cost a great deal of money. It needs to be remembered, however, that the YMCA was extremely well thought of by the whole community, not just locally. A pre-war appeal had wiped out substantial debts and a post-war appeal was also well supported, although there is a limit to people's pockets and a large overdraft had to be taken out, guaranteed personally by Major Rickerby. It took almost two years to renovate and equip the new buildings.

Once the war was over a special leaflet was produced entitled "A Great Achievement (with your help) – Cheltenham YMCA Extension". With the Marquess of Worcester as the President aided by eight Vice-Presidents including the Mayor of Cheltenham, the Bishop of Gloucester and the Principal of Cheltenham College (H.H. Hardy), an appeal was made for £6,000, being the balance of money due on the new premises on top of the £3,500 already given or promised. It should also be remembered this came hard on the heels of a nationwide appeal to build new YMCA huts across the country (see Chapter 4), and to which many people, schools and organisations had already given extremely generously.

Cheltenham was described as having "the largest shifting population of any town in Great Britain." It was a popular training ground for "shop assistants of both sexes, young clerks, apprentices and the like from all over Gloucestershire, the men and women in whose hands are the national destinies of tomorrow, for good or evil". It seems the town was regarded as having made little provision for homecoming soldiers: "Hence it is appropriate that Cheltenham Spa should possess one of the finest provincial YMCAs, the Christian social club which, to every gallant soldier was the 'Home from Home' during the Great War. In these difficult days of reconstruction, it ranks as one of the most potent and popular of agencies for the uplift of the Young Manhood of the Nation."

The ground floor was to accommodate a Reception Hall, Lounge, Restaurant, Offices, Library, Reading Room, Writing Room, Smoking Room, and Cloakrooms. The Concert and Lecture Hall on the first floor would seat 250, with adjacent Classrooms for instruction while the extensive

46

▲ *Taken shortly after the new YMCA premises were opened in the Promenade in 1921, this tranquil picture belongs to a different age. The new art-deco canopy must have seemed out of place to traditionalists.*

Billiard Room on the second floor was to have four tables. Bedroom accommodation was for 20 boarders with an asphalt Tennis Court to be an all year round attraction at the rear (later built on as the Royal Well Hut/gymnasium).

The resident campaign director was Mr. J.H.C. Gordon with Lord Kingsale and Major T.E. Rickerby acting as Hon. Treasurers. The Hon. Financial Secretary was W. Turner Long and the Hon. Secretary was Councillor Ernest Rogers. In today's money the appeal was for several million pounds and although much was willingly given, it should be noted that a separate contemporary local appeal for funds for the war memorial which now stands on the Promenade – almost opposite the new YMCA premises – fell well short of its target. In the event, the total YMCA sum of £6,000 was never realised and the 1930s economic depression later had far reaching consequences which caused part of the premises to be sold off. Nevertheless, by 1921 all was ready for a very special event.

▶ *Major Rickerby and Dr. Pruen were clearly the brains behind the move to 16, 17 and 18 the Promenade, which were seemingly purchased from private vendors in 1919 and then refurbished over the next two years.*

The *Echo* gave considerable coverage to the opening ceremony and on December 6th, 1921, published a long article entitled "Cheltenham YMCA's Great Day. Official Opening of New Headquarters by Field Marshal Sir William Robertson, GCB, GCMG, KCVO, DSO." Far from being born with a silver spoon in his mouth, Sir William started out as a Private before rising to the highest military rank (the only person ever to do so), which meant he could easily relate to the work of the YMCA and he had some sharp words for those who had promised great things after the war ended but had failed to deliver. About the YMCA, however, he was full of praise.

Appointed Field Marshal just a year previously, he had an astonishing Army career. By 1915 he had become Chief of the General Staff of the Expeditionary Force, and from 1915-18 was CIGS (Chief of the Imperial General Staff), followed by Commander-in-Chief of the British Army on the Rhine until 1920. He was greeted in a ceremony outside the new premises by a guard of honour from Cheltenham College OTC, assisted by detachments of the Red Cross, St. John Ambulance, members of the Gloucestershire Constabulary, and the band of the Gloucestershire Hussars Yeomanry.

Arriving by car from the station – although exactly which station was not specified – the Field Marshal was accompanied by the Principal of Cheltenham College, Major H.H. Hardy, whose guest he was for the occasion, and the long serving YMCA member, Major T.E. Rickerby. The general salute was sounded before various dignitaries were presented. Announced by Mr. Gordon, the HQ organising secretary, they included the Mayor (Councillor Clara Winterbotham, the town's first lady mayor, following women receiving the vote in 1918), the Bishop of Gloucester (Dr. E.C.S. Gibson), Lord Kingsale, Sir James Agg-Gardner (Conservative MP for Cheltenham from 1874-1880, 1885-1895, 1900-1906 and 1911-1928), Col. Pearson, the Deputy Mayor (Alderman Margrett), the Town Clerk (Mr. R.O. Seacome), the Rector (Rev. H.A. Wilson), President of the Free Church Council (Rev. F. Wynn), Mr. George Dimmer (former Mayor), Dr. S.T. Pruen (Chairman of Cheltenham YMCA), Mr. E.J. Burrow (YMCA) and Mr. Dyer (YMCA National Council).

The Bishop of Gloucester conducted a short dedication ceremony in the lecture hall after which the Field Marshal declared: "I have great pleasure in formally declaring these premises open, and in doing so wish every success to the good cause for which they have been provided."

This was followed by an inspection of the property when the lady superintendent (Mrs. Kite) and the general secretary (Mr. W.C. Turner) were presented to him. He also signed a copy of his new book *From Private to Field Marshal* and donated it to the YMCA library. The short distance to the local Cenotaph was then covered where Sir William laid a large laurel wreath from the YMCA National Council in London, which enclosed the red triangle, and the initials "YMCA" which had by now become accepted as the international acronym for "Young Men's Christian Association". Appended to the wreath was a large card bearing the following inscription: "This tribute to the heroic devotion of the men of Cheltenham who gave their lives in the service of King and country is placed here by Field Marshal Sir William Robertson, Bart. GCB, on behalf of the National Council of the YMCAs, December 6th, 1921."

At 3.30pm the Mayor and the Extension Committee were "at home" in the Town Hall to a great company of guests in honour of the presence of both Sir William and Sir Arthur Yapp, KBE, the YMCA National Secretary. 1,400 people were received in the Drawing Room before proceeding into the main hall where the Municipal Orchestra under Mr. Leo Dawes were "performing a bright selection of music." The guard of honour on this occasion was formed by the Cheltenham Company of the Territorials, consisting almost entirely of veterans with several medals attached to their chest. Inspected by Sir William, they were under the command of Capt. Wynter Morgan MC, and Lieut. King Higgs.

The Mayor made much of previous Military visits, citing both the Duke of Wellington and Field Marshal Earl Roberts. She pointed out the strong military ties of the town and how delighted everyone was with the visit of Sir William. He responded by saying how much pleasure it had given him to be present and mentioned the first time he had visited the town in 1876 to watch Nottinghamshire

▲ *Leaving the newly opened Promenade premises on December 6th, 1921. Following the ceremonial mace-bearer are the first Lady Mayor of Cheltenham, Clara Winterbotham, and guest of honour Field Marshal Sir William Robertson, the only man ever to rise from the lowest to the highest rank in the Army. He is just about to lay a wreath (visible on the right) at the nearby war memorial which had been built slightly earlier, although much scaled down in appearance after an appeal for funds fell short of the expected target. It was one of the greatest ceremonial occasions ever witnessed in the town with several uniformed organisations taking part. A large reception was later held at the Town Hall when Sir William warmly praised the YMCA for all the good work it had done, and said how well placed it was to influence the future for good. Among other dignitaries supporting the event were the Principal of Cheltenham College, Major H.H. Hardy; Lord Kingsale; Sir James Agg-Gardner MP; and the Chief Constable, Major Stanley Clarke.*

play cricket against Gloucestershire at the College ground. He also pointed out that no fewer than 2,000 Old Cheltonians (ex-Cheltenham College, known as OCs) had served during the Great War, prior to which many thousands more had served with distinction around the globe. Cheltenham itself had sent out between 12,000 and 13,000 [1] men to the war of whom 1,400 had made the ultimate sacrifice with their lives. Four Victoria Crosses had also been awarded.

Sir William then paid tribute to the Services work done by the YMCA from the Boer War onwards, going so far as to say that the YMCA and other similar organisations such as the Church Army, had played a major role in troop morale. Just as though the Association helped to win the war, so he thought it could help to put things right during "what we call the peace". There had been huge disappointments in post-war society and it seemed to him that the YMCA was an institution peculiarly suitable to helping things along. It was ready to extend a sympathetic hand to anyone needing help and although it realised after all that it was by righteousness that a nation was exalted, it was not everlastingly pushing religion to the front. It seemed to understand the way to a man's soul as being through his body. He therefore hoped the town would come forward and give its fullest support to the YMCA (applause).

Sir Arthur Yapp announced that £6,000 [2] was needed in connection with the establishment of the new premises. "Afternoon tea was afterwards served in the two supper rooms by George's Ltd., who had fitted up a great length of buffet to cope with the catering for so big a company." At 5.30pm the Field Marshal and Sir Arthur Yapp visited the Ladies' College and the day was rounded off by a Smoking Concert at the YMCA to which members and male friends were invited (a man's world!).

The newspaper concluded that "the whole of the arrangements of the day were organised and carried through in a remarkably businesslike manner."

In keeping with its go ahead image, a posh modern Art Deco canopy was erected over the entrance to the new premises. Supported from above by iron stanchions the semi-circular sign stated, in bold capital letters, "YMCA". There was no doubting its presence in the centre of town now!

The new billiards room was clearly a big attraction and was a natural progression from a game which proved hugely popular with servicemen during the First World War. Most YMCAs owned at least one table but it later gave way to snooker, a 19th Century activity invented by an Indian Army officer but which also faded from the scene in the face of post-war more strenuous activities.

The first enthusiastic Prospectus & Programme for the new premises was a 36 page affair published for 1921-1922. The President was the Rector of Cheltenham, Canon H.A. Wilson, the Chairman was Dr. Pruen and the Hon. Treasurer, Major Rickerby. It is to these last two men that Cheltenham YMCA must pay homage for their vision and dedication because without them the red triangle might have disappeared from the town. The General Secretary was long-serving William Turner and among the Committee of ten was George Hitchman who was also to play a significant future role. The status of the local Association was contained in the telling statement: "Most of the clergy and ministers of the town and a number of influential laymen, are Vice-Presidents, the names of whom are published in the Annual Report."

Bedrooms cost from between eight and 12 shillings per week (meals extra) with the lady superintendent, Mrs. Kite, in charge of housekeeping. The restaurant was open to members, non-members and ladies, with a wide variety of dishes costing between one shilling, and one shilling and fourpence. Vegetables ranged in price from twopence to threepence, with coffee, cocoa and cream also at threepence but tea and chocolate at fourpence. Separate "popular teas" – often referred to as "high teas" – cost between ninepence, and one shilling and sixpence.

The list of activities began with "Spiritual Development" and a quote "Men cannot live without Him and be men." In order of priority, events consisted of a Conversational Bible Class conducted by the General Secretary every Sunday afternoon at 3pm; After Church Social Hour on Sundays at 8.15pm; Bible Study Class on Tuesdays from 8-9pm; Christian Fellowship and Prayer Circle every Saturday evening at 8pm; and Family Worship which stated: "A hymn is sung and a few verses of Scripture are read every night in the Secretaries' Office at 9.30pm" – note the plural Secretaries! Popular Lectures took place once a month on Wednesday evenings; Monthly Social gatherings were posted on the notice board; a Mock Parliament was held on Mondays at 8.15pm with the Speaker (Parliamentary style) being A.J. Moxon; the Lending Library was open on Mondays and Fridays from 6-9pm; and the Musical and Song Club under the direction of Mr. L.H. Twissells was "a good opportunity for increasing musical efficiency and ability".

Billiards was practised most nights with matches played on Thursday evenings; Chess and Draughts were played in the lounge on alternate evenings (there was no radio yet, let alone television!); a game of Lawn Tennis, paradoxically on the hard court at the rear, cost two shillings an hour for four players which was a tidy sum at the time; Cricket was captained by T.B. Hitchman with E. Zebedee as vice-captain, E.J. Horlick as secretary and George Hitchman as treasurer, presided over by the all-seeing Major Rickerby. Physical Training consisted of medicine ball, athletics, aquatics and boxing under the leadership of H. Granville; Francis Knight was the Photographic Club secretary; while Table Tennis was labelled as ping-pong, a term which held sway for several decades.

The Boys' Department was still taking place at 31 Cambray under A.J. Moxon and it is not known exactly when these premises were eventually relinquished but almost certainly within the next two years. Hire of the Large Hall cost two guineas for one function and three guineas for both afternoon and evening hire. Use of the small Lecture Rooms cost between five and ten shillings with lighting extra. All in all it is clear that the new YMCA meant business on a grand scale.

****

Advertising in the 1921-1922 programme was an interesting affair and covered more than 20 pages. Apart from the local firms, space was taken by Horlick's Malted Milk, The Glasgow School of Commerce, Feathery Flake Self Raising Flour and Fry's Breakfast Cocoa. Of the Gloucestershire-based companies, only the Cheltenham and Gloucester Building Society still exists under its original name although the Model Laundry in Hatherley Road survives as the Paragon Laundry. The C. & G. proudly proclaimed it had 15,656 accounts with total assets of £1,244,964, the other companies being rather more modest about their achievements although the Laundry claimed to be one of the most up to date in the country with spacious grounds for open air drying. Not any more of course but these were the days of elbow grease and hard grind, not state of the art washer-driers and everything available at the push of a button.

Kiddieland of 401 High Street had a good selection of dolls, soldiers, trains and Meccano while the

▲ *Another picture of the new lounge*

▲ *The new lounge*

Gloucestershire Dairy had its own local farms, a headquarters in Imperial Lane which closed only recently, and three retail outlets. Alfred Mann sold various solid fuels at a time when the only means of winter heating was an open fire, often confined to one living room where all the family huddled together for warmth before making a quick dash to the outside toilet or upstairs to bed. Waking up in the morning often meant chipping ice off the inside of the bedroom windows!

A. Beckingsale of 111 High Street offered shirts of reputation, hosiery of reliability and neckwear of distinction, while Hunters of 3 the Promenade offered a fast photographic service with films delivered before 10.30am being ready the same day. How times change!

This was also a time of superb black and white line drawings, full colour publishing being almost unheard of because of the cost and difficulty involved, indeed colour photography did not come into its own until the mid-1970s. A coloured cover was about all that most publishers could manage for books and magazines at the time, although there were a few expensive exceptions. Whoever drew the YMCA interior pictures was a gifted artist because they conveyed exactly what the Association stood for, namely high standards in a refined Christian setting. Black and white they may have been but still look attractive today and must have seemed very smart at the time.

****

The 1920s are often described as the "Roaring Twenties" and this is appropriate up to a point. Lively dance music had arrived from across the North Atlantic Ocean and the BBC had begun

The YMCA was founded as a "Home from home" for young men. Indeed, several of the original 12 who met in St. Paul's Churchyard, London in 1855 were from the West Country, including the first YMCA Hon. Secretary, William Creese. Several bedrooms were built at the Promenade all of which were available for suitable tenants at reasonable prices.

could attune. True, it was for men only but that was how life was in those days with virtually every major secondary school being single sex. Many were grateful for the friendship and fellowship which the Association provided, especially those coming to Cheltenham for the first time, which was also likely to have been their first time away from home. What better place for a young man starting out on a new career?

****

broadcasting to the nation in 1922. Gramophone records were freely available and the country had metaphorically shrunk in size. However, it must also be remembered that everyone was still suffering from the catastrophic world war and there was a huge gap in society where so many of the country's young men had been either killed or badly wounded. Thus a great slice of society was disabled at a stroke. Monuments to their great sacrifice are everywhere in the land but it is sobering to reflect that the projected grandiose war memorial situated on the Promenade had to be drastically scaled down through lack of public donations. It was opened not long before the YMCA moved in nearby and was to have been adorned with angels and other expensive accoutrements. Things were therefore not quite as straightforward as history has tried to make out and for many life was very hard. There was, however, a sense of neighbourliness which has since disappeared.

The YMCA movement was at the forefront of public service and remains the oldest, and still one of the biggest, youth charities in the country. We know that Cheltenham YMCA during the 1920s was a valued enterprise and possibly the only organisation of its kind for miles around. Other similar institutions came and went but the YMCA had now been established in Cheltenham for 80 years as something tangible to which all the local public

On March 21st, 1923, Princess Helena Victoria (1870-1948), arrived to open what was described as the Junior Hall, and made a return visit on November 20th, 1935. The eldest daughter of Prince Christian of Schleswig-Holstein and Queen Victoria's third daughter, Princess Helena Augusta Victoria, she particularly identified herself with the YMCA movement as a force for good and went round the country encouraging as many people as possible. The fact that she opened a new room for the Junior Department suggests that 31 Cambray had finally been vacated, although whether this was in what became known as the Royal Well Hut situated at the rear on what had been the new tennis court seems likely but not proven.

Activities forged ahead and it is known that dances were a common event, certainly during the late 1920s. It was a time of growing optimism but financial difficulties were never far below the surface and the economic depression of the early-1930s, precipitated by the 1929 Wall Street Crash in America, proved to be a severe blow. Despite the best efforts of everyone concerned, by the mid-1930s the monetary problem was so acute that Cheltenham YMCA was forced to apply to the YMCA National Council for a loan of £3,000. Unfortunately, it was turned down and the local leadership was so upset that for a time a major rift

▲ *This artist's impression of the new main hall envisaged it would seat 250, with adjacent classrooms and lecture room for instruction. Hire of the hall cost two guineas for a function encompassing one session but only three guineas for combined afternoon and evening hire. Use of the smaller rooms cost between five and ten shillings with lighting extra. Hire of the piano was a further two shillings and sixpence (half a crown) to 5 shillings (a crown). It seems the rooms were often and well used.*

developed between the two. There was nothing else for it but to put some of the premises up for sale with number 51 quickly being acquired by Pearl Assurance. The space at the rear of the building, however, was retained which explains why the YMCA Royal Well Hut which gave such valuable service during the war years, still extended across 51, 53 and 55.

****

The stalwart outstanding leaders during the early years in the Promenade were Dr. S.T. Pruen and Major T.E. Rickerby, both well-known Cheltenham dignitaries. Their guidance and experience was invaluable. Pruen has been mentioned earlier but in conjunction with Rickerby, the duo played a massive role in the history of Cheltenham YMCA and their influence on the town was immense. Originally from the north of England, Rickerby came to Gloucestershire via Newtown in Montgomeryshire, and went into partnership with Robert Ley Wood, a fellow Christian and later the YMCA president. When that professional relationship was dissolved in 1903 he carried on alone before taking into partnership Mr. H.H. Thompson and Mr. I.D. Yeaman, renaming the firm accordingly although only the name of Rickerby has survived to the present day.

He was quite a character and threw himself into the YMCA cause early on. This is hardly surprising when one considers that his father was a friend of the YMCA founder, Sir George Williams. Elected to the Council as a Conservative for the South Ward in August 1899 he carried a motion to prohibit all Sunday concerts in public gardens and six months later defeated a suggestion to allow similar concerts in the Winter Gardens, a huge greenhouse style building situated in Imperial Gardens behind the current Town Hall. In 1902, however, he failed to stop the running of trams on Sundays. His obituary in the *Gloucestershire Echo* on February 6th, 1931 mentioned his commitment to the YMCA in detail and revealed the truth behind the move from

The cafe

Cambray to the Promenade. Not only did he deal with all the legal advice and personal services but guaranteed the overdraft on both the buildings and equipment! No figure was given but it must have been immense. It also reported that in addition to his active church involvement, he led the Sunday evening services at the YMCA for many years.

In addition to all his other commitments, he was also Chairman of CSSM (Children's Special Service Mission), eventually renamed the Scripture Union which, in addition to publishing books and Bible Reading notes, still runs children's work in schools and beach campaigns every summer. He regularly attended lunchtime meetings in Wigmore Street, Central London where he became established as a "beloved leader". Well-known locally, he lived at a house called "Hafod" on the Shurdington Road. Situated just past the Up Hatherley Way roundabout as one leaves Cheltenham, it became the Hafod House Hotel but then changed hands several times. He later moved to a house called "Lorraine" near the Pump Room in Pittville and one cannot help wondering how he travelled into the centre of Cheltenham during the 19th Century? Possibly a pony and trap.

Major Rickerby was also a member of the Territorials (originally known as the Volunteers) and was chief recruiting officer for Cheltenham during the Great War. An active worshipper at St. Mary's Parish Church, St. Matthew's and latterly, St. James, he lost his only child, Capt. J.H.E. (John Harold Ellerson) Rickerby MC from the Gloucestershire Regiment, at Holnon Wood on the Western Front but he never lost his sense of Christian purpose, even after his wife died in 1925. Born on June 29th, 1865 he lived an incredibly full life before passing away suddenly on February 5th, 1931. The Headmaster of Dean Close School, Mr. P. Bolton, paid tribute to his dedicated and visionary work as the Chairman of Governors while in another lengthy tribute, the Vicar of St. James' Church in Suffolk Square, Rev. G.W. Boothroyd, listed his many fine qualities, especially highlighting the work with his close friend Dr. Pruen. Together they regularly entertained pupils from Cheltenham College in Pruen's premises in Lypiatt Road where the doctor practised as an orthopaedic medical practitioner and surgeon. Between 20 and 30 boys willingly gathered every Sunday afternoon when the Gospel was expounded to them by these two dedicated men of God.

The lengthy CSSM obituary concluded: "Major Rickerby was a veritable Mr. Greatheart who revelled in performing deeds of kindness, the more unostentatious such actions were, the better pleased he was. It was apparent that it was the love of Christ that constrained our friend in all he did. Thus it is no wonder that he established himself in the affections of a multitude of young and old, high and lowly, so that today there are many who with saddened hearts mourn the loss of one who truly earned the name of friend."

Without Messrs. Rickerby and Pruen it seems likely that Cheltenham YMCA would have gone into liquidation either before the First World War or, if not then, probably soon afterwards. Just what their financial commitments to the Association were is unknown but we can be sure it was substantial.

****

The 1928-9 Programme and Diary spoke volumes about what had been achieved since the move to the Promenade eight years earlier. Despite the overdraft, under Chairman Dr. Pruen and Joint

Treasurer Major Rickerby, things appear to have gone from strength to strength although Rickerby now had T.G. Cooke to help him with the accounts. The Executive Committee of 11 was elected by ballot at the AGM and included future chairmen Horace Bush and Arthur Dye plus long-serving George Hitchman. The General Secretary was Norman Edwards and the Hon. Secretary of the Junior Department was A.J. Moxon, another man who gave stalwart service over many years.

▲ The hostel

The YMCA Café was described as "suitable for large parties" and was open to ladies and non-members from 10am to 10pm. On the ground floor, it had a "large and well arranged dining room, separate tables, good cooking and quick service." Morning coffee cost twopence, luncheon one shilling and sixpence (to include fish or meat, vegetables, sweet and coffee) but with cheese and biscuits threepence extra. Plain tea cost from sixpence and a meat tea from one shilling and one penny (one and a penny as it used to be called)! Suppers were provided "at reasonable charges" with minerals and cigarettes also available.

"The hostel occupies the upper floors and offers all the advantages of Association life which is debarred to those in isolated lodgings. It is comfortably furnished and only those who are desirous of sharing the community life of the Association and are in sympathy with its objects and principles are sought and accepted for permanent residence." No compromise there then!

Permanent accommodation cost 25 shillings a week for a shared room and 30 shillings for a single. Transient accommodation was available for bed and breakfast at five shillings and sixpence, with a daily rate of seven shillings. "Bathroom and general lavatories, where hot water is available are provided. No extra charge for baths." There was accommodation for motor cycles and cycles but the sting in the tail said "All residents are expected to be in before 11.20pm."

"Our object" was described as "all round efficiency, a place of companionships and fighting for character in the youth of the town. Any young man of good moral character may join as an Associate." Senior membership was ten shillings per annum and Juniors (under 17) five shillings. Honorary subscribers at one guinea (one pound one shilling) were entitled to all the privileges and could also introduce one senior and two junior members without charge. YMCA badges cost sixpence with ties from half a crown (two shillings and sixpence or 12.5p today). Blazers in registered colours were available from the office from 25 shillings upwards, this being a time when a blazer was de rigueur for the smartly dressed man with a YMCA blazer deemed especially fashionable, or trendy as it would be called today.

There were strong links with other YMCAs and fraternisation and visits were encouraged. An advert for Riley's billiard tables was placed opposite a page which said "The Association possesses one of the finest Billiard Rooms in town with three full-size tables and a smaller one." All the tables had been recovered or re-cushioned and several flying handicaps and competitions had been arranged for winter nights. Serious stuff!

In addition to the usual sports listed under Activities, were Brotherhood, Business Club, Group Correspondence Courses, Holiday Tours, Parliament, and Wireless, the latter being a big craze since the BBC began broadcasting in 1922. Mention of a gymnasium suggests that the timber framed building at the rear had already been constructed, later known as the Royal Well Hut and also the home of the Junior Department led by A.J. Moxon.

The central pages were arranged as a personal diary and adverts included the Cheltenham and Gloucester Building Society; W. Vale and Co. who gave an "unrivalled food service"; baker and confectioner D. Handcock; Leopolds the "popular confectioners"; Lipton's Tea (in the days when they were a chain of shops); ironmonger T.W. Harvey; butcher Waghorne Bros.; solid fuel supplier Alfred Mann & Son; Walkley's gramophones, records and music; Cheltenham Creamery; Paragon Laundries (then based at 22 Pittville Street); auctioneers and estate agents Cornelius & Boulter; motor cycle service depot A. Williams & Co.; butchers Holliday & Page; Wheway Cycles; jeweller Edgar Mann who gave YMCA members a 10% discount; and Blue Bird Cafes which resided at 61 The Strand and 8 Hewlett Street. It is interesting to note the many food shops, some of which were in competition with the YMCA café which clearly did not feel under any threat.

****

Although Cheltenham YMCA was obviously very active, members were also encouraged to look further afield and the 1931-2 Handbook showed a picture of the London Central YMCA building under a piece entitled "Your Place in London", listing 204 bedrooms with current prices. Correspondence Courses were encouraged and International Goodwill was linked to the 54 countries in which the YMCA operated. The YMCA's very own Red Triangle Tours would also get you there with booklets available from the Secretary. There was even a full page advert for a new book called *In the Days of Miss Beale*, a biography of the founder and principal of Cheltenham Ladies' College.

The address of the Junior Department for boys aged 13-17 was given as Royal Well Lane which was the temporary building immediately behind, situated on what is now the Council Chamber. Hours were from 6-9.30pm nightly. The lecture hall was available for hire for afternoon or evening at one guinea and afternoon and evening for £1 ten shillings (£1.50 today). Hire of the drawing room cost from between seven shillings and sixpence up to 12 shillings and sixpence, with the small room priced at five shillings. Hire of the piano was an extra 2/6d (half a crown) to 5 shillings (a crown).

Membership of the YMCA Wednesday AFC (Association Football Club) was also two and sixpence with home matches played at Whaddon Lane Recreation Ground.

In 1934 the membership was listed as follows:
Members and Associates   152
Dramatic Society (not included in above)   20
Junior Department   50
Hon. or Sustaining Members 156
Women's Auxiliary   31

Income for the year was £1062 5 shillings and fivepence halfpenny but the overall deficit was £6,475 15 shillings and one penny. This was serious money and something needed to be done about it. Major Rickerby was now dead and Dr. Pruen, although still chairman, was getting old.

◀ *The Royal Well Hut, erected during the mid-1920s at the rear of the Promenade, included a gymnasium and also housed the Junior Department.*

▲ *Another picture of the YMCA Wednesday Football Club. Taken in 1927 it shows left to right: (standing) G. Hitchman (Committee), C. Brooks; L. Phillips; F. Harris; R. Herring; J. Rainbow; J. Hayward; N. Edwards (YMCA Secretary): (sitting) D. Wallace; S. Matthews; C. Griffiths; R. Andrews; L. Hicks. Norman Edwards probably followed William Turner and continued in office until 1935 when he was succeeded by Arthur Naylor who led the Association until the early years of the Second World War.*

The visit by Princess Helena Victoria in 1935 involved a tour of the premises and a civic welcome at the Town Hall where she received purses to a value of £1,045 which, after expenses left £858 of which £429, one half, went to YMCA HQ in London. In view of this generosity HQ wiped the same sum from the debt owed to them by the local Association. However, this still left a substantial deficit for the Committee to ponder about and, as mentioned above, they eventually but very reluctantly sold Number 51 Promenade to Pearl Assurance.

The Junior Department continued to flourish with a constant membership of 48, with many more passing through. Various weekend camps took place during the summer and several gym displays were organised by Mr. J.E.F. Davey of which one was outdoors in Montpellier Gardens. The annual party was voted "the best yet" but consideration was given to the raising of the school leaving age and it was agreed that in future only boys aged 14-18 would be accepted, in other words those who had already left school! This puts clearly into focus what a boy was considered to be at the time!

Teenagers had yet to be invented and long trousers did not cover a boy's knees until usually after he was at least 14, a situation which remained well into post-war years. A.J. Moxon tendered his resignation as the Junior Dept. Hon. Secretary and although this was reluctantly accepted it was not alluded to again and he continued in office until well after the war years came along. Clearly a dedicated servant of Cheltenham YMCA, like many older men, he provided invaluable service when the younger generation went off to fight.

The hostel remained filled to capacity and the Women's Auxiliary were beavering away behind the scenes. The Dramatic Society presented three plays, *Longtails* written and produced by Mr. H.O. Barnett, the Society President; *Box and Cox* produced by Paul R. Clauss, a play later set to music by Sir Arthur Sullivan and renamed *Cox and Box*; and something entitled *E & OE* by S.C. Morris. The society also toured the villages raising money for one of the purses subsequently presented to Princess Helena Victoria.

An internal basketball league was started to promote inter-group rivalry; the 1st XI football team was promoted to the second division of the Cheltenham League; the cricket team were runners-up in the Hospital Cup but the report boldly stated that had so many players not been away on the day of the final then there was little doubt that the YMCA would have won!

Officers for 1935 included Councillor E.L. Ward as President to be succeeded the following year by Percy Smith, W.T. Cambray as Treasurer and the redoubtable Arthur Dye as Chairman, a man who became almost synonymous with Cheltenham YMCA. It is interesting to note that this report believed the Association had been founded in 1856!

The following year was sweet revenge for the cricket team which lifted the Hospital Cup and the table tennis team won the Cheltenham League for the fifth time. Billiards and snooker were less popular but part of a national trend which was not reversed until the advent of colour television during the mid-1970s. A.J. Moxon's resignation seemed to have evaporated because he was still giving "efficient leadership" of the Junior Department and J.J. Virgo the ex-World Field Secretary of the National YMCA opened the winter season's programme.

****

The splendidly-produced 1938 Annual Report, "The Times In Which We Live" gave a broad outline for the general public and is the subject of a separate chapter. The 1938 Handbook, however, was aimed purely at those interested in using the facilities. Titled "Cheltenham YMCA and Residential Home" we learn that the General Secretary was A.E. (Arthur) Naylor, whose son, John, later became a post-war National YMCA secretary. He was also separately described as the Physical Director of Training, assisted by J.E. Davey and, according to the leaflets showing white-vested and long white-trousered men going through their paces, it was jolly serious stuff. "Training is given in all branches of Physical Education – both Theory and Practice – for those desiring to become Leaders willing to render service to outside Clubs. Subjects include: History, Theory and Principles of Physical Education, Physiology, Anatomy, Hygiene, Class Teaching etc." Wow! Lectures took place on Tuesdays evenings followed by Practicals on Thursday evenings. Regular examinations were available for those wishing to take them and significant is the mention of the Hon. Medical Officer, Dr. D.E. Morley who just happened to be the Borough's Medical Officer who had already served for some time on the YMCA executive committee and continued to do so for many years.

Comments on the Hostel are also worth quoting verbatim: Under the heading "Home and Club Life Combined" visitors could read the following: "Situated on the Promenade, probably the finest in England, the Hostel occupies the upper floors of the Association building – centrally situated for all purposes. Here the stranger will find friendship – an introduction to the town and its surroundings – and amenities which cannot be found elsewhere. It is the best of home and club life combined. Those who are in sympathy with the Association's objects and principles are welcomed as permanent residents, priority being given to young men leaving home for the first time. Permanent residents must be members of the Association – cost 5 shillings per annum. A limited number of transient residents are accommodated when rooms are available."

Under a picture of a hemispherical bar described as the Buffet, we learn that the Restaurant was available to members and Associates to eat either a la carte or table d'hote at "popular prices". The Buffet, on the other hand, was open from 9am – 10.30pm providing "cigarettes, chocolates, light refreshments etc." There was no anti-smoking lobby in those days because the dangers were not appreciated, indeed it is only in the last 20-30 years that non-smoking railway carriages have become the norm whereas they were once outnumbered at least four-to-one in favour of those who expected to light up as a matter of course.

Permanent hostel residents were classified as those staying three months or more, who still paid the same amount as ten years earlier, namely between 25s and 27s 6d per week for a shared room (approximately £1.25 to £1.37 in today's currency), while single rooms retailed at 30 shilling per week (£1.50). This included room, full board, boot cleaning and baths! Before one runs away with the idea of snobbery it must be pointed out that boot cleaning was seen as an everyday part of hotel service, and great store was placed on clean shoes for both

A happy group of YMCA residents outside the Promenade on October 4th, 1936. This is now the main entrance into the Council Offices.

work and play. They had to be spotless as a new pin every day without fail! Failure was looked upon as both slovenly and bad form.

Temporary residents were charged between 37s 6d and 40s (£2) for sharing, with a single room coming out at 42 shillings per week full-board. Bath, bed and breakfast was 5s 6d with special reductions for YMCA members!

Several rooms were advertised for hire to the public. The Lecture Hall was licensed for music and dancing, and was available for social functions and meetings with a capacity of 130. Smaller rooms provided seating for 15, 30 and 60 people. The phone number was given as 4024, to which has since been added the digits 5 and 2 to transform it into 524024 today! A nice touch of continuity down the years. Anyone responding to an advert in the Handbook was specifically asked to mention the YMCA when doing so.

Page 31 was an exhortation for ladies to join the new section being opened specially for them. They were also invited to request a special brochure and tell their friends all about it. A specially produced leaflet showed just how serious the new Young Women's Section was intended to be and the winter programme included the following but with a proviso that it was likely to be extended:

Sunday 3pm Special Monthly Rally on 1st Sunday of each month
3pm Y Fellowship on 2nd, 3rd and 4th Sundays
4.30pm Tea and Conference
Monday Committee Meetings
6-10pm Badminton
7.30pm Amateur Dramatic Society
8-10pm Library open
Tuesday 7.30pm Keep Fit Classes
Wednesday 7.30-8.30pm Dancing Classes,
    Volleyball, Basketball, mixed Table Tennis
10-10.15pm The Vigil
Thursday 7.30pm Concert Party rehearsals
8pm Foreign Language groups
8-10pm Library open
Friday Popular Lectures, Junior Town
    Council, Badminton
Saturday Netball, Hiking & Cycling,
    Outings, Badminton

In addition it was noted that Table Tennis, Darts, Lounge Facilities etc. were open at other times similar to the YMCA. Debates and other activities may be suggested by members and would be provided for accordingly. The cost of all this was 5/- (five shillings or 25p). Further activities mentioned on the back of the leaflet included Camping, Canteen Work in National Emergency, Country and Ballroom Dancing, Cricket, Domestic Science, Employment Bureau, Guild of Service, Polytechnic Touring Association, and Swimming (both mixed and ladies only).

"Happy companionship, good sportsmanship, opportunities for learning, social enjoyment and spiritual enlightenment are the keynotes of the Association's programme." A trim, beaming young lady on the front waved her right arm and exhorted other young women of Cheltenham to "Come In and Join Us!"

This new branch found immediate favour but before it got into its full stride the war intervened with the inevitable result that membership during the early years was confined mainly to older people. Younger women were not to be denied, though, as we shall see later.

Meanwhile, there was a second female branch of Cheltenham YMCA known as the Women's Auxiliary. The Chairman was Mrs J.E. Webster; the Vice-Chairman Mrs. J.H. Trye (wife of the Mayor of Cheltenham); the Hon. Secretary was Mrs. W.A. Baker; the Hon. Treasurer Miss Higgins; with the committee consisting of Mrs Evans; Mrs. L.B. Fletcher; Mrs. W.J. Fowler; Mrs. P. James; Miss Jeffery; Mrs. A. Nunn; Mrs. C.G. Neat; Mrs. W.H. Thody; Mrs. Tarr; and Mrs. Wilcox. One wonders why some ladies had initials and others not? Their work is best described by the Handbook: "The Women's Auxiliary exists to help the YMCA to carry on its work, and is one of the finest in the country. New members are cordially invited to join, membership 1 shilling per annum (5p!), and non-members are welcomed at any of the social functions arranged by this section. Meetings are held on the first Monday in each month at 4pm."

The timing of this meeting is significant because the vast majority of married women did not carry out paid work, indeed it was usual to resign one's post immediately prior to marriage. Their place was firmly in the home, looking after the family with the husband as the undisputed head of the house. While this may seem strange today it was perfectly normal then and remained so until at least the 1960s. Talk of Women's Lib. would have caused apoplexy, not just among the YMCA faithful, both male and female, but amongst the whole of pre-war and immediate post-war society.

Ladies, however, performed a vital role and were natural leaders in many areas. In addition to their own homes they were especially important in social events, carnivals, fund raising, Church activities, uniformed organisations etc. Today there are always vacancies being advertised for youth leaders but in those days it was seen as a duty and, it must be added, an extremely pleasant and worthwhile obligation. One can just imagine the camaraderie among the Women's Auxiliary and how they would have been puzzled at today's acute shortage of volunteers. Scouts, Guides, Cubs, Brownies, Boys Brigade, Church Lads Brigade, Army cadets, youth groups etc. were rarely short of adult help. A vast horde of young people benefited from their experiences and one cannot help feeling that most of today's youngsters are missing out. Loyalty was a key element in society and never more so than at the YMCA.

In what was described as the "Physical Department" the 1938 Handbook gave the following quote: "Give me health and a day and I will make the pomp of emperors look ridiculous." Clearly they were an educated lot! Among the winter activities listed was Association Football (as opposed to Rugby Football), with two teams who had their home ground at Brooklyn Road, presumably what is now King George V Playing Fields where the wheel has turned full circle and the Junior YMCA football teams now play each weekend. Badminton was held at the Montpellier Baths (now the Playhouse Theatre) on Wednesdays and Saturdays from 2.30-10pm. Gymnastics, Basketball and Boxing were also on offer.

In the summer one could choose from Athletics on Tuesdays and Thursdays, or Baseball on the same nights at Brooklyn Road. There were also three Cricket teams run by three different secretaries! Camping apparently had a permanent home in Leckhampton and three grass tennis courts were

▲ *This splendid picture of the YMCA Junior Gymnastics Club was taken in the Royal Well Hut around 1938. The coach is "Pop" Davey who was hurriedly seconded to run Baker Street YMCA in early 1940. The boys' clothing speaks volumes about their social backgrounds but we can be sure it was the very best their parents and the YMCA could afford. Once war arrived, however, then it really was a case of "make do and mend".*

available at Montpellier from May to September. If that was not enough then the Montpellier Baths was reserved exclusively for the YMCA on Monday evenings. Phew! Take your pick from that lot! No? Prefer to stay at the Promenade? Well ….

Indoors we find that Billiards and Snooker was on the agenda, accompanied by outstanding results from the Table Tennis club. Darts, "an ever popular game" had the latest type of board – whatever that meant – while for the really studious both Chess and Draughts were also available in the lounge. Never a dull moment!

The Junior Department was now open to all boys under the age of 16 and showed a short-trousered and a long-trousered boy leaning against each other in a casual pose, both wearing suits. Surprising? Not really because most children had just two sets of clothes, one for school and one for best which is what they usually wore to the YMCA. "A complete programme provides for the all-round needs of body, mind and spirit." The Secretary was Mr. A.J. Moxon and new members were encouraged to join a "world-wide Christian Fellowship which exists in 55 different countries with a membership of nearly two million." Membership was the princely sum of 2d (twopence or tuppence) per week and the club was open every evening from 6.30pm. Activities were as follows:

Mondays – billiards, table tennis, draughts and house games
Tuesdays – recreational gymnastics, basket ball etc.
Wednesdays – members' surprise programme
Thursdays – general gymnastics
Fridays – indoor house games, Bible Class, family worship
Saturdays – occasional outings, football, fireside discussions, study circle and prefects' meeting
Sundays – no special meetings so that boys may be encouraged to attend their own particular places of worship.

▲ *A post-war view looking down on the back of the YMCA Promenade premises showing the roof of the Royal Well Hut which was constructed in the mid-1920s, replacing a new but under-used hard tennis court. The photo was taken from the former YMCA premises at Yates's Wine Bar, formerly the* Echo *newspaper offices.*

The officers were, President, Councillor P.T. Smith and Chairman, Councillor H.T. Bush. The junior work committee consisted of J.S. Box, J.E. Davey, G.O. Hitchman, A.H. Mace, J.W. Smith, and Mrs. J.H. Trye. with A.J. Moxon as Hon. Sec.

Every Monday evening at 7.30pm it was time for the Cheltymca Dramatic Society who put on three plays in 1938. P.R. Clauss produced Arnold Ridley's *The Ghost Train*; Councillor H.O. Barnett (also the Society's President) produced R.C. Sheriff's *Journey's End*; and Miss W. Power produced Aimee and Philip Stuart's *Nine Till Six*. The Hon. Secretary was S.C. Morris, membership cost 2/6 and the Society was "Open to members of the ladies' section"!

The preface to the Orchestra said "And the night shall be filled with music, and the cares that infest the day shall fold up their tents like Arabs and as silently steal away." It was a quote from Longfellow which would not be permissible today! The President was Arthur Cole and the Vice-President Eric Woodward. The outstanding conductor was Ronald Brown who, much to everyone's disappointment, later moved away. There were more than 20 players and new members (including ladies), were most welcome to join, also at the annual subscription of 2/6.

Under the quote "It is the duty of every man to take an interest in civic affairs" the Junior Town Council took place on the 2nd and 4th Fridays in each month. It was basically a debating society but an extremely serious one and we learn that on October 14th 1938, "His Worship the Mayor, Capt. J.H. Trye, JP, will invest the JTC Mayor with his chain of office."

Once a month on a different Friday, guest speakers were invited to give a talk. Judge Kennedy spoke on "The Citizen and the Law"; Chief Constable Col. W.F. Henn spoke on "Alexandria, the Market of Africa"; R. Consterdine, MBS, talked about "Cyprus the Golden Isle"; D. Morris of the BBC spoke about "Some Misconceptions and Difficulties in Broadcasting"; G.T. Kelson, a former Mountie from Canada discoursed on "The Trail of Adventure"; and bringing up the rear, on an unspecified date in April because of his sporting commit-

▲ *Another post-war view of the Royal Well Hut taken from across the road by the bus station. The hut was used extensively by the pre-war YMCA Junior Department under the leadership of A.J. Moxon, doubling as a gymnasium and canteen for adults. It was dismantled in 1956 and is now the site of the Council Chamber.*

ments, the world famous Gloucestershire batsman Wally Hammond was due to speak about "Cricket". "Look out for further announcements!" shouted the leaflet.

The world, however, was in turmoil during the 1930s and although political will may not have been as strong as it might have been, the Armed Forces were on a state of high alert. War was finally declared in September 1939, and by the end of the year adult membership of Cheltenham YMCA was in rapid decline. The pattern was repeated at similar institutions right across the country with young men – and later women – signing up for the Armed Services in their thousands. Cheltenham, like every other major town in the land, was suddenly stripped of its young adults. Nevertheless, the youth work, under the capable leadership of A.J. Moxon, was very strong and still expanding so, despite reduced adult membership, bigger premises were needed. It is an ill wind that blows nobody any good and when George Hitchman, also a trustee of the Baker Street Men's Institute – whose membership had been similarly decimated by wartime call-ups – came along and offered their buildings at a peppercorn rent, then Cheltenham YMCA simply jumped at the opportunity.

****

The full story of the 20 year history of Baker Street YMCA is contained in a separate chapter, as are the wartime activities.

****

[1] These figures do not tie up with accepted statistics of combatants from Cheltenham and may have included everyone who served in some capacity during the First World War. The accepted figure for those actually fighting is approximately half this amount of whom approximately 25% were killed.

[2] This figure was never substantially reduced and the 1930s economic depression made it impossible for another huge appeal to succeed.

CHAPTER 6
1938 ANNUAL REPORT

This was one of the earliest documents found during the initial search for archive material and was so well put together it deserved a chapter to itself. Recession was in retreat and, despite political unrest in Europe, there was great optimism at Cheltenham YMCA that the financial corner had been turned and that great things lay ahead. Little did they know what was about to unfold .....

In 1938, although war was very much in the air both at home and in the Far East, it was quite clear that after being forced to sell off Number 51 Promenade, Cheltenham YMCA was still in very good heart. The Annual Report was published early in 1939 and is a remarkable document for the time. Consisting of 24 pages, including seven full of photographs, it was entitled "The Times In Which We Live" and gave a glowing account of what happened during a busy 12 months.

The list of officers was a veritable "Who's Who" of Cheltenham politicians and famous local dignitaries especially among the 16 Vice-Presidents who included D.L. Lipson a well-known local councillor and mayor who had been housemaster of Corinth, the Jewish boarding house at Cheltenham College, and also the Independent MP for Cheltenham from 1937-1950. Alfred W. Martyn had succeeded his father as boss of the world famous local firm of sculptors H.H. Martyn who, among other items built the national Cenotaph situated in London's Whitehall. Another famous name was George H. Dowty (later knighted) whose local manufacturing company became a force to be reckoned with and whose apprentices often lodged at the YMCA. The executive committee was no less impressive with three future Cheltenham mayors among its ranks, Horace Bush, Arthur Dye and George Readings.

The Annual Report began as follows: "As one crisis follows another and new ideals rise to be smashed – new creeds and doctrines promulgated and fresh solutions offered to the world as a panacea for its troubles, can there be any wonder why youth is bewildered and why it finds it difficult to accept some of the standards that have given rise to the present world problems? Youth is often blamed for what it has done so little to create, when perhaps below the surface there is more good to be found when real opportunities are given for its self-expression."

◀ *This fine collection of individuals was described in the caption as "Leaders in the YMCA". They were not identified, however, so we can only conjecture as to what they did and who they were. Their appearance suggests the photo was taken at either a reception or dance but was the single white bow tie significant? It was taken for granted in 1938 that all would be well dressed for special occasions.*

Well, Cheltenham YMCA certainly gave it plenty of opportunity for self-expression, indeed it is unlikely that any other local youth organisation came even close to offering as many activities. The Report continued: "Cheltenham YMCA is a Christian organisation which believes that Christ came to show the world what God is like and what through Him many may become, and in presenting this report the officers believe that this faith has guided the Association through the turbulent days of 1938 so that today its work is flourishing as never before in its history." The building was being used to its utmost capacity and approximately 40 different activities were on offer.

Great store was made of the new Young Women's Section. 90 members joined within the first four weeks and a "good programme" was in operation. Mrs. J.H. Trye was the President and it was felt that Cheltenham should be grateful that a hitherto men-only organisation was now running mixed activities! Remember that single sex was the norm in most schools at the time and continued so for many years. So popular was the new section that over 1,000 people, mostly young ones, crowded into the Town Hall to see it open in style.

On the financial side, the budget had been met and it was optimistically stated that "1939 will be a year of opportunity." Never was a truer phrase uttered but it was to be fulfilled in a manner which was hardly what was intended or expected.

Back to 1938 …. "It is gratifying to report that the programme has been fuller and more varied than in any past year, and this in spite of tremendous difficulties of accommodation." It seems the town was so grateful that it chipped in to help. The Town Council granted the use of the Montpellier Baths (now the Playhouse Theatre but with the baths concealed underneath the floor) for gymnastics, basketball and badminton six evenings a week during the winter. Overton House School was also made available for drama rehearsals with individual members opening their homes for meetings and practices. Sunday afternoon meetings were very popular and the education side included various lectures, foreign languages classes, and a new library. There was obviously a personal link with Overton House School which was situated at 86 St. George's Road. Typical of many similar family run educational institutions in the town, in 1942 the Principal was Mrs. M.L. Maclean and it was described as a boarding and day school for girls with a preparatory section open to boys. It closed after the war and is now an annexe to The Overton hotel.

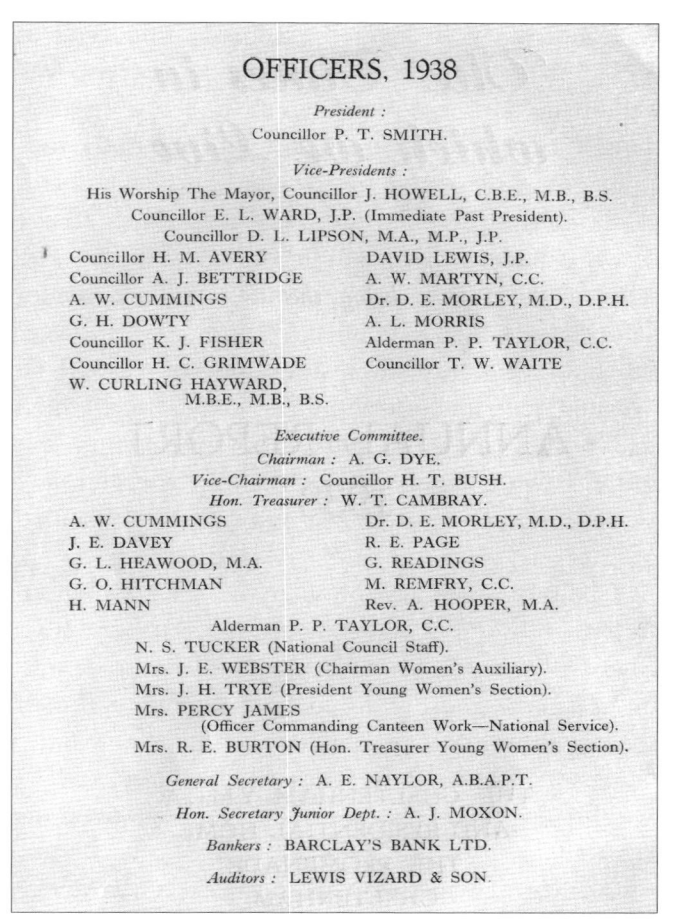

A sub-heading stated "Firm Foundations: Upon this rock I will build." A steady development of the religious programme had taken place and many members were serving as Sunday School teachers and in other church capacities across the town.

Special monthly rallies were followed by teas and conferences with numbers doubling during the year. The "Y" Fellowship met on the 2nd, 3rd and 4th Sundays in each month also with increased numbers. Meanwhile, the Fireside Fraternal met during the winter and the Study Circle during the summer. Attendance was not large but both were deemed well worthwhile with a good exchange of views. It should be pointed out that television had yet to take a stranglehold on society with only the wireless, 78rpm records, cinema going and live theatre for competition. If one wanted something to do then one went out and did it! There were no television couch potatoes for another half century!

OFFICERS, 1938

President:
Councillor P. T. SMITH.

Vice-Presidents:
His Worship The Mayor, Councillor J. HOWELL, C.B.E., M.B., B.S.
Councillor E. L. WARD, J.P. (Immediate Past President).
Councillor D. L. LIPSON, M.A., M.P., J.P.

Councillor H. M. AVERY	DAVID LEWIS, J.P.
Councillor A. J. BETTRIDGE	A. W. MARTYN, C.C.
A. W. CUMMINGS	Dr. D. E. MORLEY, M.D., D.P.H.
G. H. DOWTY	A. L. MORRIS
Councillor K. J. FISHER	Alderman P. P. TAYLOR, C.C.
Councillor H. C. GRIMWADE	Councillor T. W. WAITE
W. CURLING HAYWARD, M.B.E., M.B., B.S.	

Executive Committee.
Chairman: A. G. DYE.
Vice-Chairman: Councillor H. T. BUSH.
Hon. Treasurer: W. T. CAMBRAY.

A. W. CUMMINGS	Dr. D. E. MORLEY, M.D., D.P.H.
J. E. DAVEY	R. E. PAGE
G. L. HEAWOOD, M.A.	G. READINGS
G. O. HITCHMAN	M. REMFRY, C.C.
H. MANN	Rev. A. HOOPER, M.A.

Alderman P. P. TAYLOR, C.C.
N. S. TUCKER (National Council Staff).
Mrs. J. E. WEBSTER (Chairman Women's Auxiliary).
Mrs. J. H. TRYE (President Young Women's Section).
Mrs. PERCY JAMES
(Officer Commanding Canteen Work—National Service).
Mrs. R. E. BURTON (Hon. Treasurer Young Women's Section).

General Secretary: A. E. NAYLOR, A.B.A.P.T.

Hon. Secretary Junior Dept.: A. J. MOXON.

Bankers: BARCLAY'S BANK LTD.

Auditors: LEWIS VIZARD & SON.

Education was deemed extremely important in 1938, and rightly so! The debating society was called the Junior Town Council and had the full support of the real local council with one of the pictures showing the then Mayor of Cheltenham, Alderman Capt. J.H. Trye investing the Junior Town Council Mayor with his chain of office. The name of the latter was Alderman D. Wallace, namesake of the Chief Executive Officer 65 years later! Of the year's most interesting debates was: "That Westal Green junction should be made safer" which was carried on the floor and a subsequent letter sent to the Town Council. They obviously got their way because a traffic island was subsequently installed on this busy section of Lansdown Road!

Cheltymca Dramatic Society enhanced its reputation with three plays: *Journey's End* by R.C. Sheriff; *Nine Till Six* by Aimee and Philip Stuart; and *The Crooked Billet* by Dion Titheradge. If ever there was an ironic production then it was the latter because within 12 months Cheltenham YMCA would be billeting servicemen from all over the country.

Among the talks given during the year were those by His Honour Judge Kennedy; Stanley Rous, Secretary of the Football Association; Col. W.F. Henn, the Chief Constable of Gloucestershire; Mr. A.T. Voyce, rugby international; and Mr. S.C. Davies the racing motorist.

Finally among educational activities was the YMCA Orchestra under the direction of Ronald Brown. It was at one point the largest amateur orchestra in Gloucestershire and gave several concerts both in the YMCA and at other venues. Unfortunately. Mr. Brown left Cheltenham but it was hoped that extra accommodation would see a resurgence in interest.

Hardly surprisingly, Physical Fitness had a section all to itself with the initial comment: "It is important to realise that the effects of physical education are on the 'whole' man and not part of him. The development of character is one of its main objectives, and this cannot exclude body, mind or spirit. Fitness therefore is an ideal to be fostered, and the programme should cover as wide a range as possible, in order to include opportunities for all types and conditions of young people."

Thanks were expressed to Cheltenham Town Council "who have rendered assistance in every possible way" and also to the Higher Education Authority who, through the National Fitness Council, had appointed an instructor-leader to assist the Association's work. Hope was expressed that "in the near future a properly equipped gymnasium with ample dressing accommodation may become available". They were to be kept waiting!

Gymnastics classes were held regularly for both men and boys and an exhibition was given by the Birkenhead YMCA International Demonstration Team at the Montpellier Baths. The Leaders' Training Class also benefited gymnastic groups for St. James' Church Lads Brigade and at Charlton Kings, with assistance also given in swimming, basketball and play leadership. Basketball had several teams with one playing in the English National Championship League Division 1, great help coming from some American missionaries staying at the Association.

Two regular Football teams played in the local Cheltenham League, one of which won Division 2, scoring 129 goals and conceding only 10. Two other elevens also took to the field for those not good enough to play at a higher level.

Cricket also fielded four regular teams, including an evening team, a Saturday XI and a Junior XI. Arrangements for 1939 had been made for six teams, including a Young Women's XI.

Badminton suffered from poor lighting and Athletics was also disappointing but membership of the Table Tennis club had doubled to 40, winning eight out of 10 matches against other local clubs. In the play off they defeated Cavendish to win the Division 1 Shield.

Members of the Junior Department used the camping site at Leckhampton but there was need for more equipment to allow Seniors to take part.

It is interesting to note that Billiards and Snooker came under the heading of Recreation rather than Physical Fitness! Nevertheless, two teams took part with considerable success in the Cheltenham League. Exhibition games were given by "the well-known professional" Mr. Claude Faulkner and by the ladies' world champion, Miss Joyce Garner.

Under the direction of Basil Miller the Revelymca Concert Party gave more than 20 con-

YMCA Officials at the Town Hall Social

▶ This formal assembly includes Cheltenham YMCA President, Percy Smith, fourth from right on the front row wearing his chain of office. Next to him, also with her chain of office, is the President of the Young Women's Section, Mrs. J.H. Trye, wife of the Mayor shown in the picture below. She gave great wartime service as described in Chapter 7.

The Junior Town Council.

◀ The Mayor of Cheltenham Alderman Capt. J.H. Trye, CBE, RN (Ret.), invests the Cheltenham YMCA Junior Town Council Mayor, David Wallace, with his chain of office. Debating was a very serious business and doubtless there would have been much discussion as to whether the country ought to go to war with Germany. Twelve months later that is precisely what happened.

Cheltymca Dramatic Society

▶ This very active department put on three plays during the year. Picture here is R.C. Sheriff's First World War drama entitled "Journey's End". They also performed "The Crooked Billet" by Dion Titheradge, a well-known musical writer. It was ironically prophetic because within a very short time the YMCA were billeting servicemen from all over the country and abroad.

certs in six months, the majority in order to raise money for different charities. The Town Hall Celebration Social was especially successful, as were many other socials during the year, indeed many folk had to be turned away from the President's Opening Social through lack of space! This was the sole reason for switching the Young Women's Opening Social to the Town Hall which was just as well because more than 1,000 people turned up! Music was provided by Mr. H. Cook and his Dance Band. The New Year's Party was also a great success as was a visit from Cirencester YMCA and a special meeting to introduce Toc H members to YMCA members.

The YMCA has always provided short term accommodation, indeed that was one of the reasons that George Williams founded it, for people like him who were working in a strange town, in his case London during the 1850s. "In providing a home away from home the Hostel has met a great need." Mrs. Gerrard the housekeeper apparently worked wonders but demand always exceeded space. Nevertheless a happy atmosphere existed throughout the residential section.

The Welfare Department consisted of four sections with the Employment Bureau existing to find jobs. The National Savings Club had a small but growing number of members while the Polytechnic Touring Association existed for giving help to those desirous of travelling at home and abroad. The YMCA Friendly Society, however, had received relatively little use.

50 delegates attended the YMCA Western Divisional Annual Conference hosted in Cheltenham by the Mayor, Alderman Capt. J.H. Trye, CBE, RN (Ret).

Membership had grown from 527 in 1937 to 681. 276 were full and associate members, 159 honorary supporting members, 50 were in the Junior Department, 94 in the Women's Auxiliary and 102 in the new Young Women's Section.

Under the heading of Finance the figures today seem incredible with a budget surplus for the year of £2 11 shillings and fivepence! The overdraft on the current account was £476 13s 10d while the overdraft on the building account stood at £4,4926 9 shillings. At the end of the Annual Report was a list of all 159 honorary supporting members whose yearly subscriptions and donations ranged from five shillings to George Dowty's generous five guineas. The largest individual donation came from the Cheltymca Dramatic Society which contributed £17 15s 6d, an enormous sum for the time, the majority averaging around 1 guinea.

A substantial section of the Report focussed on Service to the Community. "The record of service rendered by members to the community is a striking tribute to the spirit existing in the Association, and one which should make those connected with it feel justly proud." The Secretary for Education in Cheltenham, Mr. W. Turner Long, had again asked the YMCA to organise a scheme of Play Leadership for children in the parks and recreation grounds during the month of August. Included in this was a sports meeting for which 700 entries were received for 25 events. 48 races were held in two hours with 80 prizes presented by the Mayor. Several other councillors and dignitaries also turned up.

Baseball was overseen by four American missionaries based at the YMCA and thanks was extended for the support of the 2nd Cheltenham Rover Scout Crew (St. Philip's). The Town Council conveyed their thanks by a gift of £20 to the YMCA with the National Playing Fields Association also recognising their work.

The Annual Party for poor children was a delightful function with over 100 boys and girls present.

The Guild of Service had carried out a number of odd jobs.

Mr. A.J. Moxon was the Hon. Secretary of the Junior Department and had clearly been very busy with activities taking place five nights a week. The average attendance was 34. The Friday evening Bible Class was described as the centre of the Club's life and had been well attended. A Junior Dramatic Society showed great promise under the direction of Mr. J.E. Davey and a successful Rummage Sale took place with support from the Women's Auxiliary who also ran the successful Annual Junior Party.

The new Young Women's Section was led by the Mayoress, Mrs. J.H. Trye with Mrs. A.G. Pite a fine Chairman of the Advisory Council which had been established on October 25th. She was succeeded by Miss M. Jennings when her husband Arthur, the

Football Club

◀ Cheltenham YMCA ran four adult teams and this picture dates from October 1937. Back row from left; unknown referee, J.W. Smith, A.J. Bray, K. Smith, R. Smith, H. Doxey, A. Daft, L.J. Marshall; front row from left; H. Cook, E. Bliss, V. Moss, A.S. Vollans. There are only 11 players because substitutes did not arrive for another 30 years. The referee is properly kitted out for the time in open necked shirt and blazer!

Cricket Club

▶ Amazingly, the YMCA ran six pre-war teams, some of which played midweek on Wednesday afternoons when, like most of the country, the town closed down and everyone went home at lunchtime. Many still had to work all day Saturday but the lucky ones played in the afternoon for a different cricket team. The twelfth man often acted as scorer and drinks waiter, but was sometimes called upon to field in the case of injury.

Baseball Section

◀ It seems that both baseball and basketball were popular during the late-1930s, no doubt an impetus coming from four American missionaries who lodged at the Promenade. Being an international organisation, the YMCA provided an easy transition for people from different continents with each Association priding itself on giving first class hospitality to visitors.

▲ Gymnastics was another sport taken very seriously, as this open air display suggests. There was no shortage of interest in YMCA activities by the general public, and this picture includes a large number of children. Training took place in the Royal Well Hut where the gymnasium was situated but outside help was also given to St. James' Church Lads Brigade and at Charlton Kings.

▲ Led by Ronald Brown, the YMCA musical ensemble was at one point the largest amateur orchestra in Gloucestershire and gave several concerts, both in the Promenade and at outside venues.

▲ *This fascinating picture of the YMCA Concert Party shows the leader, Basil Miller, fifth from the left on the back row. Next but one on his left, with glasses, is John Lott who married Whyla Williams, sitting far left. Their progeny included a daughter called Felicity who later became a famous singer and a Dame.*

new Principal of Cheltenham College, died suddenly after only a year in office. Soon afterwards she also lost one of her six children, Edward, from a burst appendix. Undaunted, she soldiered on and became Vice Principal of Cheltenham Ladies' College from 1939-1946.

The new section had its own finances with six women acting as leaders. In addition to a separate programme it was felt that the additional mixed activities promoted a better understanding of the sexes! The Town Hall Social on February 9th 1939 was followed by a Special Mixed Service at the YMCA on Sunday, February 12th. "Great opportunities lie ahead but it is essential that the work which has been so ably started should receive the support of an increasing number of public spirited people." Little did they know how true that was going to be.

The Women's Auxiliary had an exceptionally busy year under the excellent leadership of Mrs J.E. Webster (Chairman) and Mrs. J.H. Trye (Vice Chairman) – no political correctness in those days! The monthly tea meetings had been well attended with many interesting speakers. Among the activities were garden parties, whist drives, sale of work, rummage sales and general entertainments. A substantial cheque was given as a Christmas present to the YMCA and among other solid items donated was a new refrigerator. The Hon. Secretary, Mrs. Baker, and the Hon. Treasurer, Miss Higgins, were both thanked for their efforts.

The section on National Service was a premonition of things to come because it reported that many members of the Women's Auxiliary had joined the Women's Voluntary Service for Civil Defence, put aside for Canteen Work for the Fighting Services under the YMCA. Enrolment for the Cheltenham unit came under the direction of Mrs. Percy James with 60 Cheltenham women taking part. A short course of ARP Lectures was in progress backed up by a course on practical canteen classes, soon to be put to good use right across the county.

Obituaries included Fred Daldry, General Secretary of Bournemouth YMCA who trained the Cheltenham YMCA General Secretary, Arthur. Naylor, whose son John Naylor later became Secretary of the National Council of YMCAs from the 1980s to the 1990s. Daldry had a namesake nephew Fred, who succeeded Charles Belcher as the Cheltenham YMCA Secretary after the war!

▲ This Junior Department Party includes their Leader and Assistant General Secretary, A.J. Moxon (middle with bow tie) and on his right, Arthur Naylor, the General Secretary.

▲ The YMCA placed great store on training others and this collage is from a summer sports meeting organised as part of the Play Leadership Scheme on behalf of the Council.

◄ Sunday Afternoon Rallies were always well attended. There was no television, no Sunday sport, and BBC radio broadcasts were generally dull. In fact until well into the 1960s very little at all happened on Sundays. Shops, cinemas and most places of entertainment were closed so a good meeting was just the ticket. In the middle on the front row is President, Percy Smith, and on his left the General Secretary, Arthur Naylor.

Thanks were expressed to several people including the *Gloucestershire Echo* newspaper; Cheltenham College for the use of its cricket ground; the Clergy and Ministers of the Town; Cheltenham Town Council; the County Education Committee; and the Area Committee of the National Fitness Council.

The Conclusion speaks for itself: "If this report has suggested that the achievements of 1938 have been wrought by the hands of men and women then it would be misleading. The guidance to do the right things and the power to carry them out has come from God. Therefore, with gratitude to Him the Executive Committee look forward to the future with high hopes and great confidence that this work may go from strength to strength, and always be a centre to which youth can come for guidance and help." The forthcoming war saw to it that the latter part of this paragraph was carried out to the full.

****

This was the last major printed document issued by Cheltenham YMCA until 1950, when the Annual Handbook was reintroduced. The intervening years, in keeping with the rest of the country, were fraught with difficulty but, thanks to a dedicated band of volunteers and staff, the Association survived relatively unscathed. Wartime itself was a quite remarkable story.

► A very crowded Town Hall on the the opening of the Young Women's Section. Mrs. Trye, the first President felt that Cheltenham should be grateful that a hitherto men-only organisation was now running mixed activities! Single sex was the norm in most schools at the time and continued so for the next 30-40 years but so popular was the new section that over 1,000 people, mostly younger ones, turned up. It had initially been thought unnecessary to book the Town Hall but when 90 young ladies signed up in the first few days it was realised that large numbers had latched on to the new group with gusto.

CHAPTER 7
SECOND WORLD WAR 1939-1945

Although it came as no real surprise in September 1939, when prime minister Neville Chamberlain finally uttered the fateful words "This country is at war with Germany", it still sent a silent shudder down everyone's spine. The gloves were off and mobilisation quickly became the name of the game. After initial panic, when the government hastily banned all public entertainment and large gatherings, there was time for reflection. The so called "Phoney War" proved to be an uneasy truce and entertainment was soon put back on the menu, although too late to save some actors who had already enlisted.

The *Gloucestershire Echo* of January 22nd, 1940 mentioned a "YMCA Sunday Evening Concert" in the lecture hall when the YMCA Light Orchestra played "Children of the Regiment" by Herman Finck, "Bells Across the Meadow" by Albert Ketelbey, "Under the Balcony" and "Second Serenade" by Jonny Heykens, a selection from the First World War musical "Chu Chin Chow" (which had just been revived in London), and "Tres Jolie" by Emile Waldteufel. The baritone soloist was Tom Cruwys and an interval talk was given by Chairman Arthur Dye based on St. Luke, Chapter 14. Refreshments were served by members of the Young Women's Section. This kind of concert was extremely popular at the time and remained so until the late-1960s when the Light Music genre took a nose dive. Happily, it has been rediscovered and such a concert today would meet with the same favourable reception it did more than 60 years ago.

Once the phoney war was over, Cheltenham was no different to anywhere else in that everyone rallied to the cause but it was not, of course, a direct target like London, Birmingham, Liverpool, Manchester etc. It did, however, suffer considerable bomb damage with several fatalities, and it was later discovered that one of the prime targets was H.H. Martyn's Sunningend premises in Lansdown which had been mistakenly marked on the map as being those of Dowty Group HQ at Arle Court. This was not entirely surprising when one considers the Gloucestershire Aircraft Company in Hucclecote was an offshoot of Martyn's.

In a two-hour raid on December 11th, 1940 many houses in Stoneville Street were demolished with resulting casualties and fatalities, and a gasometer was also blown up at the junction of Gloucester Road and the High Street. A string of bombs also straddled Leckhampton, blowing up the Pilley Lane railway bridge. Brunswick Street was badly damaged in a separate incident on July 27th, 1942, again with several fatalities and casualties with other lesser incidents occurring from time to time. However, because Cheltenham was not regarded as a high risk area and was strategically situated geographically, it became a base for many servicemen and women, indeed Cheltenham College Chapel was even mooted as an alternative to the Houses of Parliament should the government be forced to leave London.

What was Cheltenham YMCA up to during this period of hostilities? The answer is a great deal and the Addendum to this chapter, discovered and added after the main body of the text was complete, is based around a wartime YMCA booklet published in late-1941 or early 1942. It gives a fascinating insight into the early months and is best read as a separate entity.

Centred around the Royal Well Military Canteen, the Lansdown Station Military Canteen, many smaller local and outlying canteens and Service centres, several mobile tea cars and a mobile library, the Women's Auxiliary got to work with a vengeance. Dressed in dark green uniforms similar to those of the WVS (Women's Voluntary Service) they put up a magnificent show both locally and nationally. Meanwhile, the premises in the Promenade were stuffed out as accommodation for all and sundry but particularly visiting servicemen.

Almost at a stroke the young men of Cheltenham were whisked away, either on active service or for military training. Subsequent President, Lionel Fitz, who first joined the Junior Department in 1938, mentions his wartime experi-

▶ Taken around 1940 this very busy Promenade scene shows the YMCA at the bottom right. Although theoretically a safe town Cheltenham dealt with huge numbers of servicemen and women, and was bombed on a number of occasions. The YMCA was always full to bursting with several overspill units nearby, including the Unitarian Church and Royal Well Chapel at the rear, the former now an auction room, the latter demolished.

◀ The famous Royal Well Canteen situated at the rear of the Promenade on Royal Well Road. The Council Chamber now stands on this spot. Built in the mid-1920s as a gymnasium extension, it also housed an expanding YMCA Junior Department which was forced to move out in early 1940 when it found a new home at the Baker Street Men's Institute which became Baker Street YMCA, better-known as Baker Street Boys' Club explained in the next chapter.

▲ Every conceivable means of transport was utilised during the war when petrol was rationed and at a premium. Milky Ways and Maltesers have a long history!

▲ Mrs. James (left) and Mrs. Trye, were the two major leaders of the women's YMCA wartime work.

ences in the penultimate chapter. There was, however, no diminution in the junior membership and so strong did it become – understandably when one considers the loss of fathers, general amenities and almost universal motherly protection which encouraged children to find worthwhile pursuits – it grew rapidly. It was soon homeless, however, because when the Royal Well Junior Department Hut became the Royal Well Canteen for servicemen in November 1939, they had nowhere to go.

During negotiations for the use of Alstone Baths, the town's first municipal swimming pool situated on Great Western Road (opened 1887, closed 1975 and demolished 1984), the boys temporarily moved to Clare Street Hall, the former St. Luke's church hall situated off Bath Road near Cheltenham College Junior School. Then help suddenly arrived from an unexpected source. George Hitchman and other influential YMCA committee members and trustees of the Gas Green Young Men's League in Baker Street, offered their premises at a peppercorn rent. Denuded of its members they were only too keen to keep the premises going while the leaders of Cheltenham YMCA were only too happy to accept them. Thus began the Baker Street YMCA covered in another chapter.

Meanwhile, back on the Promenade, the YMCA turned its attention to other urgent matters. Accommodation for servicemen was needed wherever there were training facilities and Cheltenham was as busy as anywhere. Later on the town also hosted American servicemen who added more than a bit of colour to the town, although not everyone was happy about their attentions to the local women! Certainly the pubs and clubs did a roaring trade when there was often little room inside even to raise a glass to one's mouth!

Inside the Promenade the rooms were quickly made available to those in need but an even greater service was performed out at the back. The Royal Well Military Canteen was rapidly created from the wooden gymnasium and served troops night and day from, September 1939 until May 1946. Full details were given in a specially prepared post-war booklet entitled *A Souvenir Tribute to the Royal Well Military Canteen*. In it we learn the inside story of just one among hundreds of similar canteens around the country. Although not specifically mentioned in the text, it must also be remembered that Cheltenham YMCA ran a second large amenity, the Lansdown Station Military Canteen which stood at the top of the slope to the left as one faces the front entrance of the station buildings today. This hut was speedily erected in late-1939 on the same site as that built in 1916 to assist troops during the First World War.

****

Let the Souvenir booklet speak for itself:

"In the spring of 1939 the Cheltenham Women's Auxiliary YMCA, like so many others, was going on with its useful, helpful work for various peace-time YMCA activities. These, indeed, it has kept up and still continues to do. But about the time of 'Munich', Mrs. James and Mrs. Trye came back from Women's Auxiliary Headquarters in London with the message that the motto up there was the Scout's one of 'Be Prepared' so a course of lectures by experts in canteen work was arranged, and when September 3rd came there was a nucleus of 20 workers trained and ready for service. Mrs. James, who had organised this, was appointed War Leader by Women's Auxiliary Headquarters, and she was joined by Mrs. Trye, whose enthusiasm, drive and resource were as invaluable as Mrs. James' powers of organisation and of administration.

Work was started at once in the main YMCA building, but as the troops poured in the place was soon crowded out, and it became evident that a service on a much larger scale was required.

The Hut which had served the YMCA as a gymnasium was taken over, and by the end of November had been put in order and equipped and became 'Royal Well Canteen'.

The work was organised from the beginning by Mrs. James and Mrs. Trye, with Miss Paice as Manageress and Mrs. Lulham as Assistant-Manageress and later on, on Miss Paice's retirement on marriage, as Manageress.

Mrs. James, as War Leader, enrolled the band of workers who came forward in great numbers, and organised a system of shifts under various leaders, who were the nucleus of Women's Auxiliary members who had already been trained in canteen work.

▶ This happy group at Royal Well would have been a motley collection of servicemen who might have come from anywhere. The YMCA's aim was simply to make life as comfortable as possible for any who sought out accommodation or refreshment. Note what is probably a colourful railway poster on the wall together with the mesh on the window which might have been a legacy from its time as a YMCA gymnasium.

THREE SCENES AT THE ROYAL WELL CANTEEN

▶ Queueing for a drink. The canteen never closed and on one monitored day alone it served more than 2,400 meals, 1,793 cups of tea and 635 cups of coffee and cocoa. On the busiest day the number of meals served exceeded 3,000! This speaks volumes about the army of volunteers who turned up each day to help the cause.

The canteen day was divided into five shifts, each shift requiring ten or twelve helpers and put in charge of a Shift Leader. Many of these, as also many of their workers, served through the whole six years of war. Every week these Leaders met under the Chairmanship of Mrs. James, and in that way constant touch was kept with all aspects of the work and free discussions were held.

Then as to finance, it was mainly owing to Mrs. Trye's generosity, and to that of her American relations and friends, that all the alterations were made and equipment provided. No general appeal for funds was made, but many kind gifts were received.

A Finance and Management Committee was set up which included the Chairman and Secretary of the Cheltenham Women's Auxiliary. With able expert help very careful accounts were kept, costs scrutinised, and the problem of keeping up standards of quality, while cutting out waste, and of leaving the profit as low as possible without financial danger, was dealt with, with more and more efficiency as experience was acquired. Most of the Women's Auxiliary Military Canteens did not have the advantage of this expert watchful local management, and were financed and controlled from HQ.

During the war years £10,000 was sent from Royal Well Canteen to YMCA Headquarters to be used for further war work. During that time five million cups of tea were sold at 1d. each, and over £78,000 in all was taken over the Canteen counters. On that large scale if there was not to be an actual loss there had to be a substantial margin of profit. However, but for the big company of voluntary workers, there would have been little or no profit, and it might be said that this £10,000 was a definite gift from them, over and above that cheerful and devoted service which gave the 'homey' friendly atmosphere which seemed to envelop all who entered Royal Well. As one of the men wrote, 'You seem to think of all the little things that cheer us boys who are far from our home surroundings.'

There are so many who did outstanding work they cannot here be named, but a word must be said of the devoted workers who came every morning at 5.45am, winter and summer, to clean, and had the place spick and span by 8 o'clock, and of those who, after a hard working day, came once a fortnight to wash down the whole of the floor, and of the band of ladies who came every morning to prepare vegetables and fruit.

Let us look at Royal Well in a peak hour. The place is packed, men of the three British Services, women of the WRNS, ATS, WAAF and Land Army, and also many of our USA allies. These last said they liked to meet our Service men and women in the friendly atmosphere of Royal Well, and they allowed that for once the British could make coffee up to the home standard. A compliment indeed! Change was to be had at the door so that exact sums could be handed over the counter, thus ensuring quick and efficient service.

What the Service men and women thought of it can be seen by the letters chosen from so many, which are reproduced at the end of this book."

****

The first letter came from Lance Corporal A.L. Bentnall who was serving in Greece but whose parents had moved to Cheltenham. He had been most impressed when he visited and commented " …. I found a comradeship which I haven't seen in other canteens." The other two letters were written on YMCA Wartime Headed Notepaper and simply signed "A Serviceman" and "A Canadian". Both gave glowing testimony to the work of the Royal Well Canteen and were obviously heartfelt thanks.

Then came a poem entitled "Royal Well Canteen" probably written for the farewell dinner which took place on June 19th 1946, the canteen having closed the previous month:

There was a canteen low and green
Where crowds of troops were always seen.
Sad our hearts to say "goodbye",
For we will love it till we die.

Tea, buns and sandwiches we served,
And carefully food control observed,
Hard work, slogging, chores did try,
But still we'll love it till we die.

Our dear old Hut, the Royal Well,
Tonight we come to say "Farewell!
Six years of work have now passed by,
But still we'll love it till we die.

▲ *Just a few of the many helpers at the Royal Well Canteen. The top picture shows Mrs. Trye in the centre (in uniform) with Mrs. James to the right. Elizabeth Trye, wife of the Mayor of Cheltenham, was an American with endless drive and enthusiasm, while Irene James was appointed War Leader by the YMCA Women's Auxiliary HQ in London. Together they made a formidable partnership and were loyally supported by a vast number of local people.*

▶ Part of the vast army of volunteers who turned up every day to help at one of the local YMCA wartime canteens. The Royal Well was the most central but an equally impressive canteen was situated at Lansdown Station on the same site as the First World War YMCA Canteen. Others were situated at St. Andrew's Presbyterian Church and the Wesleyan Chapel in St. George's Street. Cheltenham was also the central YMCA depot for the whole county. This assorted group outside the Royal Well Canteen enjoyed great camaraderie, many while their husbands were away on active service.

◀ Elizabeth Trye was a truly dynamic American who took charge of all the YMCA tea vans, at least four of which were acquired through her own personal connections in the USA. The wife of Captain John Henry Trye, the Mayor of Cheltenham in 1932-3 and 1937-8, she galvanised her troops and is seen (left) with the very first tea car paid for by women in Boston, Massachussetts.

▼ The first ceremonial cup of tea was served to the Mayor and Mayoress, Councillor and Mrs. Wilfred Waite. The van bore an inscribed plaque which read "To the women of Cheltenham from the women of Boston".

◀ This van appears to be serving cigarettes which were not recognised as a danger or health hazard for many more years. In fact they were supplied during both the First and Second World Wars as a matter of course and in huge quantities to the troops.

Note the YMCA flash on the young lady's sleeve and also the YMCA badge on her cap.

The YMCA Women's Auxiliary uniforms were believed to be dark grey in colour.

THREE DIFFERENT TEACARS IN SERVICE AT THE ROYAL WELL CANTEEN

▲ This van bears a badge on the roof over the windscreen which reads "YMCA Tea Car. No. 301 serving HM Forces".

◀ This van is serving tea and buns. Note the YMCA red triangle on the mugs. This symbol was adopted during the First World War and has been synonymous with the YMCA worldwide ever since.

There was no age restriction on women volunteers, and young and old worked together in harmony.

81

QUEEN MARY'S VISIT TO CHELTENHAM, AUGUST 5th 1942

◀ ▲ ◀ ▼ HM Queen Mary inspects war workers at the Royal Well Canteen.

▶ Queen Mary, Mrs. Trye and a tea van.

◀ The Queen being greeted outside the YMCA by Chairman, Arthur Dye. On the far left is YMCA President, Percy Smith and in the middle is the Mayor, Wilfred Waite. A crowd of well-wishers crowd the steps while several more look through the windows.

▶ Queen Mary lived at Badminton during the war and was a willing and most conscientious worker throughout the whole period of hostilities. She regularly visited West Country towns and encouraged all the different wartime services. On this visit to Cheltenham she also took the salute at a march past in Montpellier Gardens (see opposite).

▲ The collection of "purses" by Royalty was a major feature of YMCA fund raising and took place several times in Cheltenham, the recipients being Princess Helena Victoria in 1923 and 1925, Queen Mary here in 1942 and the Princess Royal a decade later in 1952. Seen above is Mrs. James handing over a purse on behalf of the YMCA Women's Auxiliary. In the background from the left are the Town Clerk, Frank Littlewood (in wig) the Mayor, Wilfred Waite (hidden), former Mayor, Daniel Lipson, and the Mayoress, Phyllis Waite.

▲ Queen Mary leaving the Royal Well Canteen supported by the Mayor, Wilfred Waite. Immediately behind him is his wife, the Mayoress, Phyllis Waite wearing her small chain of office. To her right, also wearing his chain of office, is Percy Smith, the YMCA President who became Mayor of Cheltenham from 1949-1951.

The notice below the YMCA sign says "Canteen 24 Hour Service".

A different picture of the Queen leaving through another door has the words "YMCA Beds" above it.

▲ ▶ Queen Mary takes the salute at a large march past in Montpellier Gardens. Mrs. James is leading the YMCA volunteers, each of whom is wearing the distinctive YMCA armband on their left side.

In the background can be seen Montpellier Spa Road which means the marchers are all heading, appropriately, in the direction of the Queen's Hotel!

▶ Cheltenham YMCA was very busy in its own right supporting the Armed Services but the town itself also served as the YMCA depot for the rest of the county. This picture shows the wife of the YMCA Divisional Secretary, Mrs. Swainson, opening a new YMCA hut at Bourton-on-the-Water in August 1941. The hut was attached to the Bourton United Services Club and, like all the other YMCA wartime huts, was timber-framed. She is assisted by Dr. R.B. Stewart.

District YMCA centres served by Cheltenham included Winchcombe led by Mrs. F.W. Adlard; Weston-sub-Edge by Mr. Aldred; Minchinhampton by Mrs. V. Fyffe; Cranham by Miss C.A. Simpson; Woodchester by Mrs. S.J. Verney; Guiting Power by Major Gooch; and Bourton-on-the-Water by Mrs. Courtney. In addition, the Cheltenham YMCA stores served centres at Cirencester, Gloucester, Tewkesbury, Cinderford and Chepstow, with the depot being administered by the Cheltenham Association on behalf of the National Council of YMCAs.

▶ Queen Mary resided at Badminton House during hostilities but got out and about as often as she could. Included in her trips were frequent visits to nearby Cirencester and she is seen here in July 1941 with workers and patrons of the YMCA Services Social Centre in Abberley House, now part of the Corinium Museum. It was clearly a welcoming centre as shown by the ubiquitous YMCA signs which could be found all over the country.

◀ In May 1941, Mayor John Howell (left) opened a YMCA exhibition in a specially constructed caravan sited outside the old General Post Office in the Promenade, opposite Cavendish House in what is now a pedestrianised area. At the microphone is Cheltenham YMCA President, Councillor Percy Smith, and on the right is Mr. E.E. Wickens who was in charge of the exhibition. The notice on the steps says "Admission Free - Exit Only" so once you were in then it was strictly one way traffic!

▶ The St. Andrew's Presbyterian Church in Montpellier — now the United Reformed Church — was another busy YMCA canteen, set up through Rev. W. McTevendale, an active member of the YMCA Executive Committee. Initially it was to remain independent but as the YMCA already had an infrastructure in place and was able to provide willing volunteers, it was recognised as best to link up. Mrs. McClellan took charge and a fine interdenominational spirit became apparent with everyone welcome at the church services.

◀ Lifts for Servicemen was a scheme devised by a young airman, L.A.C. Houghton, in conjunction with the YMCA. It aimed to help men and women of the Forces get maximum time on leave and make the best use of petrol by filling each car with the maximum number of passengers. Motorists called in to say when and where they were travelling and their details were then matched up with Service requirements as quickly as possible. The central meeting place was outside the YMCA on the Promenade.

▶ Another ingenious scheme was matching up the needs of servicemen and women travelling through Cheltenham in need of accommodation and sustenance. Many folk were more than willing to provide meals, especially at weekends as it was regarded by many parents as a "quid pro quo", knowing that their own offspring would be catered for in a similar manner somewhere else in the country. This blackboard speaks for itself but one wonders what the difference was between an Australian and a Colonial!

The booklet had begun with a message from HH Princess Helena Victoria, GBE, Queen Victoria's granddaughter who was no stranger to Cheltenham YMCA, having visited it twice in the past. As the President of the National Women's Auxiliary of the YMCA she sent a heartfelt message of thanks " …. for the splendid work you have accomplished during the past strenuous years."

Next came a message from The Hon. Mrs. S. Marsham, DBE, the Chairman of the Association, followed by an extract from a letter written from the War Office by General Sir Ronald F. Adam, Bart., GCB, DSO, OBE who also paid tribute to the ladies' work.

Finally, and most poignantly, came a joint message from Elizabeth Trye and Irene James, the Co-Leaders to their workers which ended: "We are very proud to have worked with you". It was obvious they meant it.

Then came the opening paragraph of the booklet which was also the epitaph to a fine effort: "On June 19th, 1946, at Royal Well Canteen, there was a farewell party to commemorate its six years and nine months' service. Three hundred people were present but many were absent. It is to the whole body of canteen workers, and to the faithful friends who through these long years in so many different ways helped to make the work successful, that this short account is addressed, in the hope that it will help to make 'Memory' hold the door."

Not surprisingly, the wear and tear on the Royal Well Hut was enormous. Following the pounding given to it by thousands of servicemen's boots, the floor was so badly damaged that the government paid for its renewal after the war was over. The hut was removed in 1956 and served for a time as St. Thomas' Mission Church situated near Thirlmere Road on the Alma estate in Up Hatherley, surviving until all the prefabs were replaced by permanent post-war housing in the early-1970s.

****

Elsewhere in Cheltenham there were a number of vans known either as Tea Cars or Mobile Kitchens and at least one Mobile Library, all connected at least in part to the YMCA (see Addendum to this chapter). The Library on wheels was donated by Mrs. Trye's American mother and with the YMCA triangular logo sitting in the middle, proudly stated "Mobile Library for H.M. Forces". Mrs. Trye herself served the first cup of tea from a Mobile Kitchen presented by the women of Boston, Massachussetts, the recipient being the Mayor, Councillor T.W. Waite whom she must have known quite well. Apart from normal duties these tea vans turned up whenever there was an emergency, such as the bombing in Brunswick Street when tea and soup were distributed to both victims and helpers alike.

On August 5th, 1942, none other than Queen Mary appeared and took the salute at a march past. She also witnessed an inspection of at least a dozen Mobile Canteens and visited the Royal Well

▲ *While Mrs. Waite pours the tea at the Lansdown Station Canteen, the soldiers can reflect on a hot cup of cocoa costing one penny, a sausage twopence, bacon and beans both threepence, and an egg fourpence. It is unlikely that the LMS Timetable on the wall would have been much use though!*

YMCA LANSDOWN STATION CANTEEN

Lansdown Station, now the only railway left in Cheltenham, was on the LMS wartime main line and saw hundreds of thousands of servicemen travelling through, many of whom had to change trains. When they were discovered sleeping rough in the vicinity a new YMCA canteen was hurriedly erected and once opened it never closed. During the Dunkirk evacuation it handled in excess of 10,000 men passing through on trains destined for all parts of the country. When they steamed off, however, they took so many YMCA cups with them that a rapid house to house search for replacements had to be undertaken!

▶ The leaders of the Lansdown Station Canteen were the Mayoress, Mrs. Phyllis Waite (left) and Mrs. E.L. Ward.

Canteen into the bargain. As she departed with the Mayor, a photographer captured her descending the steps and just behind is a notice which read "YMCA Canteen – 24 Hour Service". One cannot ask for greater devotion to duty than that!

Looking back, YMCA President Lionel Fitz remembered being a member of the ATC drum and bugle band which led the military parade. He also remembered the bomb damage affecting the unique factory of H.H. Martyn which had by then switched from ornamental iron and stonework to military matters, and also a gasholder being blown up. Even Lord Haw Haw got in on the act by claiming, falsely, that German aircraft had bombed the Cheltenham railway marshalling yards.

****

Meanwhile, back at the Promenade, the YMCA coped extremely well with whatever was thrown at it. Space was always at a premium but as many as possible were squeezed in and looked after. Ask anyone who can still remember the war and they will tell you that the thought of ever losing to Hitler simply never entered anyone's head. Once Churchill was at the helm then everyone naturally assumed that victory would come. It was just a matter of time. Activities may have been reduced in number and the gymnasium commandeered by the Women's Auxiliary but life was as normal as hostilities would allow it. Everyone simply got on with their jobs.

Anywhere deemed suitable was used for accommodation and if the YMCA was full, as it usually was, then alternative premises were sought. These included the nearby Bayshill Unitarian Church now used as an auction room, and Royal Well Chapel also situated between Cheltenham Ladies College and the bus station but demolished during the mid-1960s. Dozens of other similar properties were also put to good use.

In addition to the temporary residents, there were thousands and thousands of visitors. One of the most famous and who remembered frequenting the YMCA on the Promenade, sitting on the ground floor drinking tea and watching the world go by through the window, was Sir Norman Wisdom. Unknown at the time, and having suffered an extremely difficult upbringing, he ran away from home and begged to be allowed to learn a musical instrument and enlist. His brilliant show business career effectively began at Cheltenham Town Hall whilst a member of the wartime Royal Signals band. When someone turned his music upside down for a joke, Norman promptly stood on his head and played it the wrong way up! His later clowning came about almost by accident when he slipped during his act and provoked laughter from the audience. When he did it again they roared their approval and from then on it was the tight-fitting suit and cap, and perpetual clowning. In the words of his first hit song in 1953: *"Don't laugh at me 'cause I'm a fool"*. Norman also later admitted to regularly siphoning petrol from his CO's car which is how, much to everyone's astonishment who could not work out how and where he obtained the fuel, he managed to ride a wartime motorbike around town! So important was Cheltenham to Norman that he returned annually for a Royal Signals reunion dinner for the next 60 years!

Charles Belcher eventually succeeded A.E. Naylor and between them they faithfully held the fort throughout the war years. He was capably assisted by his deputy, A.J. Moxon who was originally in charge of the Junior Department for boys under 16. However, when the Baker Street YMCA was established in 1940, Moxon stayed on at the Promenade, his place as Youth Leader at Baker Street being taken firstly by "Pop" Davey and later by Vic Dymock.

The wartime years for Cheltenham YMCA were therefore, perhaps paradoxically, both frustrating and exhilarating. Most of the local young men had departed but in their place came hordes of other young men from all over the UK, USA, Canada, Europe and the British Empire. Women too played their role in uniform, both in the Services and in general service. For the older members of the Women's Auxiliary it was a golden opportunity to shine in the most remarkable manner – and shine they did.

Everyone did us proud and this book takes great pleasure and satisfaction in publicly saluting all those connected with the wartime effort at Cheltenham YMCA.

Well done!

▶ Possibly the best-known Cheltenham Serviceman was Norman Wisdom, seen here second left on the front row of the Royal Signals football team. He surprised everyone by riding a motorbike around town but little did his C.O. Major Knowles (back centre) know that the petrol was being siphoned from his car! Sir Norman was a regular at the YMCA and returned to Cheltenham each and every year for his Regimental dinner.

◀ Not only did the troops need physical sustenance they also needed things to fill their spare time. With no television, 78rpm records being melted down and re-used and precious little on the radio — or wireless as it was known at the time — the obvious alternative was books. The nation was keen on reading and the education system, both for children and adults, actively encouraged it. This wartime mobile library was donated by Mrs. Trye's mother in New York, long before the Americans entered the war.

▶ When the YMCA Headquarters was destroyed in London, most of the National leadership moved to Cheltenham where they were welcomed and made as comfortable as possible by the local Association. Suitable living accommodation was found at Aban Court in Malvern Road and the Criterion Temperance Hotel in Albion Street — seen here in an Edwardian photograph but since demolished — was secured for their offices. It was an interesting reconciliation following the huge disappointment of HQ turning down a request for a £3,000 loan by Cheltenham during the mid-1930s.

ADDENDUM TO CHAPTER 7

"OUR WORK FOR THE TROOPS"

Some time after this chapter was initially completed a much sought after document was unearthed at Birmingham University which holds the national YMCA archives. Its existence was known about but a local copy had proved elusive. 82 pages long, albeit more than half of which was fascinating advertising, it filled in many of the wartime gaps and rather than attempt to rewrite this chapter it was felt best to give it a section to itself. Some repetition is therefore inevitable

It was probably published in late-1941 or early-1942 because the Mayor was listed as Councillor John Howell whose term of office ran from 1938-1941 but like many wartime documents little was given away in case it fell into the wrong hands. Hostilities still had at least three years to run but what had already happened via the YMCA in Cheltenham speaks volumes.

The Foreword was by the President, Percy Smith, who commented on 200 YMCA members being initially called up to the Services. After that he paid tribute to the "loyal, enthusiastic and self-sacrificing work of hundreds of local good friends and supporters, without whom the task would have proved too much", the task being the service already provided by Cheltenham YMCA for the war effort.

Three pages were given over to listing all the wartime YMCA Personnel covering the President and 14 eminent Vice-Presidents including Councillors D.L. Lipson MP and A.J. Bettridge after whom a local school was later named, George Dowty of what later became Dowty Aerospace, and A.W. Martyn of H.H. Martyn and Son. Among the 15 strong Executive Committee was W.W. Crosweller whose local firm made its name in bathroom and shower fittings. A.E. Naylor was still General Secretary assisted by Capt. E.L.L. Webb. J.E. Davey was the Boys' Work Secretary assisted by A.J. Moxon. Mrs. W.A. Baker was the Women's Auxiliary Secretary and Mrs. N.G. Osborne the YW (Young Women's) Secretary. Capt. and Mrs. R.F.C. McDowall ran the Information Bureau and W. Dawson was in charge of the Stores. An Education Committee was headed by chairman Sir Henry Gooch JP with Canon J.B. Goodliffe, the Rector, as his vice-chairman.

It was obvious that a Services canteen must quickly be brought into action, but where? The initial solution was conversion of the Royal Well Hut into the Royal Well Canteen. The Boys Department moved out, initially to Clare Street Hall and then to the Baker Street Institute described elsewhere. However, it is clear that a 24-hour YMCA service had already been in operation from the moment war was declared, although food was always a problem and all wartime institutions, including boarding schools, had great difficulty finding enough supplies for the large numbers of people they catered for.

Almost from day one the Royal Well Canteen proved too small to meet the needs of all the servicemen passing through the town because it was always full and particularly busy at weekends. On one monitored day alone it served more than 2,400 meals, 1,793 cups of tea and 635 cups of coffee and cocoa. On the busiest day the number of meals served exceeded 3,000! What could be done to ease the situation?

The matter swiftly came to a head when soldiers were found asleep on benches in Queen's Road while waiting for railway connections. It was resolved to do something at once and the result was a second YMCA hut established at Lansdown Station, on the same site as the First World War hut mentioned in the 1914-1918 chapter. The LMS Railway immediately gave permission for the project and a local firm was entrusted to build it, which they did very speedily. Successful from the outset many thousands of men and women had reason to be thankful for its friendly welcome.

The management was in the hands of Mrs. E.L. Ward and Mrs. T.W. Waite (wife of the Mayor) and since its opening in January 1940 – a date which shows just how quickly it was erected – it never closed its doors. During the Dunkirk evacuation it handled in excess of 10,000 men passing through on trains destined for all parts of the country, who were supplied with free tea, sandwiches, biscuits and cigarettes. The main problem was getting the cups returned because trains did not wait long and hundreds were carried away to unknown destina-

▶ *An early view of the Lansdown Station Canteen before it was extended. Initially erected in a great hurry when servicemen were found sleeping overnight on benches in the street, it soon found itself as busy as the Royal Well Canteen. Most of its visitors were short term, however, unlike other YMCA canteens in the town. The central location of Cheltenham and its strategic importance as a railway junction meant that many of the troops spent several hours waiting for a connection.*

◀ *These are boys from the Baker Street YMCA, or Baker Street Boys' Club as it was more commonly known locally. Everyone did their bit and the youngsters are collecting salvage for the war effort, an extremely important occupation. Many of the railings in the town were taken down and used for scrap with anything aluminium of vital significance for, among other things, making new aeroplanes for the RAF.*

▶ *This small boy had a day to remember when he presented a "purse" to Queen Mary in Montpellier Gardens. Dozens of local organisations vied with each other to collect cash for the event and many made great sacrifices. "Make do and mend" was one of the wartime phrases which stayed the course into post-war austerity although the sarcastic joke "There is a war on, you know" gradually faded from the public vocabulary.*

tions. At one point it proved necessary to make a house to house collection to keep the supply going. The LMS (London Midland Scottish) Railway Company also gave practical help by loaning two railway carriages to provide extra sleeping accommodation for men stranded on their travels.

A third YMCA canteen was to be found at St. Andrew's Presbyterian Church, set up through the good offices of Rev. W. McTevendale, an active member of the YMCA Executive Committee. Initially it was to remain independent but as the YMCA already had an infrastructure in place and was able to provide willing volunteers, it was recognised as best to link up. Mrs. McClellan took charge and a fine interdenominational spirit became apparent with an open invitation to the church services being taken up by many. The busiest time of day was in the morning when breakfast was served to men who had spent a night in one of the many bed centres when it was a case of all hands on deck. This excellent morning repast cost ninepence, a treat which nobody wanted to miss. In addition to the main hall equipped for meals and games, there were two quiet rooms for reading and writing letters around a cosy fire. A lecture room was also available for evening prayers and meetings.

A further YMCA canteen was known as the Wesley on St. George's Street under the leadership of Mrs. W. Nicholson and Mrs. P.B. Hayman, admirable premises which included quiet rooms for reading, writing and recreation. Opened as a Methodist chapel in 1840 it closed in 1971 and became a warehouse, later converted into flats. District YMCA centres served by Cheltenham included Winchcombe led by Mrs. F.W. Adlard; Weston-sub-Edge by Mr. Aldred; Minchinhampton by Mrs. V. Fyffe; Cranham by Miss C.A. Simpson; Woodchester by Mrs. S.J. Verney; Guiting Power by Major Gooch; and Bourton-on-the-Water by Mrs. Courtney. In addition, the Cheltenham YMCA stores served centres at Cirencester, Gloucester, Tewkesbury, Cinderford and Chepstow, with the depot being administered by the Cheltenham Association on behalf of the National Council of YMCAs.

Cheltenham was among the first in Gloucestershire to provide a mobile canteen and later ran several. They went anywhere and everywhere, whenever the need arose. Later in the war they attended bomb damaged parts of the town, providing sustenance to injured and rescuers alike. Soldiers off the beaten track were grateful not just for refreshments but also for bootlaces, postage stamps and even braces.

Mrs. Trye was the brains behind the scheme and enlisted the support of her two sisters in America. Mrs. Sewall from Boston sent £190 raised from a party at her house and Mrs. Jaffray of New York sent £279 raised from a single afternoon's Bridge at the Women's Republican Club! The first mobile canteen was joined by several more and by 1942 there at least eight operating around the district, a number certainly exceeded by the end of hostilities. Served by a stores depot in Pittville Street and staffed entirely by volunteers the fully equipped canteens were presented by Mrs. Hoseason, Mrs. W.H. Bagnall (two vans), and Mrs. R. Trye (credited with no fewer than four!). The leaders were Mrs. Bagnall, Miss Bagnall, Mrs. Adlard, Miss P. Gough, Mrs. Matheson, Miss Anderson and Mrs. Trye.

The success of the mobile canteens led to the introduction of an equally appreciated Mobile Library carrying a cargo of both light and serious books. This time the donor was Mrs. Trye's mother in New York. Readers of the booklet were encouraged to provide "fiction, thrillers, detective and adventure stories, biography, travel, drama, popular science and any contemporary books on current affairs". The receiving depot was at 13 Pittville Street.

Sleeping accommodation was a major problem. Up to 100 men were catered for at the Promenade premises, albeit on armchairs, settees and even on the floor once the hostel and lecture hall had been filled to capacity. Bayshill Church offered their lecture hall where 40 beds were installed but still the supply was inadequate. The Mayor and D.L. Lipson, the town's MP, were then partially responsible for organising a further 70 beds in the Royal Well Chapel.

Nine months experience of the war proved that a properly organised scheme was essential to deal with enquiries and so an Information Bureau was established. Run by Mr. and Mrs. McDowall with assistance from the Young Women's Section in the

▲ ▶ In a two-hour raid over Cheltenham on December 11th, 1940 many houses were demolished with resulting casualties and fatalities. A gasometer was also blown up at the junction of Gloucester Road and the High Street. These two pictures show the aftermath in Stoneville Street with several YMCA rescue workers on hand. A YMCA tea van can also be clearly seen back right on the picture above. It was never clear whether the raid was intended on the town.

◀ Brunswick Street was badly damaged on July 27th, 1942, again with several fatalities and casualties. These publicity pictures were taken soon afterwards and capture the YMCA Women's Auxiliary teams at work with their tea vans. Although the recipients and donors are all smiling, the reality was very different. Both Mrs. James and Mrs. Trye appear to be in the picture above and we can be sure that wherever and whenever there was a need these two remarkable ladies would not have been very far away.

evenings, it was open seven days a week from 9.30am to 9.30pm helping with accommodation, postage stamps, cinema and theatre bookings, guides, lifts to various places etc. The standard of efficiency was high and thousands of servicemen and women were helped in numerous ways.

Lifts for Servicemen was a scheme devised by a young airman called L.A.C. Houghton in conjunction with YMCA officials and began with a two-fold objective:

1. To help men and women of the Forces to get the maximum time on leave with a minimum of expense.

2. To make the greatest use of the country's petrol by filling up each car with its maximum number of passengers.

Motorists were encouraged to call in at the Enquiry Bureau and say when and where they were travelling, details which were then matched up with Service requirements as quickly as possible, the central meeting place being outside the YMCA on the Promenade.

Another clever idea was the Host Scheme where, instead of Forces being accommodated in a communal setting, they were invited out to a meal or sometimes for a whole weekend by host families. Again through the good offices of Mr. Houghton, the Rotary Club joined the YMCA in getting this scheme off the ground, later transferring direct to the Enquiry Bureau. It was reported that Christmas (presumably 1941) saw more than 200 men catered for in this manner.

At the suggestion of the National Council of YMCA's Education Department, the General Secretary and Sir Henry Gooch, former Chairman of the London County Council who had come to Cheltenham for the duration of the war, conducted a survey to see what might be required in the town. The result was a series of lectures, as many as 50 a month, given on various educational topics. Lecturers gave their time free and often paid for their own transport, the Women's Voluntary Service coming to the rescue when necessary.

In a section entitled Social Work for Members of H.M. Forces were listed Concert Parties where the loss of Basil Miller to the RAF was regretted but whose place had been ably taken by Miss Mollie Bose. Saturday Evening Dances were arranged by Mr. H. Cook with the Royal Well Hut filled to capacity. Only a week before Christmas Day 1941 it was suddenly realised that no provision had been made to entertain all the local Service people and that the cinemas and theatres would be closed. A huge Christmas Day Social was therefore staged at the Town Hall by the YMCA, Women's Auxiliary and the Martini Concert Party. More than 1,000 men and women enjoyed five hours of non-stop entertainment, hosted by the YMCA Young Women's Section, Toc H and the Central Brotherhood. Refreshments were nearly all home made by the YMCA domestic staff and served by the Canteen workers organised by Mrs. P. James. As several members of the Forces put it: "What should we have done without Cheltenham YMCA?" Many other socials were also held at the Town Hall.

Under the heading General Welfare Work were included various items. Gifts of equipment included wireless sets, gramophones, pianos, books, games, knitted woollen comforts, furniture for rest rooms, rugs, pillows and beds. Bible New Testaments and hundreds of thousands of envelopes and sheets of notepaper were also distributed. Washing and lavatory facilities had been greatly improved by a grant from the National YMCA War Service Fund and a Lightning Repair Service was working well, with clean socks and garments repaired within 24 hours if left in a box at the Enquiry Bureau. Parcels for Members on Active Service included comforts knitted by the Women's Auxiliary and Young Women's Sections.

The Baker Street Boys Club is dealt with in a separate chapter but merited six pages of text and photographs in the booklet. It was regarded as an important future part of the local YMCA and in time, so it proved. J.E.F. Davey, who had given valuable voluntary service at the Promenade, was appointed in charge with the now ageing A.J. Moxon who had run the Boys Department for many years, still looking after the younger end, although younger in those days meant 13 year olds, not primary school age like today.

A Youth Service Squad was formed which acted as messengers for the WVS (Women's Voluntary Service) and the YMCA generally, as well as up to six boys gardening at the Emergency Hospital each

▲ *It's all over! The servicemen may still be in uniform but for the YMCA Women's Auxiliary it is the end of an era in which they distinguished themselves in every conceivable manner.*

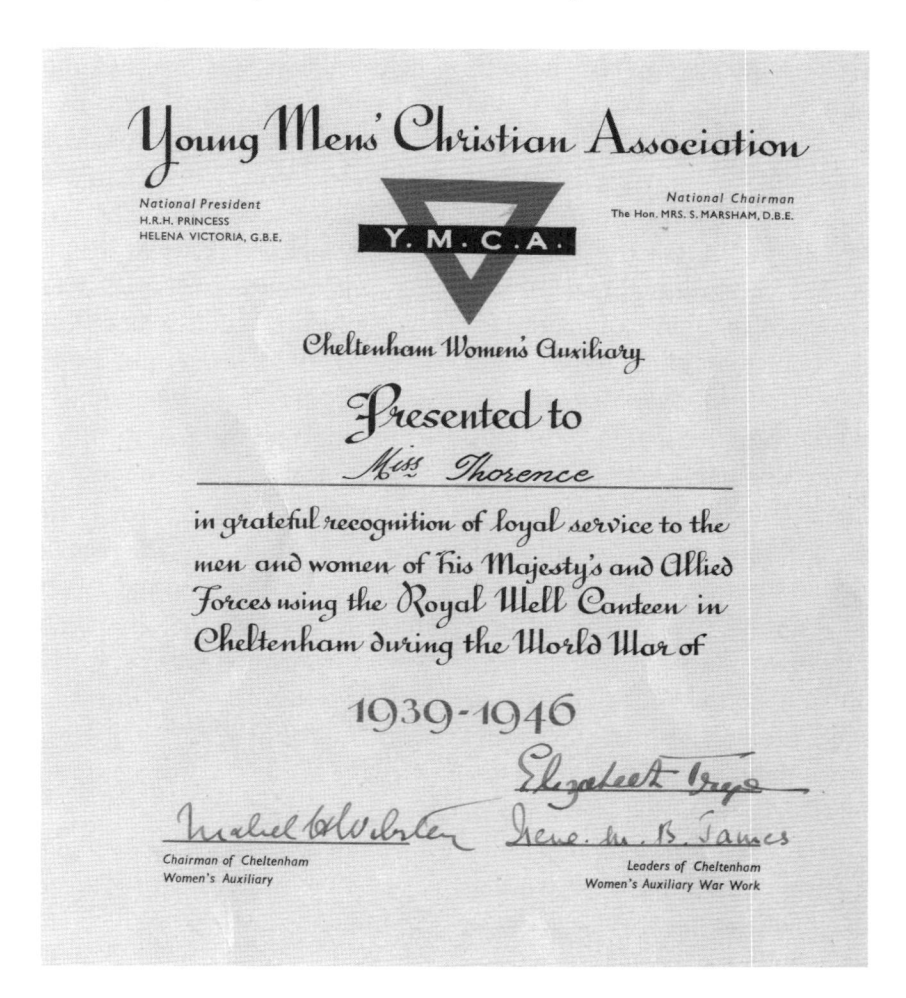

Young Men's Christian Association

National President
H.R.H. PRINCESS
HELENA VICTORIA, G.B.E.

Y.M.C.A.

National Chairman
The Hon. MRS. S. MARSHAM, D.B.E.

Cheltenham Women's Auxiliary

Presented to

Miss Thorence

in grateful recognition of loyal service to the men and women of His Majesty's and Allied Forces using the Royal Well Canteen in Cheltenham during the World War of

1939-1946

Chairman of Cheltenham
Women's Auxiliary

Leaders of Cheltenham
Women's Auxiliary War Work

evening. This was situated in the former workhouse which reverted to the Public Assistance Committee in 1943, later becoming St. Paul's Hospital. They also helped with collecting salvage. The orchestra under Mr. P. Britten-Austin numbered 12 players and was congratulated on various concerts. Miss Laird and Miss Brant were singled out for their work in the canteen and mention was also made of the visit of the Duchess of Beaufort to the 1940 December Bazaar.

The Women's Auxiliary and the Young Women's Section were both doing valuable work all over the town with the latter consisting of girls from all walks of life. It was regretted that Mrs. Osborne was to retire as Secretary but we know that Mrs. Webster remained in charge of the former throughout the war, assisted by Mrs. W.A. Baker and Miss Higgins. Well done the fair sex. You did a fantastic job throughout the war.

The Hostel in the Promenade was incredibly overworked with the lecture hall turned into a Services dormitory. The camaraderie was obvious, however, because a letter from a member of the Home Guard enclosed a cheque for two guineas being the balance from his usual hotel which he had foregone in preference for the YMCA!

Membership was compared between 1939 and 1940 with a significant growth from 50 to 140 in the Boys Club, and 130 to 220 in the Women's Auxiliary. The Young Women had declined slightly to 237 with Men (Associate and Full), and honorary supporting male members remaining roughly the same at 347 and 149 respectively, very satisfactory given the numbers who must have gone off to fight. 90% of the YMCA young men were in uniform with free membership granted during their time of service for the duration of the war. Just how long it was going to be they had no idea at the time.

When the London Central YMCA offices were bombed, several members of the National Council, under the leadership of General Secretary, Frank Willis, and much to the delight of the local Association, chose to come to Cheltenham. They were accommodated in Aban Court in Malvern Road with offices in the Criterion Temperance Hotel at 3 Albion Street. It seems they worked closely with the local YMCA which did its best to ensure their enforced stay was a profitable one.

There was a small surplus of income over expenditure but constant wear and tear on the premises meant that repairs and renewal of fittings was a serious business. After the war was over the floor of the Royal Well Canteen was so badly damaged that the government agreed to replace it. A special vote of thanks went to the Free Churches who combined in making collections for local YMCA funds.

A joint Cheltenham and National Council YMCA Appeal resulted in £3,600 of which £2,400 was for a hut and £1,200 for mobile canteens. Thanks were due to the Mayor, John Howell, the Chairman of the Cheltenham War Service Fund Committee and Arthur Dye (YMCA Chairman) his deputy. They led a "splendid committee of leading public men and women" who were important in the appeal's success. A further sum of £550 was contributed by the Women's Auxiliary via the Royal Well Canteen.

More than 1,000 people co-operated to make the booklet possible and it is clear that a great deal of self sacrifice was made in the process. Of the 55 adverts, which included several private hotels, was the Stanhope Steamship Company, who had bases at London, Cardiff, Hull, Newcastle upon Tyne and amazingly an inland branch at 81 Promenade, a clear reflection that Britain's shipping was vital to the wartime economy. The only advert still recognisable today was for Martin the Jewellers, still in the same premises near the Clarence Lamp.

Publishing such a booklet must have taken a great deal of time and effort, especially under arguably the most dangerous period in our country's long history. Later, in the war the Americans came to town and were also made very welcome at Cheltenham YMCA. Slowly the tables were turned and by 1945 it was all over. Rebuilding was now the order of the day and Cheltenham YMCA was ready to open another chapter.

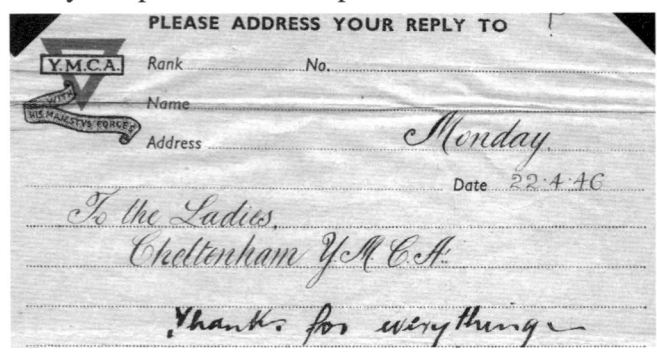

MESSAGE FROM H.H. PRINCESS HELENA VICTORIA, G.B.E.

AS President of the National Women's Auxiliary of the Y.M.C.A. I send you this message of heartfelt and sincere thanks for the splendid work you have accomplished during the past strenuous years. I have followed all your varied activities with keen interest and am very proud as well as deeply gratified for your devotion to the work you carried out so admirably.

Now that your war work has come to a close may I express the hope that I can rely on you continuing your loyal service for the welfare of the youth of this great country, as you gave to its fighting men.

Again I thank you from all my heart and wish each one of you, my workers, happiness and prosperity.

Helena Victoria

The farewell dinner for all wartime helpers at the Royal Well Canteen was held in the same premises on June 19th 1946. There were 300 present but many absent for unavoidable reasons. The mesh on the windows showed it was now back in use as a YMCA gymnasium with the government having agreed to put in a new floor to replace the one irreparably damaged by the constant wear and tear caused by servicemen's boots! The top table above includes from left: Mrs. Webster, Mrs. James, Mrs. Trye, Mrs. Lulham, unknown, unknown, Mrs. Waite and Mrs. Baker.

CHAPTER 8
BAKER STREET YMCA 1940-1967

When war arrived in Autumn 1939 the Royal Well Hut at the rear of the Promenade was immediately commandeered for a Services canteen. The Junior Department therefore found itself homeless and moved briefly into Clare Street Hall off Bath Road. Formerly rented in 1860 for St. Luke's Church by Baron de Ferrieres and Mr. H. Roper, and bought outright in 1878, this building was used for mission and outreach to the poorer parts of the parish before being sold in 1933. The YMCA saw it as only a stop gap, however, and negotiations quickly took place with the Council for the use of Alstone Baths in Great Western Road. Before any conclusion could be reached, however, there was a most interesting turn of events.

Pre-Second World War there was an extremely strong sense of local community when parochialism was still at its height. Most churches were relatively well attended and many town suburbs had their own well-supported community centre. One such was the Gas Green Young Men's League in the St. Paul's area of Cheltenham. However, when war arrived in 1939 membership of such institutions plummeted dramatically and the organisation in Baker Street suddenly found itself with outdated buildings in need of renovation and almost no occupants of what had recently been a thriving concern.

One of the trustees was George Hitchman who was also on the executive of Cheltenham YMCA, and he suggested that the YMCA President, Horace Bush, should contact the Baker Street Chairman, Rev. Herbert Clarkson and Secretary, Douglas Beckinsale with a view to taking over the premises as a youth club. Although YMCA adult numbers had also plummeted dramatically the youth work was going extremely well and the committee knew they were about to play a key role within the town doing voluntary war work and billeting soldiers. This decree had, naturally, come from on high via YMCA England in London when everyone was exhorted to play their part. While Cheltenham YMCA in the Promenade was therefore looking ahead to a busy but totally different future, the need to cater for the youth of the town was seen as an extremely important factor, especially in view of the acute shortage of fathers and father figures who were elsewhere pursuing service on behalf of their country. The request was therefore gratefully accepted and on December 28th 1939 Cheltenham YMCA moved its youth work to Baker Street YMCA at a peppercorn rent of £2 per annum.

At the time there was a strong national movement called the Association of Boys Clubs which reflected the fact that virtually all senior schools were single sex, a situation which did not change radically until the 1960s, and for many areas not until much later than that. Thus it was that Cheltenham YMCA took possession of the Baker Street premises with an official opening on January 20th 1940, celebrated with a suitable supper attended by several boys and a platform party consisting of ten YMCA committee members. It was quite normal for senior members of any institution to be seated on a raised dais with a collection of willing helpers, nearly all ladies, beavering away behind the scenes doing the preparation and serving. Everyone happily accepted the status quo and their position within it.

The Junior Department Leader at the Promenade was A.J. Moxon, an older man, and it was decided he should stay put and help the overburdened town centre premises. A youth leader called J.E. "Pop" Davey, who had previously run the Junior Dramatic Society, was therefore appointed from within and successfully established a thriving work which prospered for the next 27 years. A fine gymnast himself, he wasted no time in forming a gymnastic team, and even managed to field two league football teams in his first year of tenure, the Cheltenham Youth Division for 1940-1 showing membership for both Baker Street YMCA 'A' and 'B' teams, the only club to do so. The other teams that year were Whaddon Sports Club, the eventual champions who had a long history as the Whaddon Boys' Club which was originally established by

▲ *The whole essence of Baker Street YMCA Boys' Club is captured in this splendid photograph taken in 1964. Although relatively late in its 27 year lifespan it shows the dedication which went into making it the premier youth club of its time, an important part of which was the 1st Cheltenham Company of the Boys' Brigade which Captain Vic Dymock (left centre) founded as early as 1943. Right centre is Bill Gibbins, Bandmaster of the Company which won many prizes down the years. This picture was taken to celebrate first place in the trumpets and bugles section of the National Band Contest held at Hornchurch in Essex.*

Cheltenham College; 125 Squadron Air Defence Cadet Corps; St. Mary's (Charlton Kings) Juniors; 1st Cheltenham (St. Paul's) Church Lads Brigade; St. Stephen's; Cheltenham Technical College and Woodmancote Juniors. By the 1944-5 season most of the youths were young men and Baker Street YMCA had gravitated to playing in Division Two of the Works and Services League.

In July 1940 a conference was held for county leaders of youth work to which boys and helpers were also invited. In May 1941 the Boys' Club was adopted by St. Paul's Training College, whose members offered their services as leaders for various activities. Later in the year, an Open Week was arranged for November 17-23, into which was packed an incredible amount, including the opening of the new gymnasium by the Mayor of Cheltenham, Councillor Wilfred Waite. Among the activities mentioned were physical training and gymnastic displays, table tennis, a handicrafts exhibition, drama concert, film show, a social and dance, and the dedication of the chapel. The week culminated on Sunday afternoon with a special rally and tea.

Among the various dignitaries who attended were Councillor H.T. Bush (President of Baker Street YMCA); G. Hitchman (Chairman); A. Adams (Vice Chairman); Councillor P.T. Smith (President, Cheltenham YMCA); A.E. Naylor (General Secretary, Cheltenham YMCA); Councillor G.B. Compton; Anthony Adams and Anthony Thomas (both National Association of Boys Clubs); Rev. D.E. Leavey (Chairman, Cheltenham Federation of Youth Organisations); J.H. Duthie (Hon. Secretary, St. Paul's Adoption Committee); and two gymnastic judges, A. Riley (St. Paul's College) and H. Starmer-Smith (Gloucestershire P.T. Organiser). An epilogue concluded all the activities from Monday to Thursday evening.

▲ *These early pictures of Baker Street Boys' Club taken at the opening party on January 20th 1940, tell us a great deal. The management committee (top) consists of left to right back row; A. Adams, D. Wallace, W. Chaplain, H. Barter, and J. Yates: front row; H. Bush, A. Dye (YMCA Chairman), G. Hitchman (Boys' Chairman), A.J. Moxon and G. Heawood. The boys numbered 60 in total and are all in their best clothes. Cheltenham, like the rest of the country, was extremely parochial and the lads would all have been local, the club being a major attraction in the area for the next quarter of a century.*

A printed leaflet in 1941 called "Everything a Boy wants to do" listed the following available activities: Art and Drawing; Amateur Dramatic Society; Basketball; Bible Study; Camping; Canteen; Boys' Weekend Conferences; Chess and Draughts; Cricket; Concert Party; Film Programmes; Fireside Talks; Football (three teams); Gardening; Gymnastics; Handicrafts; Leaders' Training Classes; Library; Midweek Services; Popular Lectures; Rambling; Socials and Dances; Sunday Afternoon Rallies; Swimming; Service Squad; Table Tennis; and Tennis. Amazing! No wonder Baker Street YMCA was well supported. A footnote said: "Leadership in activities arranged by St. Paul's College, Hon. Secretary J.H. Duthie; Canteen arrangements by Miss H.M. Laird and YW Section, YMCA, with the co-operation of St. Mary's College." The latter was the local women's teacher training college which later amalgamated with the men to form The College of St. Paul and St. Mary, now officially the University of Gloucestershire. The work of the YMCA women's sections is well documented in the wartime chapter.

In 1943 Pop Davey moved away to take up a new appointment as Physical Education Director for the North East Region of the YMCA and was succeeded by Vic Dymock who was to broaden the scope of the work considerably and take it on to new heights. In 1944 the table tennis team won the senior Cheltenham League but as they were lifting various trophies so the first report of loss of life came through. Older men from Gas Green had

▲ A publicity photo taken in 1941 on the "adoption" of the Club by St. Paul's Training College

already made the ultimate sacrifice but to them were now added the names of two Baker Street boys, Reg Baldwin and Doug Holtham. This would also have been mentioned in the *Baker Street YMCA Gazette*, a regular publication at this time.

****

There had certainly been three editions of the *Gazette* by March 1945, printed on the Roneo system where wax masters were stencilled on a typewriter and then placed on a rotating drum of ink which, when turned with a handle, pressed the ink through the stencil on to the paper. Most typewriters had three settings with the mechanism dictating where the keys hit the carriage, either the black or red section of the ribbon, or by missing it altogether which was the stencil cutter. Primitive drawings could also be made manually on the master copy, some of which included physical training activities with a note that everyone was looking forward to the display at the Town Hall on April 5th.

Wartime jokes abounded, particularly at the expense of the Americans who were by now a very visible presence in the land. Two went as follows:

"An American and British sailor were arguing about the size of their flagship. The British man said his was so big the chef had to drive round it in a car. The American said his flagship was so big that the chef had to go through the Irish stew in a submarine to see if the potatoes were done!"

"An old lady on a bus sat watching a nearby American chewing gum. When she got off she said 'Thank you for trying to talk to me but I'm stone deaf'!"

Trips out of Cheltenham were a rare wartime event and a poem was printed about a sortie to Bristol YMCA which speaks volumes:

At the station we didn't have long to wait
For our train was only two hours late.
When it arrived there was a shuffle of feet
And we were left standing without a seat.

We arrived at Bristol with no time to waste,
So to Colston Street we made great haste.
The dinner they served us was very grand,
After we'd finished we could hardly stand.

Of goals our United had their fill,
They won their game by eight goals to nil.
Also our Nomads had great fun
They won their game by eighteen to one.

Then we went to the room to wash and dress
And we had quite a job to wash off the mess,
The water they gave us was very nice
But we had quite a job to break the ice.

When we arrived home to our club we ran
For at seven thirty our dance had began.
When we got there the dance was quite slow
But the twenty five of us made things go.

All of us think we had a good day
And on behalf of the footballers, I would like to say
Thanks to the persons who did the job,
To make our trip pleasant and well worth two bob!

The poem may not have won any prizes for rhyme and rhythm but the sentiments were quite clear. Two bob was two shillings, 10p in today's money but a great deal in 1945. Colston Street was another name for Bristol YMCA where Colston Hall is still situated.

NEW WEEKLY PROGRAMME

		GYMN	GAMES ROOM	CANTEEN	LOUNGE
Mon.	6–7.30	P.T. & Games	Crafts	Billiards	7.15 Prayers
	7.30–10	T.T. Matches	T.T.	R'ments & Blds.	Discussion Grp.
Wed.	7–10	Basketball General Games	Crafts T.T.	Billiards Refreshments	Members' Rcds. or T/V 9.45 Wed. Sp.
Thurs.	6–7.30	P.T. & Games	Crafts	Billiards	T/V
	7.30–10	F'ball Training	T.T.	R'ments & Blds.	Variety or Skiffle Group
Fri.	7–10	General P.T. and Games	T.T. Darts	Billiards Refreshments	Records or T/V
Sat.		Competitions, Camping, Expeditions, Adventure, Sport, Conferences, Dances, etc.			
Sun.	8 p.m.			Chatabox	
	9.15 p.m.			(Fortnightly)	Chatabox "Quiet $\frac{1}{4}$"

Note—Juniors (12–13 years) will only be allowed in the Club from 6–7.30 p.m. on Mondays and Thursdays. Seniors (14 years upwards) will not be allowed in the Club during the Junior Sessions.

Among the club jottings was reference to a visit from the YMCA Regional Secretary Mr. R.H. Swainson (notice how everyone had two initials in those days) who was "very impressed with the happy atmosphere prevailing in the club".

There was also a message from Rev. de Courcy Ireland, the Town and County Councillor for the St. Peter's area of Cheltenham and a letter from a former member, Jeff Davis, who had moved to Eastbourne but eulogised about his time at Baker Street and said how much he missed everyone.

The Club Gossip page was just that with a suggestion that a shelter be built outside for waiting girl friends! Overheard in the canteen was the following gem:

Member: "I haven't reached any Spam in this sandwich yet."

Mrs Newland from the kitchen: "Have another bite son."

Member after taking another bite: "None yet."

Mrs. Newland: "Sorry son, you must have passed it!"

Spam was of course the staple diet during the last war. The acronyms either stood for "spiced ham" or "scientifically produced artificial meat". Take your pick but it was – and still is – rather like luncheon meat but we eat rather less of it today than we did then!

Five members of the services were mentioned by name and best wishes extended to them all. Sports reports took in football, table tennis and athletics with a special appeal to anyone who had not returned their special gym display shorts to do so at once.

Among the questions on the puzzle page were the following:

1. How many 7.5 pence in £1 million? Actually it said how many seven and a half pence because decimalisation was decades away!

2. If it takes two men six days to dig a hole, how long would it take one man to dig half a hole?

3, The first of first is first, and the last of last is last, and there is twice nothing, which is still nothing, in between. What is it?

Does anyone know the answers?

In 1950 the first Cheltenham YMCA Handbook was issued since 1938 and three pages of it were devoted to Baker Street Boys Club and the 1st Cheltenham Company of the Boys Brigade. It made splendid reading.

The premises were described as comprising a gymnasium, canteen, workshop, games room, showers, dressing room etc. A big project was underway to build a new lounge measuring 24 feet by 16 feet which was to present greater scope for educational work. In connection with this a radiogram had been constructed by the members at a cost of £16, a huge sum of money but the motto was: "It can be done – it will be done – it is done". Also being built was a new Secretary's office, entrance, cycle sheds etc. All the work was voluntary with gifts of furniture and furnishings gratefully received.

Activities were varied and catered for the "Spiritual, social, physical and mental welfare of all boys". Many honours and trophies had come their way but these were not judged as a measure of success, only that of the loyalty, enthusiasm and team spirit of members.

Table tennis had enjoyed success, winning both the 4th and Junior Divisions of the Cheltenham League. There were two football teams, the senior one winning the County NABC (National Association of Boys' Clubs) Junior Award. A new rugby section was opened by Denis O'Brien and one of the two cricket teams won the Cheltenham Youth Shield. The cross country team won the NABC Junior County Trophy and also the Cheltenham Youth Cross Country Dowty Cup. Membership was limited to 150 with renewal for everyone taking place in September when any vacancies were offered to new members. The gym section was popular, as was the basketball. Even the handicraft group which specialised in "covering, carpentry and plastering", won a runners-up plaque at the Cheltenham Youth Exhibition. Photography was a new group and a full programme of films was shown. Socials and dances were supported by an excellent canteen run by parents and friends.

▲ *Baker Street, like many other youth clubs of the time, placed great importance on physical fitness with gymnastics being a particular favourite. However, anyone trying to indulge in activities like this in the street today would quickly be run over by a car!*

A separate page about the Boys' Brigade explained how it linked up with the YMCA during wartime, having so much in common that the two were seen as complementary. The BB object was "The advancement of Christ's Kingdom among boys, and the promotion of habits of obedience, reverence, discipline, self respect and all that tends towards a true Christian manliness." Drill was seen as an important part of discipline as was Bible Study. Activities included Drum and Bugle Band, First Aid, Athletics, Swimming, Camping, Signalling, Wayfaring, Firefighting, and Educational Study.

Self-supporting financially the BB won the County Band, County First Aid, and County Camp Cup, all three from 1948-1950, and also the County Football, Cricket and Cross Country!

****

The football section in particular was always strong but until the 1970s there were no younger children's leagues in the town. However, in 1948

Baker Street YMCA first team joined the newly formed Cheltenham Youth League, which they won in 1950-1, 1955-6, 1956-7 and 1957-8. Apart from this local success they also lifted the Gloucestershire County Youth Shield three times, in 1951-2, 1955-6 and 1957-8.

This remarkable achievement was a genuine team effort but it must be said that among the squad were the two sons of the former Cheltenham Town football manager, George Summerbee, once a professional with Aldershot and Preston North End but who was sadly to die young at the age of only 40, the victim of Addison's Disease, a rare ailment which shrivelled the kidneys and was not diagnosed. At the time the more likely of the two boys was thought to be John but it was Michael (Mike) Summerbee who went on to greater heights, firstly with Swindon Town then on to Manchester City where he won winners medals for the League, the FA Cup, the League Cup and the European Cup Winners Cup. He also won eight caps as a full England international under his friend and World Cup winning captain, Bobby Moore (later Sir Bobby), to add to an earlier Under 23 international cap. John was all for his younger brother succeeding and after Mike's initial success never again thought about a professional career for himself.

Cricket was also a popular sport during the summer months when more time was available than today to make this equipment-based activity viable. Sadly, owing to the high costs and problems of maintenance, cricket at youth level has now become almost the sole preserve of grammar and public schools. 50 years ago almost everyone played it in the street and local parks but it is something of a rarity today, although a few senior clubs do run thriving youth sections.

On November 19th 1952, Baker Street YMCA was honoured with a visit from the Princess Royal, Victoria Alexandra Alice Mary, the only daughter of King George V, who had married the Earl of Harewood. Usually known as Mary, after her mother Queen Mary, she would doubtless have been encouraged by what she saw as an excellent example of a spiritual, social and physical rebuilding job going on all around the country. She was accompanied by the Duke of Beaufort, and the Mayor and Mayoress of Cheltenham. A proud Vic Dymock conducted them round the premises.

****

So integral did the Boys' Brigade become with Baker Street YMCA that it merited a separate mention in the 1959-60 Cheltenham YMCA Annual Handbook which quoted from a letter by Vic Dymock which went as follows: "As I write this paragraph, a vivid picture comes before me. After a wonderful period of camping at Penally an optional service of thanksgiving and re-dedication was held. 95% of those attending camp were present. At the close of the service a request to remain behind was made to those boys wishing to have a further knowledge of how to become a Christian. 30 boys remained.

This picture illustrates our work, to stimulate interest in, and create Christian manliness. That is why the YMCA and Boys' Brigade must continue to work together and why these two great movements have so much in common. Our Company continues to maintain its high standard of giving a boy every opportunity of becoming a citizen of the highest order, incorporating all aspects of life."

Among the Baker Street events listed in the same handbook were a Club Flag Day, an intriguingly titled Who's the Best?, a Fathers Challenge Night, a Soap Box Derby and Cycle Polo. One wonders what happened in the last two events and how many buckled wheels resulted?

****

The 1950s and early-1960s at Baker Street were a buzz of excitement and a typical week in 1964 listed the following activities:

Sunday   – 11.15am Boys' Service
      – 8pm Social Hour (monthly – films, music, discussion)
Monday   – 6-7.30pm Juniors (12-14 years)
      – 7.30-10pm Table Tennis matches, Crafts
Tuesday   – Boys Brigade
Wednesday – 7-9.45pm Games
      – 9.45pm Prayers
Thursday   – 6-7.30pm Juniors
      – 7.30-10pm Football Training

▲ *A poor but important image of the The Princess Royal with the Mayor of Cheltenham, Councillor T.L. Thompson. She was a big champion of the YMCA movement and on November 19th 1952, visited Tewkesbury YMCA, Baker Street YMCA (above), then the Central YMCA in the Promenade, after which she went to lunch in the Town Hall. Accompanied by the Duke of Beaufort and various Cheltenham civic leaders, she received a remarkable total of 95 purses containing a total of £3,448 raised on behalf of the YMCA Appeal.*

Friday   – 7-10pm Games, Basketball
Saturday   – Football, Camping, Expeditions, Conferences, Dances etc.

In addition to the above programme, table tennis, billiards, darts, chess and draughts were available. A television, record player and piano were also available for members' use.

****

Another significant notice for 1964 read as follows:

YMCA work with the youth of Cheltenham is carried on at the following centres:
   Baker Street YMCA Boys Club
   St. Thomas's YMCA Youth Club
   Pilley Lane Boys Club
   Central YMCA Boys Department

St. Thomas's was the mission hut daughter church to St. Mark's situated on the Alma estate in Up Hatherley, previously the Royal Well Hut and canteen which was re-erected in 1956 as described in an earlier chapter. Pilley Lane was attached to Pilley Lane Baptist Church while the Central YMCA was based in the new headquarters at Vittoria Walk. All in all it was a pretty impressive line up of youth work conducted by Cheltenham YMCA throughout the town (see Satellite Youth Work in Chapter 12).

****

1964 was also a big year for the Boys' Brigade whose band won first prize in the trumpet and bugles section at the National Band Contest in Hornchurch. The proud picture of the immaculate band taken outside their Baker Street HQ would have looked good in colour but black and white

◀ *In 1944 the Baker Street Boys' Club were the Cheltenham Table Tennis champions. Judging by the trophies on display it seems they won more than just the league.*

With limited movement for everyone during the war, sport took on a more serious dimension and we can be sure that the table tennis would have faced stiff competition from other local clubs. However, as most of the "boys" practised several nights a week they would have certainly kept their eye in.

Other sports were equally competitive but the "win at all costs" attitude which developed later had no place in amateur sport then.

photography was not to be displaced for another decade. Below the large noticeboard and YMCA red triangle was a smaller noticeboard which listed everything on offer at the club:

"Baker Street YMCA Boys Club

The aim of this association is to develop Christian manhood by providing activities of a physical, social, educational and religious nature. Membership is open to any boy 14-16 years and the Club is open each night from 6.30-10pm (subject to alteration).

Activities according to season:
Athletics, Art and Drawing, Army Cadets, Basketball, Billiards, Boxing, Bible Study, Camping, Cycling, Concerts, Draughts, Drama, Film Programmes, Football (3 teams), Tennis, Gardening, Library, Lectures, Rambling, Socials, Swimming, Service Squad, Shooting, Table Tennis, Boys Brigade etc. Physical Training Monday, Tuesday, Thursday 8-10pm. For details of membership and enquiries see the Boys Work Secretary any evening at the club."

****

Baker Street YMCA became almost a life's work for Vic Dymock who quickly became involved with the nearby Gas Green Baptist Church where he established the Boys Brigade in 1943. In time he became the regional BB chief but in the short term expanded activities to such a pitch that in 1966 he asked to become autonomous. Cheltenham YMCA had by now moved from the Promenade to Vittoria Walk and, as indicated above, had youth work running elsewhere so, in deference to all the hard work put in by its leader, the request was agreed to and Vic was warmly applauded for all his efforts.

The official hand over took place on January 11th 1967 when Baker Street Boys Club was renamed the Gas Green Youth Centre with Vic Dymock as its leader, assisted by Dave Bell and Richard Hyett. The peppercorn rent of £2 per annum remained in place.

On November 30th 1980 Vic Dymock was awarded the MBE from HM The Queen at Buckingham Palace, for services to youth work and the Boys Brigade in particular. He died on January 24th, 1993 after a short illness, aged 85, just two months short of the 50th Anniversary of the 1st Cheltenham Company of the Boys' Brigade which he founded on March 13th 1943.

There are many members of Cheltenham who still fondly remember their days at Baker Street YMCA which consisted largely of what today would be described as an old-fashioned gymnasium but in those days was as good as most schools could offer. In effect it was a large hall fitted with wall bars and ceiling ropes. Other equipment included a vaulting horse and springboard. In these premises took place most of the activities, a veritable treasure

▲ *The all-conquering Baker Street YMCA football team which won several trophies during the 1950s. Among its members was Mike Summerbee, later to find fame with Manchester City.*

trove of goodies which ran under the auspices of Cheltenham YMCA from 1940 to 1967. Mothers and helpers came in to serve refreshments on a regular basis with one of the favourite dishes being beans on toast. They were happy days indeed for all those fortunate to have taken part in the general camaraderie! One feels that everyone also benefited enormously.

Let its epitaph be a quote from the Cheltenham YMCA Handbook for 1959-60: "This club is closely linked with the Central YMCA and is open to all boys of any denomination between 12 and 18 years of age. The aims and guiding principles of the Club are uniform with those of the parent Association, i.e. the building of the whole personality – Body, Mind and Spirit."

◀ *On November 30th 1980, Vic Dymock attended Buckingham Palace to receive the insignia of a Member of the British Empire (MBE) from Her Majesty the Queen. It was a proud moment but tinged with sadness that his late wife Lilian was not able to be present. He was, though, supported by his two sons and daughter-in-law: from left to right, Tony, Hazel and Colin. It was formal recognition of his lifetime's devotion to youth work, and in particular that of the 1st Cheltenham Company of the Boys' Brigade. He was also the Battalion President for the BB and attended numerous functions across Gloucestershire. He died in January 1993, aged 85.*

CHAPTER 9
THE PROMENADE 1945-1956

Once hostilities ceased then it was back to business. With the youth wing now firmly established at Baker Street YMCA, special attention was given to renewing and renovating the Promenade. A personal account of this period may be found in Chapter 13 where the President in 2005, Rev. Lionel Fitz, looked back over 60 years at Cheltenham YMCA.

Charles Belcher succeeded Arthur Naylor during the war and capably held the fort aided by his deputy, A.J. Moxon, but there was much to do in the period of inevitable austerity which followed. Young men were keen to get on with things and between 1945-1951 attendances at professional football matches in Britain reached their peak. This was also reflected on the field of play with many teams keen to participate, indeed it was quite normal to play or train on Saturday morning then go to watch your local professional team during the afternoon. If your match clashed in the afternoon, however, then that naturally came first and which is how Lionel Fitz found himself back playing for Cheltenham YMCA after a break in the RAF. En route to watch Cheltenham Town he was drawn into a match on the adjacent Whaddon Rec. and was persuaded to rejoin as soon as he was demobbed in 1947. Having been a member of the Junior Department from 1938 he was only too happy to get going again and before long found himself as the members' representative on the Executive Committee, which had by now realised it needed a younger man onboard.

In charge, was Arthur Dye, Head of Naunton Park School and a well-known and respected local Councillor. As the Chairman, he knew exactly where he was going and after retiring from education in 1950 devoted a great deal of his boundless time and energy into the well-being of Cheltenham YMCA. Other committee members included Councillor H.T. Bush (later the Mayor of Cheltenham), Dr. Morley (the Borough Health Officer), George Hitchman (owner of a tailor's shop), and Vic Dymock (a local builder). The last two were also heavily involved with Baker Street YMCA where Lionel later became the chairman.

****

1950 saw the reintroduction of the Annual Handbook, the last printed document of this kind being the impressive 1938 Annual Report entitled "The Times In Which We Live". It had held out high hopes for Cheltenham YMCA but these were almost immediately dashed by the war years and then by the grey post-1945 austerity period which lasted well into the 1950s. Money

◄ *Second on the right with the 1946-7 Junior Charities Cup winning team, in hat and coat, is Charles Belcher, who took over from Arthur Naylor as YMCA Secretary during the war. He donated the President's chain of office when he retired in 1950 which was later worn by Lionel Fitz, standing next to him in football kit.*

▲ *This panoramic summer view of the Promenade is easily dated by the flags and bunting for the 1953 Coronation of Queen Elizabeth II. The letters "YMCA" can be clearly seen in the middle behind the banner.*

was tight, industry was literally in need of rebuilding, as were much of the big urban areas. There was also a general food shortage and people brought up during this time never threw food away which was considered wasteful in the extreme. "Waste not, want not" became a real issue and catchphrase.

The local YMCA, however, did an extremely good job with a dedicated staff working hard to put the Association back on its feet. Under the driving force of Chairman, Arthur Dye, Secretary Fred Daldry and Boys' Work Secretary, Vic Dymock, the Executive Committee set out their stall right from the start. As the 1950 Handbook put it:

"The YMCA seeks …."

The directing of young men and boys to Jesus Christ as the Way, the Truth and the Life; the provision, in an atmosphere of friendship, of amenities and activities which will enrich character and develop manhood; the education of young men and boys in the responsibilities of citizenship, and the fitting of them for tasks of personal service."

The element of service was key in all Christian work at the time and had been for generations. Only later in the 20th Century did it slip from the agenda when a more liberal society and a "me first" and complaint infested culture arrive on the agenda, making genuine service much more difficult to uphold in a litigation conscious atmosphere.

Membership was still divided into two. Associates were effectively general members while Full Membership was open to anyone who had been a member for at least three months and was desirous of being "a disciple of the Lord Jesus Christ" and who sought to be of Christian service within the Association. Little has changed since then. Membership for all was 15 shillings per annum (75p in today's parlance).

Page 5 began "And now …." stating what had happened since the last pre-war Handbook was produced; of how Baker Street YMCA had been acquired and developed; and what new facilities had been installed in the Promenade, among which were new showers. Standard today, showers were a rare luxury 50 years ago until post-war school improvements saw them installed en masse in secondary schools. It is unlikely that anyone over the age of 60 in 2005 will remember having a shower as a child at home although possibly at school. Baths were

◀ *This was a very welcome sight in the Promenade for many visitors, residents and Servicemen during the years 1921-1956*

109

the norm with the water often shared within the family, sometimes at the same time!

These improvements were all in keeping with the post-war vision at Cheltenham YMCA where the Executive Committee of ten men was determined to move ahead. A Chapel (or Quiet Room) was created where "amid the rush and whirl of life, you are welcome to turn aside to find quiet and rest for meditation and prayer."

It went on … "And now …. don't stand on the brink of things. Come right in. We would like to help you – and we believe you can help us."

The busy week's programme was enough to attract a full house with table tennis and drama on Mondays; football training and evening prayers on Tuesdays; sound films, lectures and snooker matches on Wednesdays; gym, basketball and billiards matches on Thursdays; table tennis and Bible studies on Fridays; table tennis, football and socials on Saturdays; and rallies, conferences and after church socials on Sundays. Other special events were also regularly held.

November 1950 saw a visit from the National Secretary, Sir Frank Willis, and many other meetings were listed in detail, A full fixture list was published for both football teams and it was remarkable to find sex education on the agenda more than once, a subject which was virtually taboo for two more decades. The Women's Auxiliary had Mrs. J.E. Baker as its President and Mrs. W.A. Baker as it Chairman, being a "a band of ladies who back up the YMCA in all its activities." Meetings were held each Monday at 3pm in the upstairs lounge with new members cordially invited.

Among the sound films from October to December (in private hands silent films were still the norm) were three on athletics, and one each on football and yachting. Outdoor pursuits were very much the thing but as there was an acute shortage of swimming pools nationally, public or private, the swimming section had not yet recommenced. Only in the last 25 years has there been an explosion in public pools whereas 50 years ago anyone living outside an urban area was unlikely to learn to swim unless they went on holiday.

An interesting innovation was the founding of the C-Club which replaced the former Bible Study and Discussion Group, with the aim of underlining

▲ *Cheltenham YMCA, Senior Division Charities Trophy Winners (Dimmer Cup), Season 1951-2. There are 12 individual trophies but only 11 men in kit because substitutes were still 20 years away. Back row, left to right: Ivor Newland, Joe Stone, Gil Chivers, Bob Frost, Bill Newland, Len Champion, Geoff Stanford, and YMCA Secretary. Fred Daldry. who later moved to Kingston-upon-Thames YMCA. Front row, left to right: Ken Cross, Ken Stone, Dave Hall, Arthur Ainger, Lionel Fitz, Vic Pearce and Ken Hopkins (Football Secretary).*

◂ *Cheltenham YMCA were Champions of Division 2 in 1949-50. Note the referee's official outfit.*

the "C" in YMCA. Thursday evenings between 9-9.40pm included "real fellowship, straight talks, live singing and full opportunity for questions and discussion". Within two years, however, it was renamed the Christian Fellowship Group.

Advertising was used as a means of paying for the publication and included: Elm Farm Dairy; Tandy Electrical (eye-catchingly upside down, presumably deliberate); A.C. Hands bakery in Painswick Road; the YMCA Restaurant, where lunches cost two shillings; W.A. Woof, the long established local sports outfitters and supplier to Cheltenham College; the Cheltenham Steam Laundry of Great Western Road; the Bible Depot in Winchcombe Street; fruiterer and florist C.V. Berry; the Cheltenham Crisp Company of Worcester Street; and a full page about the danger of road accidents sponsored by the Cheltenham Accident Prevention Council.

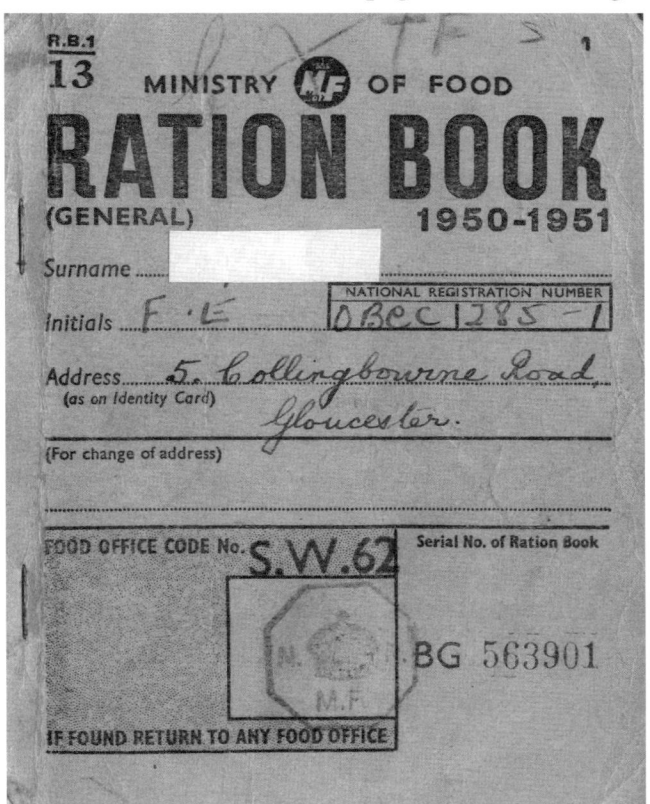

The football teams had great success right up until the move to Vittoria Walk in 1956 by which time anno domini, girl friends and family commitments had caught up with most of the players. Meanwhile, the Promenade was a home from home for quite a sizeable number of local young men who spent most of their evenings playing billiards and snooker, table tennis, football training, drinking coffee and generally messing about.

They were joined in the early-1950s by a significant collection of apprentices from Smith's Industries among whom was a young man from South Wales called Brian Burrows, who later served for more than 30 years as a deacon at Cambray Church, including a brief spell as secretary and a much longer one as assistant secretary. Away from home for the first time, he arrived in August 1950 on a three-year student apprenticeship at Bishops Cleeve. His room overlooked the Royal Well taxi rank and he remembered early-morning breakfasts prior to starting work at 7.30am! His transport was a Sturmey Archer 3-speed bicycle kept in the basement along with several others, all of which were dutifully carried up the steps every morning in all weathers. Brian also remembered the Chapel in the front of the basement.

◂ *Wartime ration books continued well into the early-1950s, especially for such items as soap, tea, sugar and sweets.*

Like many of his contemporaries, he spent two happy years at the YMCA and was soon drawn into their activities. Many of the group had close links with nearby Cambray Church and after gravitating there as well and, under the influence of his new-found friends, committed his life to Christ in 1952. Having married a local girl from the church he later returned to work full-time in Cheltenham and celebrated his Golden Wedding in 2005. It is of note that the Christians among this group openly shared their faith at the YMCA, a fact which impressed Lionel Fitz at the time.

Among the grey post-war years, Cheltenham YMCA was like a beacon in a fog. There was little for young people to do in those days and any form of evening activity was a welcome relief to what was for many, a dull repetitive day at work. Apart from the sporting scene there was popular and classical music to enjoy every week and once a month a dance was organised by the football team. Highly successful in every way, these events added considerable cash to the coffers and provided a major attraction for much of the town. Undesirables, however, were not allowed to spoil the fun and the equivalent of modern day bouncers made sure there were no unwanted gatecrashers.

Central in location and uncompromisingly Christian in approach, Cheltenham YMCA's years in the Promenade were extremely eventful. With so many influential local people running the Association it is hardly surprising that it had such a high profile but post-war expansion called for a radical rethink and overhaul. What actually happened, however, was somewhat unexpected, and the answers can be found in the next two chapters.

****

What better way to close the YMCA's 35 busy years in the Promenade than by looking at the visit of the Princess Royal on Wednesday, November 19th, 1952. The *Cheltenham Chronicle and Gloucestershire Graphic* (incorporating the *Cheltenham Looker-On*) was a large broadsheet and on the following Saturday gave huge coverage to the event, its front page being filled entirely with pictures at various stages of the proceedings. Unfortunately, the quality of cheap post-war newsprint was dreadful and reproduction of the images virtually impossible.

The Princess was a big champion of the movement and after visiting Tewkesbury YMCA, Baker Street YMCA, and the Central Cheltenham YMCA in the Promenade she went to lunch in the Town Hall. Accompanied by the Duke of Beaufort and various Cheltenham civic leaders, she received a remarkable total of 95 purses containing a total of £3,448 raised on behalf of the YMCA Appeal. They came from all corners of the town, indeed the paper commented that nearly every family in Cheltenham had contributed. YMCA Chairman, Arthur Dye, read out each donor and the amount raised, at the end of

OFFICERS AND COMMITTEE MEMBERS

Patron:
Lt. Gen. Sir John Evetts, C.B., C.B.E., M.C.

President:
P. T. Smith

Vice-Presidents:
Mr. W. H. Bassett-Green,   Mr. B. Haviland,
Ald. A. J. Betteridge,   Ald. D. L. Lipson,
Mr. H. Burroughes,   Coun. A. W. Mann,
Sir G. H. Dowty,   Mr. A. G. Moxley,
The Rev. Canon   Ald. G. Readings,
    J. B. Goodliffe, M.A., Mr. H. Alwyn Smith,
        Revd. G. R. Woodhams.

Chairman:
Councillor A. G. Dye

Hon. Treasurer:
D. I. Wainwright

Executive Committee:
Ald. H. T. Bush, O.B.E., J.P.,   B. J. Lloyd,
W. H. Baggs,   Dr. D. E. Morley,
A. Birt,   W. Morley Manaton,
L. Fitz,   (Nat. Council of Y.M.C.A's)
H. A. Cousins,   S. A. G. Owen,
The Rev. Canon   E. C. W. Phillipson,
    E. C. Hanson, M.A.,   E. Whittaker.

General Secretary:
Kenneth C. Williams

Assistant Secretary: *Boys Work Secretary:*
R. J. Farr.   V. P. Dymock.

◀ *If anyone was ever in doubt as to the influence of Cheltenham YMCA within the town then they only have to look at this 1955 list of Officials which includes five Mayors of Cheltenham: Daniel Lipson, Horace Bush, Percy Smith, George Readings and Arthur Dye. Canon Goodliffe was the Rector of Cheltenham and Sir George Dowty was a big benefactor.*

▸ Cheltenham YMCA and many other local youth organisations were regular members of the Cheltenham Carnival procession, boldly stating their Christian commitment and helping build a better post-war society. It was one of the few occasions when the grey feeling of austerity was temporarily put to one side.

which the Rector of Cheltenham, Canon Goodliffe, dedicated the money to the work of God through the YMCA. All the local Association leaders were present as were the National Secretary from London, Sir Frank Willis, and his Chairman, Winston Jones.

It was an auspicious occasion and Alderman Bush, who welcomed the Princess on behalf of the West of England Division of the YMCA, related previous Royal visits when purses had been presented, namely those to Princess Helena Victoria in 1923 and 1935, and to Queen Mary in 1942 during the war. The latter lived at Badminton House during hostilities and was a regular visitor to Cheltenham and other West Country towns,, always keen to encourage especially where there had been bombing and loss of life.

Everyone understood their place in the 1950s. A Royal visit was a big event and everyone was united in a desire to improve mankind in general. The war was still vivid in the memory of most adults and although children knew very little about it, they naturally followed their parents' hopes and aspirations. Church going was still respectable and membership of an organisation like the YMCA very respectable indeed. Nothing, however, lasts for ever and Cheltenham YMCA was in for a big shock towards the end of 1955.

It has been argued by some that the international YMCA profile remained largely

▸ Meet the 1955 Cheltenham YMCA Volunteer Activity Leaders. Barry Lloyd ran "Music Calling" for 50 years and Arnold Wills, a local school teacher who influenced future international Mike Summerbee, went on to become Chairman of the Gloucestershire Senior Schools Football Association.

unchanged until the pop group "Village People" made their famous – or infamous, depending on which way you look at it – 1978 recording of "YMCA". The truth is rather more complex, however, because the Swinging Sixties rewrote a great social chapter in our history. By then, however, Cheltenham YMCA was established in new premises not far away round the corner.

DO YOU KNOW THESE PEOPLE?

They have accepted responsibility as Secretaries or Leaders of activities, and if you want an introduction ask one of the Secretaries.

BASKET BALL	Ron Farr
BILLIARDS	Joe Phillips
BOY'S CLUB	Vic. Dymock
CAMERA CLUB	General Secretary
CHAIRMAN	Coun. A. G. Dye
CHESS	W. G. Oliver
CRICKET	Stan Owen & Joe Dymond
CYCLING	A. Holland Avery
"55" GROUP DANCE BAND	Terry Scott
DRAMA GROUP	Don. Richardson
FILM PROGRAMMES	Arthur Birt and Claude Fowler
FOOTBALL	Arnold Wills
FULL MEMBERS GROUP	General Secretary
JUDO	Ken Allen & Brian Lewis
LECTURES AND TALKS	General Secretary
MUSIC CALLING	Barry Lloyd and E. C. W. Phillipson
OVERSEAS WORK FUND	Ron Farr
POPULAR MUSIC GROUP	Ron Farr
PRESIDENT	P. T. Smith
SNOOKER	Peter Thomas
SWIMMING	Bob Hawkins
TABLE TENNIS	Peter Cruwys and Alan Knight
LAWN TENNIS	Arnold Wills
TREASURER	D. I. Wainwright
WHIST	Les. Neale
WOMEN'S AUXILIARY	Mrs. Baker & Mrs. Webley

CHAPTER 10
CENTENARY MOVE FROM THE PROMENADE

In keeping with its go-ahead image and to commemorate the Centenary of its foundation, in November 1955 Cheltenham YMCA put forward an ambitious new plan to extend the rear of their premises in the Promenade. The plans were drawn up by architect Barry Lloyd, later to become Chairman and Vice-President of the Association. The three storey block would face out towards Royal Well, a planning application which would have no hope of succeeding today! At the time, however, it was seen as a replacement for the long-serving YMCA hut which had stood on that very location for many years and given valuable service, firstly as a pre-war gymnasium and then as a Services watering hole during the war itself.

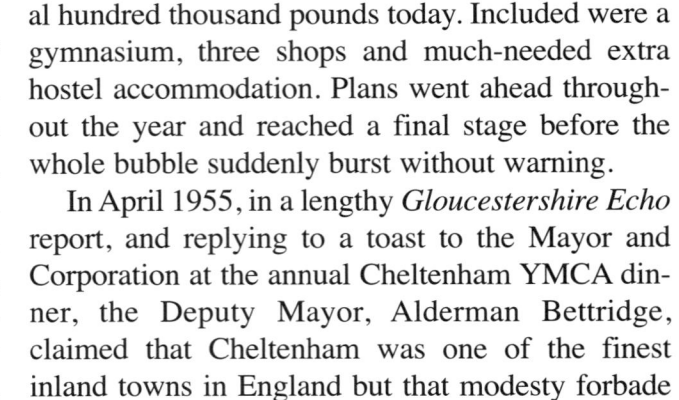

The new building was estimated to cost up to £25,000, a substantial sum the equivalent of several hundred thousand pounds today. Included were a gymnasium, three shops and much-needed extra hostel accommodation. Plans went ahead throughout the year and reached a final stage before the whole bubble suddenly burst without warning.

In April 1955, in a lengthy *Gloucestershire Echo* report, and replying to a toast to the Mayor and Corporation at the annual Cheltenham YMCA dinner, the Deputy Mayor, Alderman Bettridge, claimed that Cheltenham was one of the finest inland towns in England but that modesty forbade him from adding that it also boasted one of the finest councils! The future, he said, depended on its young people.

Mr. A.G. Moxley proposed the toast to Cheltenham YMCA and spoke of his own experiences at home and in America where he had been welcomed by various YMCAs. In reply, Alderman P.T. Smith said how fortunate Cheltenham YMCA was with its supporters. He compared England in 1855 with how it had developed since and expressed the view that the

This year the Y.M.C.A. in Cheltenham celebrates the completion of 100 years work for the young men and boys of this town. A great forward movement is planned and, to commemorate the Centenary, the hostel is to be extended, and a really first class gymnasium is to be provided, and both housed in the new building in Royal Well Road (as shown above).

The Worshipful the Mayor of Cheltenham (Alderman Lt.-Col. C. W. Biggs, O.B.E., J.P.) invites you to hear all about it at

The Council Chamber, Municipal Offices
on
Tuesday, November 22nd, 1955, at 6.0 p.m.

R.S.V.P.
The Mayor's Secretary,
Municipal Offices,
The Promenade,
Cheltenham.

◀ *If the YMCA extension plans had gone through in 1955 then this is what the area of Royal Well Road now occupied by the new Council Chamber would have looked like. Ironically, the Mayor, Lt.-Col. Biggs, invited everyone to attend the unveiling of the project in the old Council Chamber. Three shops, a new gymnasium and 13 new bedrooms were all on the drawing board but when the rateable value went up overnight by 900% then everything was hurriedly scrapped.*

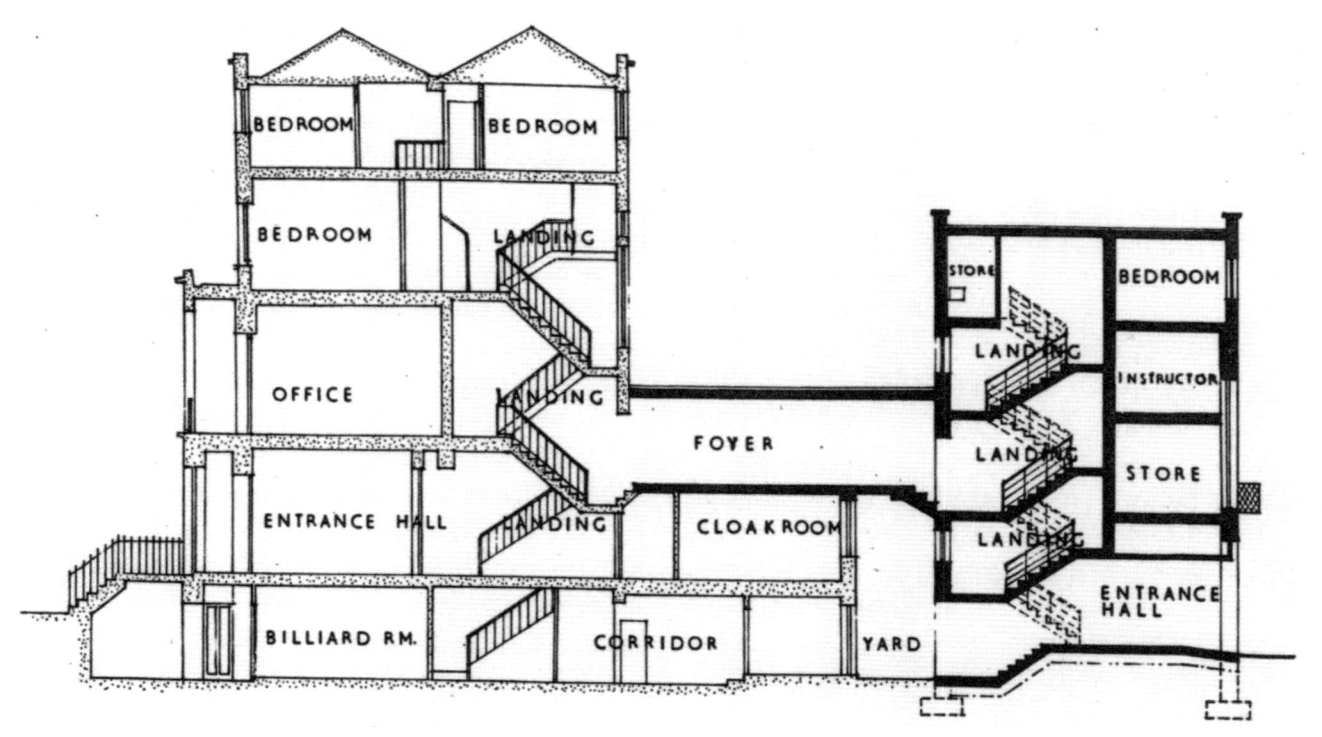

▲ *The impressive looking cross-section of architect Barry Lloyd's plans for the aborted 1955 extension of the YMCA in Royal Well Road. The Promenade main entrance is to the left of the picture by the railings.*

local YMCA was not standing still but forging ahead. The Chairman, Councillor Arthur Dye, also replied and said he and his committee hoped within two years to have the finest equipped gymnasium not just in the town but in this part of the country. He asked all supporters and members to double their subscriptions during the coming year.

Mr. Lionel Fitz, proposing the toast to the guests, said how pleased he was to see so many people in attendance. He announced that the billiards team had won the Preston Cup, the 2nd XI football team hoped to win promotion and the table tennis team had won Division 1 of the Cheltenham League. Overseas guests were welcomed and Mr. J.L. Goulder praised Mr. Vic Dymock and Secretary Mr. Ken Williams for their work at the Baker Street Boys' Club and Promenade premises respectively.

The next *Echo* report was in late September when the President informed everyone that they had £2,200 in the bank and a great deal of faith! "We shall continue to pursue a progressive policy and to strive for conditions and a standard that will be in keeping with the importance of our work." Vic Dymock described how the Boys' Club had won the Cheltenham Table Tennis League, the Gloucestershire Association of Boys Clubs Senior Football Cup, the Cheltenham Youth Cricket Shield, the Cheltenham Youth Band Shield and a camp trophy. They had also won awards at the national competition held in London.

When Mr. J. Cooper spoke on behalf of the men's football teams he commented on the lack of changing facilities at King George V Playing Fields. Chairman Arthur Dye said he was speaking to the right person because he was personally on the Parks and Gardens Committee. However, the cost would be between £8,000-£10,000 – an enormous sum equivalent today to several new houses – and that if they were not careful then their rates would be as high as Charlton Kings!

Mrs. W.A. Baker, Chairman of the Women's Auxiliary group said they planned to furnish one of the bedrooms in the new extension while the Secretary, Ken Williams, reported on other activities which included athletics, billiards, snooker, tennis, secular and church socials, dances, a Harvest Festival, youth orchestra, gramophone recitals and Sunday tea table talks. It was also reported that Lionel Fitz, later Chairman and President, had set a new record aggregate number of runs in the cricket team.

On Tuesday, November 22nd at 6pm in the Council Offices, the Mayor of Cheltenham Alderman Lt.-Col. C.W. Biggs, OBE, JP, invited

Handbook of the ..

CHELTENHAM AND DISTRICT YOUNG MEN'S CHRISTIAN ASSOCIATION
1955-56

Headquarters: The Promenade. Tel. 4024
Boys' Club: Baker Street. Tel. 2720
General Secretary: KENNETH C. WILLIAMS.

everyone to hear all about the proposed new YMCA extensions. Included on the invitation was an architect's impression of the new extension and most imposing it looked!

At the appeal, Cheltenham was reminded of the wartime canteen at Lansdown Station – situated on the site of the only remaining Cheltenham Station today but at the time there were several others – which was sponsored by Cheltenham YMCA and which never closed. Many of the volunteers were there to hear this and comments which suggested the extension would considerably improve the look of Royal Well Road and also "give the Council a lesson in good planning"! Also launched was Alderman H.T. Bush's little booklet on the history of Cheltenham YMCA entitled 100 Years Young. It had been compiled "with assistance from the Echo, Chronicle and Graphic." Among the many dignitaries present was Sir John Evetts, President of the Western Division of the YMCA who presented Bibles to Alderman Smith in recognition of his 20 years Presidency, Councillor Dye for his 35 years

▶ *Horace Bush, Mayor of Cheltenham from 1946-9, was a great asset to the YMCA. As a young man he wrote about the local Association in the 19th Century and followed it up with this small booklet to celebrate the Centenary in 1955.*

◀ *A final goodbye to the Promenade ....*

active membership, and Alderman Bush for his 30 years membership. The Mayor said how much he hoped the Appeal would be successful.

By early January 1956 the old timber and corrugated iron YMCA hut was demolished and re-erected as St. Thomas' Mission Church on the Alma estate in Up Hatherley, for which a dedication service conducted by the Bishop of Tewkesbury, the Right Rev. E.B. Henderson, took place the following October. The *Echo* reported "Entirely without external ornamentation other than a simple wooden cross, the church stands completely in harmony with the prefabricated houses and their neat gardens, by which it is surrounded." It stood on the corner of Windermere and Thirlmere Roads, serving as a YMCA youth centre, church and scout hut until the prefabs were replaced a few years later.

No sooner was the YMCA Royal Well Hut down, however, than the bombshell dropped! The Appeal Committee discovered to their horror that three major obstacles lay in their path:

1. The cost of the new extension had risen from £25,000 to at least £30,000 and possibly £35,000.

2. The rating reassessment had gone up from £112 to £1,120 – a 900% or 10 fold increase!

3. Although the main part of the building would receive financial concessions from the Council this would not apply to the shops.

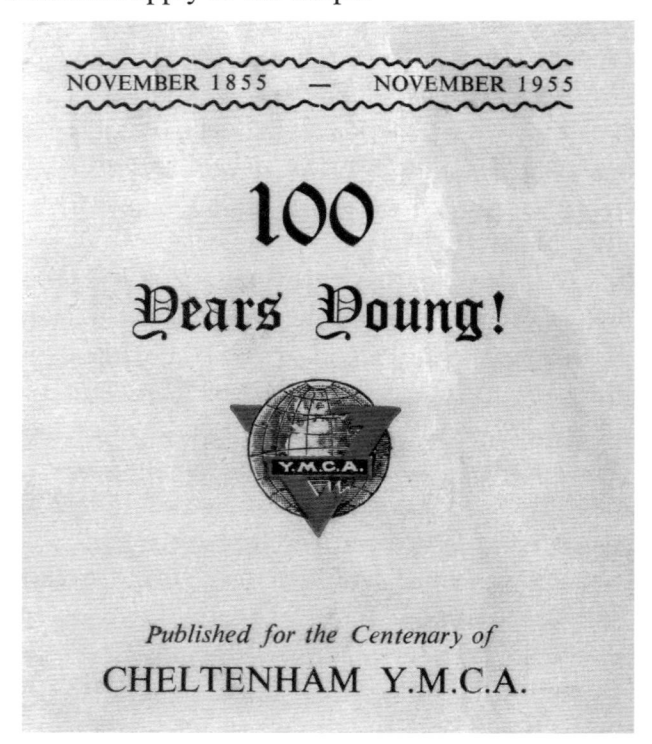

NOVEMBER 1855 — NOVEMBER 1955

100 Years Young!

Published for the Centenary of
CHELTENHAM Y.M.C.A.

and .... hello to Vittoria Walk! ▶

Faced with a yearly bill for rating and a loan repayment much larger than anything they had anticipated the committee members endured several sleepless nights.

The Chairman, Councillor Arthur Dye, acted quickly. Calling together his YMCA Board one lunchtime he announced he had put a deposit on a building in Vittoria Walk. Farnley Lodge, a large Regency building, had been put up for sale by Cheltenham Ladies' College and was purchased for £12,500. The YMCA premises at 53 and 55 Promenade were then put up for sale, together with the land at the rear of Number 51. It was bought by the Council for £27,500 thus leaving a sizeable amount of money for redevelopment in Vittoria Walk where the most suitable suggested new name was "Centenary House". This was never taken up, however. Meanwhile, the space left at the rear of the Promenade by dismantling the Royal Well Hut became the site of an extension to the Council Offices which now includes the Council Chamber.

In Chapter 13, Lionel Fitz describes the amazing circumstances which caused Arthur Dye to act so quickly and how the Council was then persuaded to more than double its original offer for the YMCA premises in the Promenade. Part of the sequence of events is worth repeating here, however.

When the members arrived they were informed by Arthur Dye that he had dreamt the previous night that they had bought Farnley Lodge and so that morning had put in an offer on their behalf! Previously a Ladies' College boarding house in it had been acquired by them in 1882 and proved extremely popular, even growing much of its own vegetables in the grounds. Requisitioned during the Second World War it was handed back fairly quickly but by 1949 the Ladies' College Council decided it was too dangerous for girls to cross the Promenade to and from lessons, and alternative accommodation was therefore sought. The board trooped round to inspect the building which, although old fashioned with huge dormitories upstairs and kitchens in the basement, was much bigger than the Promenade premises. In addition it had a fair amount of ground for extensions. There and then the whole committee endorsed the chairman's decision to purchase it.

CHELTENHAM Y·M·C·A

HANDBOOK 1956 - 1957

Meanwhile, Cheltenham Ladies' College kept the name Farnley Lodge and transferred it across the town to a former boys' prep school called Glyngarth, opposite Christchurch in Douro Road. Although they had acquired it in 1949 it took several years to renovate, hence the sale of Farnley Lodge which was put on the market in 1955, just at the right time for Arthur Dye to have his prophetic dream!

Cheltenham YMCA had moved to the Promenade premises in 1921 which were at least the thirteenth set of buildings to be occupied in its 100 year existence. The next 50 years, however, were to be spent in the newly acquired accommodation at Vittoria Walk where extensive renovations, extensions and redecoration soon took place.

The new premises were officially opened at 3pm on Monday, December 10th 1956, by The Mayor of Cheltenham, Alderman George Readings. Yet another local dignitary who had been actively connected to the YMCA, George had served on the executive committee since before the war and later had a street, George Readings Way, named after him off Hesters Way.

CHAPTER 11
VITTORIA WALK

This chapter paints an overall view of events at Vittoria Walk and should be used in conjunction with Chapter 13 "A President Looks Back" in which further detailed information may be found. It also needs to be mentioned that colour print photography did not become widespread until well into the 1970s and that although colour slides were common before this there was no cheap or easy way of converting them into prints. Although the chapter contains only black and white illustrations the colour supplement should be treated as an extension of it.

The move to 6 Vittoria Walk was a significant milestone and no time was wasted in adding substantial annexes to the building. Sadly, two of the stalwarts behind the move did not live long enough to see all the developments take place.

The first to go was President and former Mayor of Cheltenham, Percy Tyler Smith, who died in August 1957, aged 77. "PT" as he was known, spent 40 years in the town and became an Alderman in 1946, coming to prominence during the war by spearheading the local "Dig for Victory" campaign. He became President of Cheltenham YMCA in 1936 and was a generous benefactor, as he was for the town, spending much of his own money putting the dignity back into the role of mayor and civic occasions during the period of post-war austerity. A splendid framed picture of him in his ceremonial robes hangs in the conference room.

The next to go, in January 1958, was much more unexpected. Alderman Horace Trinley Bush, OBE, JP, another former Mayor of Cheltenham and dedicated YMCA supporter for more than 30 years, died from a brain tumour aged only 56. He had previously lost his wife and 12-year-old daughter, plus the lady driver of their car in a road accident near Winchester in June 1947. Now remarried he left a 5-year-old son. Thus, Cheltenham YMCA had lost two Presidents in five months, the latter being a particularly sad blow not just because of his age but because he was also President of the Baker Street YMCA Boys' Club, Chairman of the Western Divisional Council and a member of the National Executive.

In lieu of flowers donations were requested for the work of Baker Street YMCA, or Boys Club as it was more affectionately known. These came from all quarters in the form of more than 30 letters, including the local MP Major Hicks-Beach, both the Conservative and Labour Parties, several individual councillors, Pate's Grammar School for Girls, Pate's Junior School, Rotol, St Paul's College, Cheltenham Municipal Officers Guild, the Hotel and Caterers Association, and the District Allotments and Gardens Society. Horace Bush had influenced many people and was indeed a sad loss.

The driving force over the next few years was the Chairman and later President, Arthur Dye whose framed picture also hangs in the YMCA conference room. It was he who displayed the necessary vision and, using his considerable powers of persuasion through his high office as an Alderman of the Borough, and cajoled many outside bodies to support the ongoing work. Cheltenham YMCA will forever be indebted to this great man whose living memorial is the primary school which bears his name. A brief resume of his time in Cheltenham is certainly not out of place here.

Arthur Dye came to Cheltenham in 1919 after service during the First World War with the 18th Battalion of the London Irish, and made such an impact teaching at the Central School that after three years he was appointed headmaster of Naunton Park School, where he stayed until his retirement in 1950. He then became an Independent councillor and chairman of the Gloucestershire education committee, as well as belonging to the Cheltenham Lions, the United Nations Association, the Dickens Society, the Cheltenham Bowling Club and many others, in all of which he took an active role.

His death on Boxing Day, 1971, produced much coverage in the *Gloucestershire Echo* which also mentioned he had been nominated for an OBE just before he died and, because he was aware of the honour, it had therefore been awarded posthumously. The paper also reported that in 1956 he had been awarded the Gold Order of the Red Triangle for 50 years service to the YMCA and that the Borough's latest primary school in Springbank Road would be named in his memory. YMCA Secretary, Wilf Pearson who took office in 1957 having previously been at Hoylake YMCA in Cheshire, later bore testimony to Dye's unstinting efforts at fund raising for the new Vittoria Walk premises. He often accompanied his chairman to meetings with local businessmen, where he just sat back and watched Arthur persuade them of the worthwhile nature of the YMCA cause. They usually gave both willingly and generously.

Wilf later moved on to become Secretary of Liverpool YMCA and, apart from the major building work during his time in Cheltenham, forged a link with Philip Wragge, a peripatetic lecturer employed by the YMCA National Council who wrote a booklet entitled *Youth and Changing Times*. In it was a chapter called "The YMCA in Church and Society" based partly on Philip's regular visits to Cheltenham two days a week when he liaised with Wilf on meetings with local apprentices and industrial firms. The whole project was part of an organisation called "Youth in Industry" which subsequently held a conference near Lake Constance in Switzerland, to which Wilf Pearson was invited. Wilf eventually retired to Cheltenham and became a Vice-President of the local Association.

On completion of the contracts for the move to Vittoria Walk there followed a period of urgent activity. Plans had to be quickly prepared, both for the new building itself and for the first phase of an expansion project. Architect, Barry Lloyd, later Chairman and Vice-President, was the professional brains behind it.

Farnley Lodge was built as a private house between 1824-1828, probably by J.B. Papworth who was invited to Cheltenham by Dr. Shoolbred in 1824. The rear was extended around 1890 and the Italianate tower added in about 1928. The building was given Grade II listed status on May 5th, 1972. What is now the reception area was a brick-vaulted wine cellar, which was initially converted into a billiards and snooker room with two tables, a third being positioned under what is now the lecture room. The vaulting was replaced by a central steel beam and new flooring joists and the area later housed a tiered television theatre, which was itself removed for the Training Agency around 1980.

▲ *This is what Vittoria Walk front entrance looked like in 1956 but, along with the conservatory immediately behind, it was later demolished as unsafe.*

The dormitories were adapted into smaller rooms, although not very many were converted into sole occupancy. As fashions changed again, though, some of these were partitioned into singles.

The original entrance, opening straight on to the pavement, was a glazed conservatory fronted by Ionic stone columns but was deemed unsafe.and soon demolished. It was replaced by an early 1960s office block extension leaving a more modern entrance set back from the road (see pages 180 and 188). Immediately behind the facade a wide flight of stairs gave access to reception, a typist's office and small coffee bar servery. which is now the Sheila Green Rooms comprising a residents television lounge and coffee bar. The dining room was situated in what is now the foyer to the new dining room. Food was brought up from the basement kitchen via a hand-operated service lift.

The first major project was the creation of a sports hall, although this term did not come into common use for another 20 years. At the time the

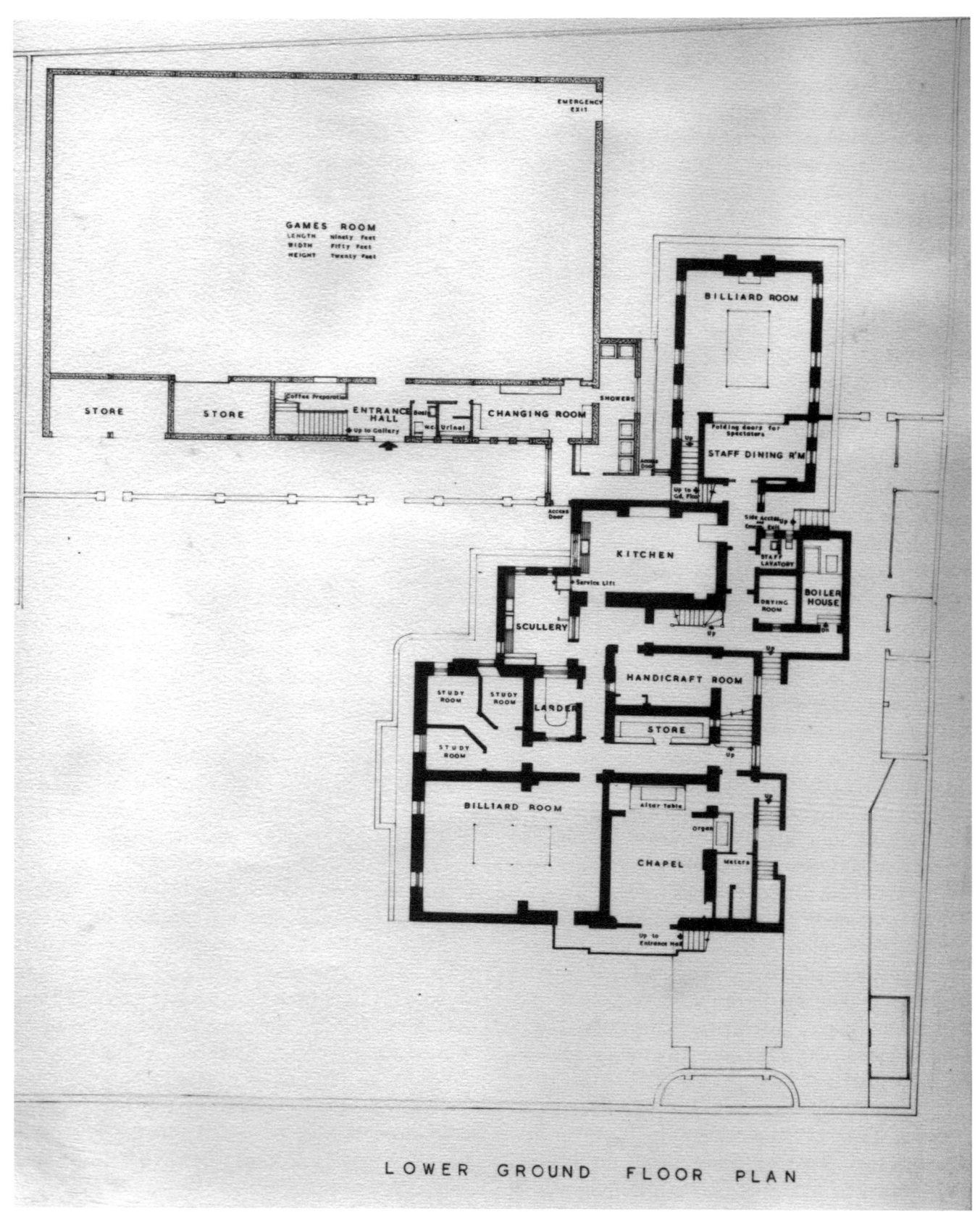

▲ *Part of architect Barry Lloyd's new plans for the development of Cheltenham YMCA at Vittoria Walk. The Billiard Room closest to the road is now the Reception area, the Chapel remaining untouched in its current location for half a century.*

GROUND FLOOR PLAN

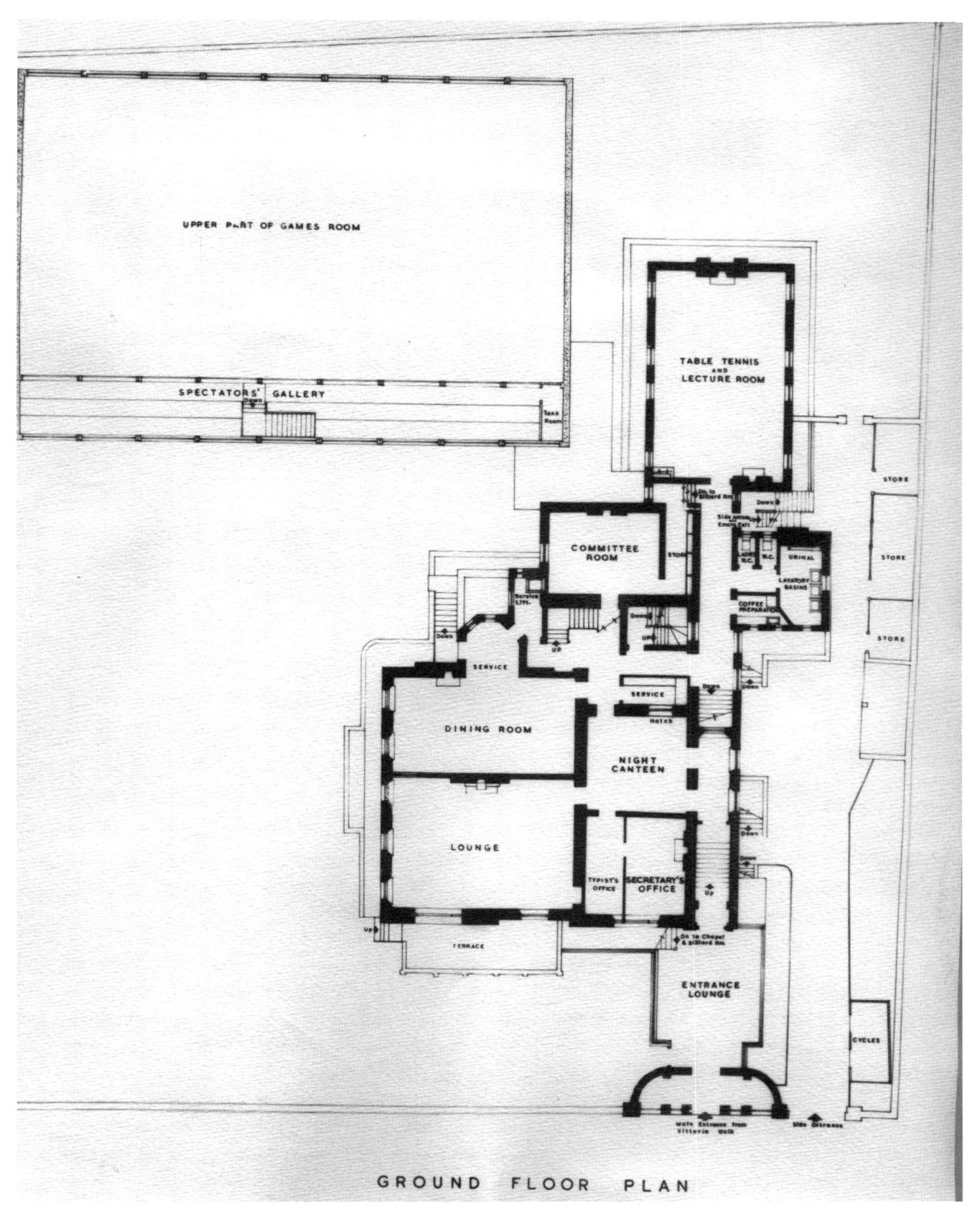

▲ Entry to the YMCA was through the old porticoed Entrance and Entrance Lounge (later demolished), then up the stairs to a Reception area shown as the Night Canteen, Typist's Office and Secretary's Office. The Lounge is now the Conference Room but the Lecture Room remains. Note the plans for what was described as a Games Room, later a Sports Hall, now referred to as the Gym.

FIRST FLOOR PLAN

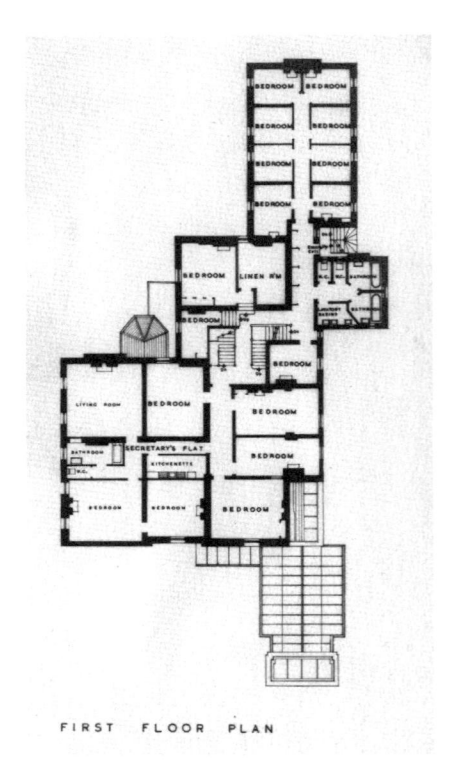

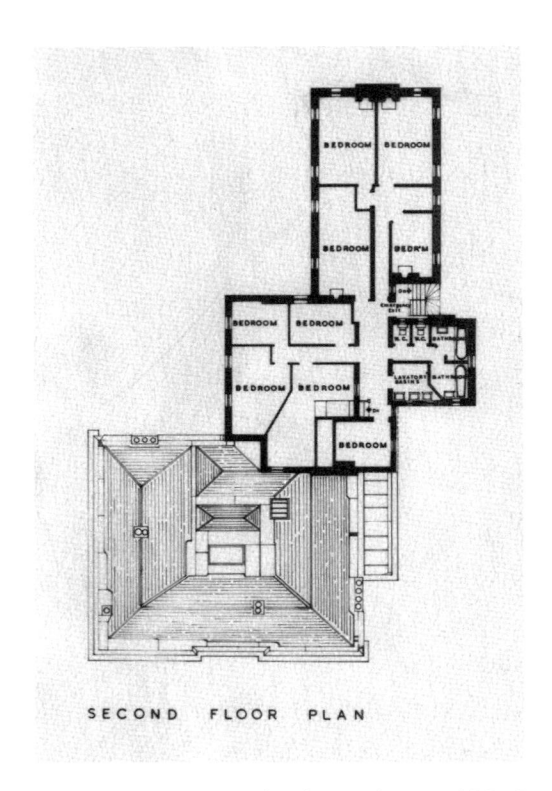

SECOND FLOOR PLAN

▲ *These views are of the South Wing incorporating the Italianate Tower built in about 1928. Part of this area is used for offices with other rooms used for the passing bed and breakfast trade.*

new structure was the biggest in the south west which is remarkable when one considers that by today's standards it is considered too small! At first it was intended to construct a timber building but it was later agreed to build a permanent hall in two phases. The first incorporated a temporary end with open access to a single door in one corner. When funds permitted the hall was extended to its full length but with a first floor set above the extension to allow more activities to be carried out, now the fitness room. The two sections were joined together but with wooden folding doors which would allow the whole hall to be opened up as an indoor cricket school. Unfortunately, they demanded to use it every night of the week which was totally out of the question so the expensive netting was never purchased. Connecting corridors were also built at this time.

During the 1960s came a strong demand for student accommodation to meet a rapid government expansion in higher education. The existing south wing rooms were unsuitable so in 1963 plans were made for a new north wing complete with dining room. A new form of building was used called load-bearing brickwork with the outer wall of 11-inch cavity construction, thus greatly reducing cost. Most of the inner walls were also load-bearing. A total of 28 study bedrooms were built, including two linen rooms which were later converted to bedrooms. The estimated cost, for which a local appeal was launched, was £41,000 towards which sum the Council made a generous grant of 50%.

The existing servery was enlarged alongside the new dining room supported on pre-stressed concrete slabs set over a warden's basement flat which is now occupied by Listening Post. Meanwhile, the original dining room was converted into a coffee bar staffed by volunteers with the original coffee bar becoming the reception area.

In fullness of time the programme facilities were enhanced by the erection of two squash courts with a first floor balcony and an auxiliary room. More recent improvements have included refurbishing the north wing and a new main entrance and reception area. The old entrance extension was demolished thus leaving the whole building more in keeping with the original architectural style. This particular improvement was highly commended in the 1997 Annual Civic Awards. The *Gloucestershire Echo* of Monday, March 3rd read:

"In the category for the restoration of a period building, Cheltenham YMCA in Vittoria Walk was commended. Judges praised the vision in restoring the building's frontage, saying it had 'restored the spirit of the original.' Cheltenham YMCA Chief Executive, Adrian Sharpe said: 'It's important we should retain the town's Regency heritage. It was more elaborate than the original plans but we're delighted with the end result of the building and with the award'."

A purpose built reception desk was added and a new staircase leading from the foyer to the dining room, now known as the Café Y, formerly the Tuck Inn. Instead of being hidden away, the chapel was now visible to all who came through the main entrance. The original basement kitchen became the ladies' changing room, the men's changing room having been extended earlier.

The renovation of the north wing formed part of a major contract. Individual flatlets were created on the top floor where it was possible to remove original partitions. Pipe work and original heating installation was replaced by a computer controlled electrical system and the original furniture was also replaced. The Café Y was also refurbished to a high standard.

****

Soon after it opened Vittoria Walk established a new pattern of residential accommodation which was tantamount to a large extended family. Mike Hunt arrived in 1961 and stayed for 14 years. Typical of the period he came as a 15-year-old apprentice to a firm of cabinet makers in Charlton Kings, with most of the other residents consisting of fellow apprentices or students who got on extremely well together. In addition there were later a number of overseas students, particularly from Africa. They also came from South America and Europe and all, apart from the Greeks according to Mike, fitted in brilliantly. A small number of disabled employees from GCHQ (Government Communications Headquarters) were also resident for whom money was raised to buy chairmobiles designed by Lord Snowdon. Unfortunately they kept breaking down!

TWO CHELTENHAM YMCA PRESIDENTS

▲ *Alderman Percy Tyler Smith, affectionately known as "PT", was Mayor of Cheltenham from 1949-51 and President of Cheltenham YMCA from 1936 until his death in August 1957, aged 77. He did much for the town as well as for the local Association.*

▲ *Councillor Horace Trinley Bush, OBE, JP was Mayor of Cheltenham from 1946-49 and succeeded Smith as President. Sadly, he died five months later in January 1958, aged 56. A dedicated Cheltenham YMCA supporter for 30 years he wrote two historical accounts of its work.*

◄ The death throes of the Royal Well Hut. Erected during the mid-1920s to the rear of the YMCA at 51, 53 and 55 Promenade, it served as a gymnasium and Junior Boys Department before being requisitioned as an important Wartime Canteen run by the YMCA Women's Auxiliary (see Chapter 7). It was dismantled in 1956 and re-erected as the St. Thomas Mission Church on the Alma Estate in Up Hatherley where it served as a joint YMCA youth centre, church and Scout hut.

▶ The dedication of St. Thomas' Mission Church among the prefabs of Up Hatherley. An offshoot of St. Mark's, it stood on the corner of Windermere Road and Thirlemere Road, and in the early-1960s regularly attracted more than 100 youngsters. It survived until the mid-1970s.

All the accommodation was originally in the South Wing which consisted mainly of shared rooms with many residents staying for years at a time, indeed Mike believed that one person stayed more than 30 years! It was not surprising that the YMCA, according to the local paper, turned away hundreds of residents a year through lack of space.

▲ Secretary, Ken Williams, oversaw the move from the Promenade to Vittoria Walk, even transferring furniture on a hand cart!.

It was all one big happy family which was further enhanced when the north wing opened in 1965 because although most of the rooms were singles and numbers almost doubled overnight, there was regular fraternising every evening, particularly in the dining room and coffee bar. A craze at one time was a game called Tip It which involved a shilling piece concealed on a bench and then tipped off by one side but skilfully concealed in someone's clenched fist. The other side had to then work out where it was amid much bluffing and bantering. All good clean harmless fun – and fun it was. Sunday morning was also a time when residents enjoyed an impromptu game of volleyball in the gym. The residential managers at this time were Mr. and Mrs. Charles Peters who lived in a flat downstairs.

In 1964 a Motor Club was founded which was registered with the RAC and ran for about six years during which time there were rallies and various other related activities. Meanwhile, the cricket club played on the Market Street playing fields near what is now Tesco's. Secretary, Des Willcox and his wife Pearl, often organised international evenings for residents and friends when everyone came dressed in their national costumes. Use was also made of Vic Dymock's lorry for displays in the Cheltenham Carnival, one of which was "Jonah and the Whale".

At the age of only 19, Mike Hunt was appointed to the Board as the Residents' Representative and stayed on this governing body for the next 40 years! In addition to various secretaries, Mike remembered good work done by assistants Derek Harper, Mike Russell and Jim Black. It was a period when about two thirds of the residents were students and when general camaraderie was at its greatest. Group spirit and esprit de corps meant everything and the closely knit YMCA residents community was a far cry from how society later evolved with more emphasis placed on individual rights compared to natural service within the community.

****

It is impossible to do justice to everything which happened at Vittoria Walk but a brief glance at the first 20 years of operation tells us much of the flavour of the time before computers and mobile phones shrank the world. In the mid-1950s life was still fairly parochial and remained so until the end of the Swinging Sixties when increasing social liberalisation, growing mobility, and the move to comprehensive schools broke down much of the old order. In theory this seemed laudable but in practice it did not work out as planned and half a century down the line Cheltenham YMCA found itself serving a very different community from the one it served when it moved into Vittoria Walk in a blaze of publicity in 1956.

The Secretary at the time of the move was Ken Williams and he soon found himself a busy man because the accommodation immediately doubled from 23 to 45 residents. Arthur Dye, the brains behind the move, was awarded the YMCA's highest accolade, the Gold Order of the Red Triangle presented by Lt. Gen. Sir John Evetts, President of the Western Division of the YMCA and also Cheltenham's Patron. In his address at the opening of Vittoria Walk, the Mayor, Alderman George Readings spoke of his debt to the YMCA in that he had made good use of a YMCA hut near the fighting at Ypres during the First World War, by writing to a young lady who later became his wife and was sitting in the audience!

▲ *The new games room/sports hall/gymnasium under construction. It suffered from an identity crisis at the time and has done ever since. When it was opened, however, it was described as the biggest of its type in the south west of England!*

In March 1957 the new chapel was dedicated by the Bishop of Gloucester, Dr. W.M. Askwith and a rider added that it was open for use by any church in Cheltenham. In August the same year there was a visit from England batsman Tom Graveney and his Gloucestershire colleague George Emmett, who demonstrated their skills in the new cricket nets. In September there was a large garden fete, including dancing and a barbecue and in October Ken Williams moved on to be Assistant Secretary to the North Midlands Regional Area of the YMCA, to be succeeded by Wilf Pearson. In November the local paper stated that it was hoped the new gymnasium would help to offset the town's "gang problems", the facility itself being opened by the Earl of Romsey on December 12th. In his speech the Earl reported there were more than four million YMCA members worldwide.

On February 25th, 1958 there was a special service to dedicate a new lectern and Bible and an Open Week from May 2-9, 1958 listed several activities open to the general public, including an orchestral link with Cheltenham Grammar School for Boys who put on a complete weekend concert. As stated in the 1958 Handbook, it is interesting to note that this period of time involved Cheltenham YMCA working very closely with the Local Education Authority, Schools (especially Naunton Park, where Arthur Dye had been headmaster until 1950), Colleges, Industry and Churches. The YMCA was known throughout the town as a force for good and many members of the Council were still listed as Vice-Presidents.

The 1958 Handbook also listed the hostel full board prices rising from £3 sharing a treble room, £3 2s 6d for a double and £3 5shillings for a single, with accommodation specifically for 44 young men working in the district. There was also a drive to enlist 1,000 Friends of the YMCA who were invited to fill in a form and pledge an annual sum.

The Luncheon Club "in a friendly and informal atmosphere" was 3 shillings daily (15p in today's money). Tea or coffee was extra but included in the price was "use of a comfortable lounge, daily newspapers and certain weeklies, participation in main Association events" and, perhaps somewhat surprisingly "cigarettes, chocolates etc. can be obtained from the shop". Cigarettes were already a killer but it was not generally recognised as such. Membership of the Luncheon Club cost men 15 shillings per annum but women only 10 shillings. Shades of discrimination which at the time was perfectly normal but today would be wholly unacceptable.

The shop was described as an important part of the Association and was open Mondays to Saturdays from 7.30-9.30pm and on Sundays from 9-10pm. In addition to cigarettes and chocolates, "toilet requisites" were also on offer which consisted of soaps, shampoos etc. not toilet ducks or loo brushes as one might expect the term to mean today. The shop was manned by voluntary lady helpers from both the Parish Church and Bethesda Methodist Church Young Wives Groups, another example of female assistance which was greatly valued. Open membership for ladies gradually crept in around this time and soon grew to equal membership in all departments.

Vic Dymock had by now become heavily immersed in the work of Gas Green Baptist Church and asked to be released from some of his Baker Street YMCA Boys' Club duties. Peter Roberts was appointed with a brief to assist him but also to work across the other three boys club for which the YMCA had responsibility, namely St. Thomas' in Up Hatherley which operated on Tuesday evenings with 100 members, Vittoria Walk or Central as it was called at the time, and Pilley Lane Baptist which was open on Mondays and Fridays and run largely by Ken Gilbert and Arnold Cryer. The same year saw Arthur Dye become President of Baker Street with Lionel Fitz as the new Chairman.

Other significant 1958 events were an Autumn Fayre, a Young People's Orchestral Concert, and the Annual Dinner on September 29th at which Major K.G.W. Shennan was appointed the new President in succession to Horace Bush who had died on January 14th after only a short term in office.

Peter Roberts put a great deal of effort into Baker Street and, wearing a false moustache, top hat, tie and tails, in a non-stop piano playing marathon lasting 6 and a half hours he raised £28 10 shillings for its funds. Locally-based Tom Graveney again appeared on the scene but this time supporting England and Essex all-rounder Trevor Bailey, who gave a cricket film lecture on behalf of the Gloucestershire Cricket Council.

****

Annual Reports at this time were produced on the time honoured Roneo-Gestetner machines described earlier in the book, and which held sway well into the 1970s both in schools and in the general workplace. To the expert they presented no problem but to the novice they often meant inky fingers or worse! Photocopying was a product of the mid-1970s prior to which actual printing had to be done by a professional company.

Colour copying on a Roneo machine could only be achieved by changing the drum, red being the only real alternative to black. Banda copiers on the other hand, were a similar kind of machine but liquid spirit-based on which different colours could be used. These also became obsolete with the birth of photocopiers although the colour variety of the latter only arrived around the turn of the 21st Century.

PROGRAMME	
Monday	
Women's Auxiliary	3.00 p.m.
S.Y.M.C.A.	6.00 p.m.
Junior Judo	5.45 to 7.15 p.m.
Judo	7.15 p.m.
Fencing	7.30 p.m.
Trampoline	7.30 p.m.
Tuesday	
Kendo	7.30 p.m.
Badminton	7.30 p.m.
Music Calling (fortnightly)	7.30 p.m.
Table Tennis	
Christian Fellowship	8.00 p.m.
Evening Prayers	9.00 p.m.
Wednesday	
5-a-side football	7.00 p.m.
Films (monthly)	8.15 p.m.
Thursday	
Netball	7.00 p.m.
Junior Judo	5.45 to 7.15 p.m.
Judo	7.15 p.m.
Volleyball	8.00 p.m.
Cheltenham Camera Club	7.30 p.m.
Friday	
Basketball	7.00 p.m.
Table Tennis	
Saturday	
Junior Club	10.00 a.m.
Football	afternoon
Badminton	7.00 p.m.
Discotheques (as announced)	8.00 p.m.

VITTORIA WALK, CHELTENHAM
OPEN WEEK
MARCH 2nd to MARCH 9th, 1958

CHELTENHAM YMCA

You are Invited to attend the following:

SUNDAY 2	10 a.m.	Prayers in the Chapel
	6.30 p.m.	Church Visit
	8 p.m.	Social Hour
MONDAY 3	7 p.m.	Table Tennis Match
	7.30 p.m.	JUDO AND FENCING Demonstration
TUESDAY 4	7.30 p.m.	Badminton League Match CHELTENHAM I versus GLOUCESTER I
WEDNESDAY 5	7 p.m.	SNOOKER MATCH
	7 p.m.	"Music Calling"
	8.15 p.m.	Debate
THURSDAY 6	7.30 p.m.	JUDO AND FENCING
	9 p.m.	Basketball Match
FRIDAY 7	7 p.m.	PHYSICAL TRAINING and Gymnastic Display
SATURDAY 8	7.30 p.m.	SOCIAL Rhythmic Entertainment
SUNDAY 9	8 p.m.	Musical Entertainment by Pupils of Cheltenham Grammar School

▲ *Two publicity programmes. The one on the left dates from 1957 and "SYMCA" stood for "Schoolboys' YMCA", the Junior Department being a quite separate work at this time.*

The 1950s also saw an upsurge in Christian outreach and the YMCA archives mention a Youth Squash, a popular term at the time for an open invitation to a talk usually followed by refreshments. In November 1958 the squash took the form of the popular Radio Programme "Any Questions" which is still going strong nearly 50 years later. The idea of the name was to attract people along in large numbers, i.e. to pack them in. It was a short-lived term, however, and had largely disappeared by the following decade.

Anther innovative change was the switch to more modern translations of the Bible. The YMCA chapel in the 1950s was mentioned in the Handbook with the words "Come ye apart" which in more modern parlance meant come and be quiet, away from the noise and bustle of the everyday routine. The King James or Authorised Version had held sway for four centuries but with the advent of the Revised Standard Version (usually referred to as the RSV), J.B. Phillips' paraphrase and the New English Bible, the situation changed very quickly. Then, during the 1960s Billy Graham championed the Living Bible, since when a whole crop of new translations have vied for our attention. It is hard to believe that only 50 years ago Christians wrestled daily with the King James translation, made easier with the use of Bible Reading Notes, especially those produced by Scripture Union, an international organisation with London offices in which Cheltenham YMCA kingpin, Major Rickerby, played an important role until the 1930s.

The 1959-60 handbook listed subscriptions as 10 shillings for 15-17 year olds; 15 shillings for 18-20 years olds, and 21 shillings (one guinea) minimum charge for those over 21. Younger Juniors of 12-13 years were only allowed on the Central premises from 6-7.30pm on Mondays and Thursdays. 1960 also saw Cheltenham host the national finals of the YMCA table tennis competition in which Wimbledon defeated Doncaster. The YMCA's very own Ian Harrison was at the time the

▲ *May 4th 1962 saw the opening of the new Sports Hall. Pictured here is the platform party, from left: Wilf Pearson (YMCA Secretary); the Duke of Beaufort (who opened the premises); Arthur Dye (YMCA President and Deputy Mayor of Cheltenham); Major K.W.G. Shennan (Lord Lieutenant of Gloucestershire); and Lt.-General Sir John Evetts (President of the Western Division of the YMCA).*

country's number one player and he was pictured playing in a doubles match. The two part-time youth workers were Norman Knight and a teacher at Arthur Dye's old Naunton Park School, Arnold Wills, who later became Chairman of the Gloucestershire Senior Schools Football Association.

The Young Wives Group were busy making preserves and holding whist drives, while Peter Roberts was editing a monthly magazine called "Vittoria Talk". Women and girls over the age of 16 were also now participating in a wide range of activities which would shortly give rise to full equality across the whole spectrum. Times were changing!

****

Martin Wray came to Cheltenham YMCA in 1963 in order to gain experience of youth work prior to being ordained into the Anglican ministry and soon found himself working at the satellite YMCA youth work at St. Thomas' mission church in Up Hatherley. The wheel eventually turned full circle because, after serving in several different parts of the country he became Vicar of St. Philip and St. James, Up Hatherley during the late-1990s through into the early 21st Century. During his three year stint at Vittoria Walk he saw many exciting activities develop including the Fri. In (a pun on Friday and Fry) youth club which ran discos on Friday evenings in the lesser hall which attracted up to 400 youngsters. On one occasion the owner of a local night club came and complained the YMCA had taken away all his customers! One major spin-off was the inclusion of girls for the first time, although not everyone was happy that the formerly all-male bastion had finally fallen to feminine charms, who now held YMCA membership to prove their existence.

Ballroom dancing was taught by Martin and Pearl Willcox, wife of General Secretary Des Willcox and the establishment of a coffee bar opening for long hours steadily increased the membership to more than 2,000, a huge percentage rise. The youngsters themselves were given extra responsibilities which brought about many new activities. The sports hall became a centre for 5-a-side football competitions for the whole town; smaller local youth clubs regularly came along to see a bigger one in full flow; trips to London theatres were arranged; a visit took place to a Billy Graham rally in Birmingham; camping occurred at the YMCA Lakeside cabin complex near Windermere; and training weekends were established at both Cowley Manor and Sandywell Park near Dowdeswell.

Mention must also be made of a stalwart behind the scenes worker, Phyllis Walker, who came soon after the war and served for many years as the secretary to the General Secretary. Another tower of strength was Barry Lloyd who, apart from designing the Sports Hall, Lesser Hall and North Wing, came in early every day and never left until late in the evening, always creative and then looking for jobs to finish. A glutton for hard work he persisted with a punishing personal schedule until well into his 80s.

The SYMCA stood for Schoolboys YMCA which met twice a week and encouraged different sports along the lines of the Duke of Edinburgh's Award Scheme. Local Youth Officer, Ruth Campbell, worked closely with the Association and was responsible for a minibus being acquired which proved extremely useful for trips of all kinds. Another local liaison worker was Peter Minal, the Diocesan Youth Chaplain for Cheltenham who was heavily involved at the YMCA with Sunday evening youth work, bringing in youngsters from several churches, including St. Mark's, St. Peter's, Emmanuel, Charlton Kings, St. Stephen's and local Methodist chapels.

Women's basketball began in the mid-1960s and in athletics Cheltenham won the YMCA Regional Championships held at Bristol. St. Paul's College were regular users of the sports facilities for their young men and female students from St. Mary's were also sent along for practical experience.

Of particular interest was some detached youth work which began in the Tiffin Café near Royal Well and developed into the Cossack Motor Bike Club, where members were taught how to look after their bikes, some ending up helping on the so-called Blood Run between Birmingham and Bristol hospitals. A key founder was John McKenzie, a YMCA resident.

Other interesting residents included several from abroad who were placed at Cheltenham on a regular basis by Mary Cobb from the British Council. With visitors from as far afield as India, Hong Kong, Malaysia, Uganda, Kenya, Nigeria, Sudan, Jordan, Lebanon and nearer to home, all points in Europe, there was a real international flavour. Various events were organised including special dinners when everyone wore their national costume.

At this time the YMCA also ran a regional Youth in Industry scheme, overseen by Frank Dyer from Bristol who, after he went off to run the YMCA Lakeside Centre in the Lake District, was succeeded by Len Compton. Further links with industry came in the form of a close relationship with Smith's Industries, Dowty, and Walker-Crosweller, all of whom were generous benefactors.

The Sixties were certainly swinging at Cheltenham YMCA. Women and girls were now on the menu and both new and refurbished facilities were coming on stream.

A new weekly programme included a Sunday event called Chattabox, a response to an ever growing national demand for people to discuss their faith and in May, 1962 the now completed sports hall, consisting of the original gymnasium plus lesser hall and balcony, was opened by the Duke of Beaufort. On February 23rd 1963 the new facilities hosted the first ever British Junior Men's Gymnastic Championships.

In October 1963, Wilf Pearson moved to Liverpool YMCA and was replaced by Des Willcox. The Bishop of Gloucester, Rt. Rev. B.T. Guy answered questions at an event called the Chaplain's Forum and in 1965 the basketball team became the British Junior SW champions. Meanwhile, the Women's Auxiliary kept up their brilliant financial support and on March 26th, 1965 the new North Wing hostel was opened by Viscount Amory, specifically to cater for the increased numbers of students being encouraged to train as teachers at the local College of St. Paul. The Freedom of the Borough of Cheltenham was conferred on Arthur Dye on November 11th 1965.

Much opportunity had been taken by the YMCA nationally and Cheltenham YMCA locally, to include an international element with overseas students positively encouraged to stay. Several exchanges took place with Germany, including Cheltenham's twin town of Gottingen and at Hildesheim in the Harz Mountains. More than one dinner was held at which participants were encouraged to attend in their national costume.

In 1968, the Mayor of Cheltenham, Miss May Dent, launched a much-needed appeal for funds which was backed by several firms, especially Dowty's and Smith's many of whose apprentices lodged at the YMCA. The Cheltenham Lions were involved as was Naunton Park School where a sponsored walk was arranged by Chris Young who did much for other charities in his relatively short life which was prematurely curtailed by a brain tumour in 1993. One young man, a Malayan student called David Yeap, even managed a sponsored walk on crutches!

1969 saw Des Willcox move to Plymouth and was succeeded by his deputy, Roger Hunt. A ski party also drove to Oberau in the Austrian Tyrol. Meanwhile, other regular activities continued apace and included: Basketball, Bible Study, Billiards and Snooker, Boys Club (four locations), Camera Club, Chess, Cricket, Cycling, Dancing, Drama, Film Programmes, Football, Judo, Lectures and Talks, Music Calling, Overseas Work Fund, Popular Music Group, Swimming, Table Tennis, Lawn Tennis (at Montpellier), Whist and Women's Auxiliary. The latter played a major supporting role throughout most of the 20th Century before finally closing in 1992 when it became superfluous. There was also a Full Members Group for those specifically committed to their Christian faith.

The year 1969 was auspicious in that it was also the 125th anniversary of the YMCA movement with a splendid floral display mounted in Montpellier Gardens. A special booklet was produced showing local YMCA activities accompanied by excellent cartoons and amusing write-ups. Not without its more serious moments, this excellent publication also contained news of the international YMCA with thought-provoking reports from abroad.

In season 1970-71, after a gap of more than 20 years without any form of trophy, the men's football team did the treble, adding the County Intermediate Cup and the Junior Charities Cup to the Division 3 League title. Guest of honour at their annual dinner was Tony Book, captain of the all-conquering Manchester City team who had previ-

▲ Des Willcox succeeded Wilf Pearson as Secretary of Cheltenham YMCA in 1963 and stayed until 1969 when he moved on to Plymouth YMCA. After retirement he became a volunteer and, as Treasurer of the South West YMCA Regional Trust Fund, oversaw the award of charitable donations to many worthy causes over a period of several years.

▲ *March 26th, 1965 saw the new North Wing hostel opened by Viscount Amory, specifically to cater for the increased numbers of students being encouraged by the government to train as teachers at the local College of St. Paul. In time it was used by local apprentices and latterly for housing support. The platform party, from left are: Sir John Evetts; David Morris (Mayor of Cheltenham); Viscount Amory; Arthur Dye (YMCA President); J. Gayford; Percy Gardner(YMCA Chairman) and Morley Manaton (YMCA SW Region).*

ously been connected with Bath YMCA. He charged no fee and stayed over at the Carlton Hotel, congratulating everyone on their efforts and achievements which "Nobody can ever take away from you".

1971 also saw the visit of England table tennis coach, Bryan Merrett, on the occasion of Cheltenham YMCA hosting the Midland Area finals. A further unusual fund raising activity was a clay pigeon shoot at Stoke Orchard.

Arthur Dye's high profile continued with him appearing regularly in the *Gloucestershire Echo* stating on one occasion that young men's spare time must be filled to avoid boredom. His remarkable reign came to an end on Boxing Day, 1971 when he died aged 83.

1972 saw camping in Cirencester Park, an exchange with a church from Berlin and a major Charity Week event from May 12-20, one popular item of which consisted a car wash by a group of bikini-clad young ladies. In December a sponsored 24-hour five-a-side football match resulted in Cheltenham YMCA beating Prestbury Rovers by 749 goals to 620! Not all was sweetness and light, however, because the weekend discos had to be closed down after violence erupted.

January 1973 saw the donation of five chairmobiles to handicapped people, one of whom was an eight-year-old boy. Designed by Lord Snowdon (the husband of Princess Margaret), these apparently proved unreliable. In the summer another exchange took place with young people from

▲ *England international batsman, Tom Graveney, a local man who lived literally around the corner from Cheltenham YMCA, was the natural choice to open the new cricket nets at Vittoria Walk.*

Gottingen. 1974 saw the table tennis team again become the local champions and a summer exchange with a young people's group from St. Jacobi's Church in Berlin. The popular folk group called The Settlers were booked by the YMCA for a concert at the town hall round the corner and the Ladies netball team became the National Association of Youth Clubs county champions.

1975 saw the YMCA host 20 disabled French students from Paris and a group went off camping in the Lake District.

Social change was now under way, although political correctness was at least a decade away from rearing the first of its many ugly heads. Up to the 1970s, apart from the time honoured uniformed organisations such as Scouts, Cubs, Guides, Brownies, Boys Brigade, Girls Brigade, Army, Navy and Air Force Cadets, there were few activities for younger children who were still fairly happy with their own company. Church youth groups existed for older teenagers but there was not much for the pre-teens. This all changed quite rapidly and by the early-1980s there were junior football leagues all across the country. The age of the teeny bopper had arrived. Cheltenham YMCA changed to meet the perceived needs but it was not until the late-1990s that the age range crept down to infant stage. If it was to survive then the Association had to keep abreast of its competitors.

Bill Sargison arrived at Cheltenham YMCA in January 1976 and during the next nine years transformed everything, always closely supported by his wife Miriam. Philip Dawson was the Residential Secretary and Brian Chamberlain the Youth Worker but after they left Bill put in place a new management structure which was one of the best in the country. His two assistants, Richard Gooch (Residential) and Richard Pascall (Programme), worked closely and well together and were complemented by Jenny Miller the Training Centre Director and Linda Burley the YTS Co-ordinator. Other notable employees at the time included Keith Thomson, Hamish Raynham and Bruce Forrester. This group was ably assisted by Martin Doulton (Health and Fitness), Penny Le Besque (Junior Youth Work) and Adrian Sharpe who instigated the training work at St. Paul's and later became Chief Executive.

How did all this come about? Bill had an eye for youth work but expanded it in conjunction with various government training schemes, so much so that as each new initiative came out Bill was ready to embrace it. The culmination was a full blown Cheltenham YMCA Training Centre which proved to be a creditable alternative to Gloscat and only closed down when government funding was withdrawn, and made it impossible for the YMCA to continue by which time the Association had increased in size and stature within the town. The scheme employed more than 50 staff in its heyday. Part of Vittoria Walk was given over to classrooms but these were supplemented by buying two outside properties, 33 Rodney Road and 4 Wolseley Terrace. Included in the training, scheme, aimed primarily at unemployed young people, were catering, carpentry, office administration, general maintenance, painting, decorating, building and gardening.

On the activities side, Bill immediately formed a junior football section followed by a junior cricket section in 1980. With the help of a grant from the MCC, nets were purchased and laid out down the full length of the sports hall with as many as four teams taking the field at weekends. Table tennis, judo, basketball and netball were also very strong.

The North Wing accommodation block, which had been built with a substantial grant from the

Two former Secretaries of Cheltenham YMCA On the right is Roger Hunt who succeeded Des Willcox in 1969, and Phil Willerton joined in early-1985 following the departure of Bill Sargison.

British Council, continued to see many overseas visitors and a member of the Council served on the board of management for many years. Many students also started their undergraduate careers as residents of the YMCA and a lease arrangement was agreed with the Church Housing Association for the use of Ardwell House on Evesham Road which was used during the 1980s as next stage move-on accommodation. A similar property was leased in Lypiatt Road during the latter part of the same decade, in both cases the YMCA being responsible for the upkeep of the premises in return for a favourable rent.

In November 1984 Sargison moved on to become YMCA Secretary for the South West Region, regularly travelling as far afield as Cornwall. From 1996-1999 he became Assistant National YMCA Secretary for the South of England, thus having served at every level in the YMCA movement. His 40 years of service culminated with a surprise retirement lunch organised at the Carlton Hotel. The look on his face when he arrived and saw more than 100 people seated for what he thought was a family event was a picture to behold. He was also Secretary of the Association of Secretaries of YMCAs for Great Britain and Northern Ireland which later changed its name to the Association of Professional Staff of YMCAs for England, Scotland, Ireland and Wales. He was their President in 1990, a fitting climax to a lifetime of service with the YMCA movement.

****

Tony Hampson arrived as the Programme Manager in 1988, stayed until 1996 and his retrospective comments neatly summed up what took place between these dates. He joined a large YMCA with a reputation for strong foundations in traditional activity areas, and which was innovative in riding the Health and Fitness boom. Activities were available from first thing in the morning until 10pm at night, seven days a week.

There was a real commitment to the holistic approach to personal development, and choices included classical music, martial arts, racquet sports, ball sports, children's activities and aerobics/circuit training. There was also a busy Y-CARE group that fund-raised to support International programmes.

The succeeding time saw a broadening out of the programme to extend children's and 50+ programmes, and an extensive development of the exercise programme and fitness facilities. Day Camps were initiated using the YMCA's own facilities and staff, and included trips out, Cadbury's World being a favourite, especially on a hot day! Julie Hunt and Dave Tizzard played a big part in this work, along with an enthusiastic group of Junior leaders, most of whom had previously been participants in Junior and Youth programmes themselves. Julie was prominent in a thriving Ten-Sing group that adopted a Norwegian YMCA programme of music, dance and drama with a clear Christian focus. Dave also developed a thriving Saturday afternoon junior basketball programme.

For the very young there was pre-school gymnastics class.

Rosemary Harris had a real expertise in Badminton and Table Tennis, and with Fitness qualifications, she more than doubled the 50+ activity programme. This included weights-based programmes, and few prisoners were taken over a wide range of activities, including short mat bowls. The Exercise to Music programme expanded up to twenty-five classes a week, with a wide range of styles, some with a heavier circuit training emphasis, others being less vigorous and emphasising conditioning.

One significant change was substantial investment in a combined fitness room above the smaller hall, overlooking the sports hall. Opened in 1992 it contained new exercise bikes, rowers, joggers and weights facilities, giving a choice of thirty-five pieces of equipment. The later introduction of air conditioning was part of an ongoing commitment to re-invest income to ensure quality at accessible prices. These changes meant the profile of the membership changed with more over 50's and for the first time, more women than men. Members were also encouraged to have their say and shape future directions, often leading to lively debate between those who wanted the YMCA to develop a strong position as a health and fitness organisation, and the core activity and team based programmes run mainly by volunteers, many of whom had developed their leadership skills within these activities.

The development of the fitness room, the building of a new women's changing facilities, an outside changing room for the junior football teams, and the introduction of air conditioning, were all founded on members' surveys or solid committee work between professional staff and member representatives. Cheltenham YMCA had thus become a major "mover and shaker" within the South West area, having a sustained commitment to regional activities and supporting other YMCAs.

****

Following Phil Willerton's departure to Watford YMCA in December 1990, the Board of Management turned to a man with a literally safe pair of hands whom they already knew well because he had been active locally for several years. Adrian Sharpe originally joined Cheltenham YMCA in August 1981 as a Project Supervisor on the Youth Opportunities Programme, a government sponsored scheme to train unemployed young people for work. He supervised one of the groups carrying out painting and decorating, and building projects for needy organisations such as village halls, scout huts and community schemes which the YMCA operated under the name of Y Force. In 1983 he went on to become the manager of the St Paul's Skills Training Centre, where young people were instructed in catering, carpentry, glass fibre laminating, and clerical skills, as well as managing three project groups. This later became the Youth Training Scheme including motor mechanics and bricklaying.

As the government's youth training policies developed so Cheltenham YMCA became involved in the employer-led Mode A scheme while continuing with the former scheme which became known as Mode B. It was a great period of development for the YMCA as investment was made in two additional properties to accommodate the expanding schemes, one being 4 Wolseley Terrace and the other 33 Rodney Road which was later sold off to an Employment Agency as surplus to requirements. This development of the YMCA Training Agency, as it became known, enabled Adrian to move on as Operations Manager and Health and Safety Officer from 1986-1988.

He then became Deputy to Secretary, Phil Willerton, becoming more involved in mainstream YMCA operations and in December 1990 became the first designated Chief Executive. Early on a decision was made to transfer the operation of the Training Agency to Intec Colleges with proposed changes to fund the schemes in arrears and on the basis of the qualifications achieved by the trainees. The Board felt this was too risky and were proved right when Intec Colleges failed to make a go of it. However, training in computer and clerical skills continued in Wolseley Terrace under Newbury College until 2001.

1994 was the 150th anniversary of the YMCA nationally and Adrian tried to get a flower bed similar to the one laid by the Council for the 125th

HOW QUICKLY TIMES CHANGED IN THE 1960s

◀ *This late-1950s picture is a YMCA Sunday morning outing to Bibury Church. Everyone is dressed in their finery, be it a suit, best frock or, in at least one case, a school blazer.*

▶ *This photograph from the early-1970s shows boys and girls dressed as each other for a friendly cricket match. At the time it was considered simple harmless fun and very much a part of the general YMCA camaraderie. Back left, with the parasol, is former resident and long-serving Board member, Mike Hunt, while next to him is future Chairman and President, Lionel Fitz.*

anniversary in Montpellier Gardens. Unfortunately, this did not materialise but a bench in Sandford Park was placed to commemorate the event. The same year saw a big publicity event called Breakout which involved groups of people travelling as far round the country as they could within a given time limit, collecting stamps from various YMCAs along the way. Although successful in making good newspaper and local television coverage it was less successful in raising funds, most of which were swallowed up by the professional costs involved.

The idea, however, was very clever and a great challenge for competitors to visit ten YMCAs beginning with the initial letters from the word "Cheltenham", namely Cambridge, Hornsey, Erdington (Birmingham), Liverpool, Taunton, Exmouth, Norwich, Halifax, Abertridwr (Monmouthshire), and Maidstone. Among the prizes were a long weekend on the Isle of Wight for the person raising the most for YMCA funds; free tickets for a day out at Eureka, an animated children's museum in Halifax for the most money raised by a team; an Icelandic Air holiday in Iceland for the fastest individual on private transport; £100 of free shopping at Cavendish House for the most enterprising dash by a team; a day at Butlin's Somerwest World at Minehead for the fastest team using public transport; four VIP invitations at Alton Towers for the fastest journey by a team using private transport; a £100 clothing voucher from Ciro Citterio Menswear for the best fancy dress in all categories; a long weekend for two at the Queen's Hotel, Cheltenham, for the most enterprising journey by an individual; and a weekend in Wales for the fastest individual on public transport.

Much of Adrian's time as Chief Executive was spent in major repairs and development work. Repairs to the roofs and re-rendering work were undertaken as well as the creation of a new reception area on the lower ground level which involved a complete alteration to the frontage which received a Civic award. Later re-wiring and heating systems were installed in the older part of the building and a complete refurbishment of the 1960s wing included the provision of some self contained accommodation. Much of this was done with the help of grant aid from the Housing Corporation. Co-operation with the Cheltenham & Gloucester College (now the University of Gloucestershire) to provide move-on accommodation for first year students, led to the purchase of Balcontan House in Tryes Road but as needs changed this property was sold in 2004.

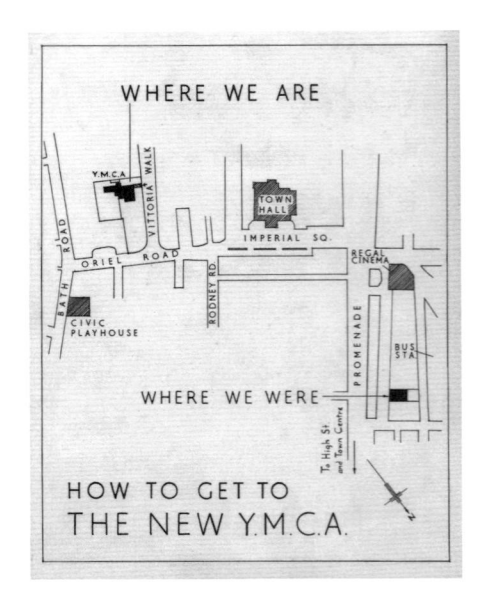

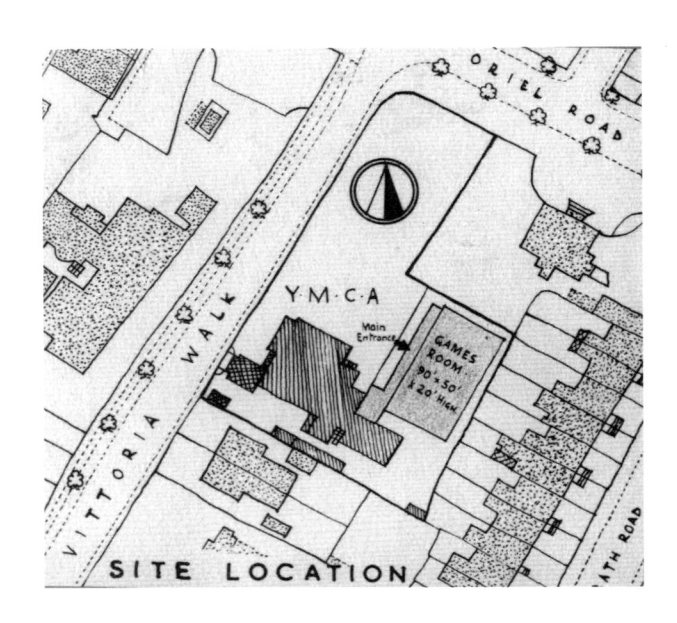

NEW WEEKLY PROGRAMME

	GYMN	GAMES ROOM	CANTEEN	LOUNGE
Mon. 6–7.30	P.T. & Games	Crafts	Billiards	7.15 Prayers
7.30–10	T.T. Matches	T.T.	R'ments & Blds.	Discussion Grp.
Wed. 7–10	Basketball General Games	Crafts T.T.	Billiards Refreshments	Members' Rcds. or T/V 9.45 Wed. Sp.
Thurs. 6–7.30	P.T. & Games	Crafts	Billiards	T/V
7.30–10	F'ball Training	T.T.	R'ments & Blds.	Variety or Skiffle Group
Fri. 7–10	General P.T. and Games	T.T. Darts	Billiards Refreshments	Records or T/V
Sat.	Competitions, Camping, Expeditions, Adventure, Sport, Conferences, Dances, etc.			
Sun. 8 p.m.			Chatabox	
9.15 p.m.			(Fortnightly)	Chatabox "Quiet ¼"

Note—Juniors (12–13 years) will only be allowed in the Club from 6–7.30 p.m. on Mondays and Thursdays. Seniors (14 years upwards) will not be allowed in the Club during the Junior Sessions.

▲ It is a pity the two maps above had the north sign at almost 180 degrees to each other! Nevertheless, the YMCA was keen to let people know where it had moved to from the Promenade.

◀ A comprehensive programme from 1960, reflecting society's then very different approach to children's work. Only boys at senior school were allowed to take part but this soon changed. A notable absentee is the Women's Auxiliary which gradually ran out of members. Reinvigorated in the mid-1930s it gave terrific service to the YMCA, especially during the war.

▲ Local resident and BBC celebrity Bill Hartley opened the fund raising Autumn Fayre in 1958.

▲ This is what the old Royal Well Hut looked like when it became St. Thomas's Mission Church in Up Hatherley in 1956. It lasted about 15 years as a church, scout hut and YMCA youth club.

▲ It would be hard to over-estimate the importance of Chairman, and later President, Arthur Dye whose boundless energy and enthusiasm benefited the whole of Cheltenham. He gave service in many areas but particularly strongly to the YMCA, both at local and national level. He was awarded their highest honour, the Gold Order of the Red Triangle, and also received a posthumous OBE after his death on Boxing Day 1971, aged 83.

◀ It is not clear who is being presented with a radio in 1966, nor why but the personnel are, from left to right, Percy Gardner (Chairman), Arthur Dye (President), Des Willcox (Secretary) and Derek Harper (Youth Leader). Harper had just arrived to succeed Martin Wray who left for ordination.

**CHELTENHAM YMCA CAR CLUB
(APPOINTED)
NIGHT HIKE
RESCUE CAR**

▲ A thriving Car Club ran at the YMCA during the early-1970s and this is an official marshall's pass alerting the Police to the fact they were engaged in a bona fide nocturnal activity!

▶ Tony Hampson was a very busy Programme Manager from 1988-1996 before being promoted to Taunton and then Bridgwater YMCAs. He was the brains behind a generally more professional fitness approach which included aerobics, step aerobics, circuit training, spin cycling and a well-used multi-gym.

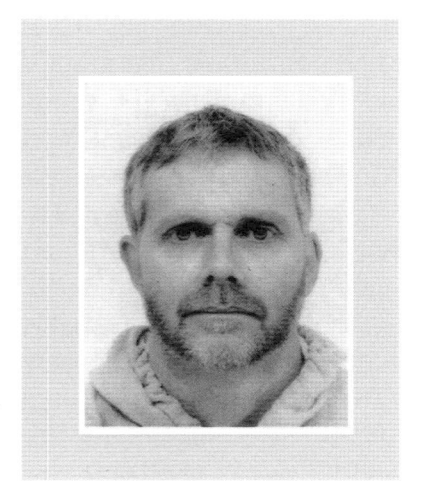

The Programme and activities were continually developing over the years with particular emphasis on exercise to music and fitness training. Such innovations as step aerobics were introduced as well as spin cycling. The fitness room was expanded and regularly updated to keep up with the times. Adrian retired in 2001 and, after thorough interviews, was succeeded by David Wallace, formerly Chief Executive at North West Kent YMCA.

Another important worker from this period was Linda Burley who was first associated with Cheltenham YMCA in 1979 as a part time Youth Programme Leader. Two years later she became a part time Field Tutor for the National YMCA's Youth at Work service which involved some work teaching Life and Social skills to the trainees on the Youth Opportunities Programme. In 1983 General Secretary, Bill Sargison, asked her to head up the new employer led Mode A Youth Training Scheme, a full time post. In 1985 she become the Director of the YMCA Training Agency with the responsibility for both training schemes.

Linda left Cheltenham YMCA in 1988 to pursue her career in training and people management elsewhere but supported the National Council of YMCAs by sitting on their National Programmes Committee and later on the Personnel Committee where she became chairperson and occupied a co-opted position on the National Board. Their close working relationship eventually led to Adrian and Linda becoming Mr. and Mrs. Sharpe!

****

In 1997 Paula Hannaford completed a written student assignment on Cheltenham YMCA. Entitled "Historical and Comparative Aspects of Sport" which touched on sporting changes in the period 1956-1996, some enforced, some planned.

Membership after the move to Vittoria Walk in 1956 was given as 300 men. There was no Sunday activity, indeed few people of any kind played sport on Sunday let alone committed Christians. It just didn't happen and even casual ball games in parks with church connections were positively discouraged by park keepers. Internally, the YMCA ran billiards, snooker, judo, with football and cricket played outdoors. The latter was enhanced by the provision of a new outdoor pitch parallel to Vittoria Walk but the land was subsequently sold to finance other projects.

In 1957 the football team lost its training ground and the judo club moved to Pittville Circus because of lack of accommodation. The basketball team also had to play all its fixtures away! This was simply not good enough and dynamic Arthur Dye stepped in with a scheme to find 1,000 people willing to donate £1 each a year which would be enough "to keep a boy off the streets and stop him from becoming a teddy boy". "Teds" dressed in what they thought was a loose Edwardian style and were the perceived scourge of the mid-1950s, with velvet suits, drainpipe trousers and carefully groomed long swept back hair giving rise to the myth they were all delinquents. They weren't but many of their hangers on certainly were, hence Arthur Dye's heartfelt plea.

During the early-1960s the demand for billiards and snooker declined so the room was converted into a television lounge. Ironically, it was the advent of colour TV a decade later which brought about the rebirth of snooker but by then other things had happened at Vittoria Walk and there was no space left for what had once been a key activity. Judo increased in numbers and its members chipped in with 50% of a new mat which cost £140, big money 40 years ago. Overall YMCA 1967 membership stood at 375 men of whom 285 were under 21, and 291 women of whom 263 were under 21. The target of going mixed a few years earlier had paid handsome dividends and the proportion of younger members, although surprisingly by today's standards, reflects a time when older people had yet to develop a fitness habit.

Volleyball came to the fore during the 1970s, a time when family membership was being developed as an important step forward. Perceptions of single sex activities were now regarded as outmoded and mixed activities were actively encouraged. Adult football was in decline but junior football was very much in the ascendancy, although still confined almost entirely to senior school level. Two squash courts were also added around this time.

The 1980s witnessed big changes with the development of a fitness studio and multi-gym, the aim being to promote general fitness and well-being within the Cheltenham area. So popular did this become that the changing rooms were upgraded and enlarged. Several similar private fitness centres subsequently opened their doors with the YMCA becoming the victim of its own success as newer and more sophisticated equipment became available. It was an expensive path which the local Association had chosen to tread and remained so well into the 21st Century.

Membership rose rapidly from around 1,000 in 1980 to a peak of 2,419 in August 1983, since when it remained around the 2,000 mark although many of these were juniors. In conjunction with the Sports Council Cheltenham YMCA devised an initiative called "Programme on the Move" which included running normal activities in local premises within a 10 mile radius, such as church halls and community centres. The sports hall balcony was renovated into a short-lived indoor bowls court but was in turn was superseded by new Powercam equipment.

Rugby League was programmed in 1984 but was ahead of its time and only lasted two years. It made a local comeback during the late-1990s but not at the YMCA which by then was firmly committed to junior football only. As stated above, the programme manager was Tony Hampson who later went on to work at Taunton and Bridgwater YMCAs, who steered everyone towards a more professional fitness programme. Aerobics, step aerobics, circuit training, multi-gym and spin cycling were all part of this scheme. A casualty, however, was volleyball because what had once been hailed as the biggest sports hall in the south west of England was now clearly too small. How times change!

▲ *Bill Sargison revolutionised Cheltenham YMCA between 1976-84, during which time he introduced off-peak activities, junior football and cricket sections, a huge self-supporting YMCA Training Agency, and many other new initiatives. He left to become YMCA Secretary for the South West Region and is pictured here in 1990 wearing the chain of office as President of the Association of Professional Staff of YMCAs.*

The increase in health and fitness related activities led to a new pricing structure with concessionary off-peak charges to encourage all-day use of expensive equipment. This was also reflected in a technology-based computer age by more sophisticated booking techniques.

In hindsight, the decision to opt in to both Sunday and daytime activities was more than vindicated as Cheltenham YMCA sought, and still does, to meet the many and varied needs of its own members and the local general public. The work at Vittoria Walk continues apace.

CHAPTER 12
YMCA ACTIVITIES

As with the previous chapter about Vittoria Walk this section should be used in conjunction with both the next chapter "A President Looks Back", and also Chapter 15, the pictorial supplement which is a natural extension of the activities described here.

It is important to remember that physical and social activities have changed dramatically down the years. Where there was once great emphasis on team games and esprit de corps this has since given way to more individual sports and pastimes. Until the post-Edwardian period, especially in rural areas, society was extremely parochial and often almost silent save for the sound of a horse and cart or distant steam train. Enjoyment was what could be found close at hand, so the visit of a member of Calne YMCA on a bicycle intent on preaching the Gospel would have been seen as a major event (see Chapter 3). Cheltenham was a good deal more advanced than that but until the advent of the motor car it too was largely parochial but in a different way.

It is hard for the younger generation to appreciate what it was like before most people had a television or phone, never mind a car, but until the 1920s nobody had a radio either! How different life was in those days and it is not hard to see why Cheltenham YMCA was much more a part of the town's everyday social structure than it is today. People went out to find entertainment such as the theatre, cinema or music hall, but they also went out to the YMCA in a similar manner.

In 1956, when the local Association moved from the Promenade to Vittoria Walk, it immediately embarked on a building programme which included a new sports hall – a term not in common use until the early-1980s – which was described as the biggest in the south west of England! Since then it has been dwarfed by an explosion in much bigger sports halls, and also found itself in competition with new fitness centres in the town. PE equipment has also changed out of all recognition and whereas a vaulting horse was once seen as an essential item it is now more a matter of the latest technological invention which automatically measures heartbeat and goodness knows what else.

Set against this historical background it is interesting to see what has occurred down the years, although it is inevitable that some activities have been omitted through ignorance, error or lack of available information.

****

Residential Accommodation – For the first 50 years of its existence, Cheltenham YMCA concentrated on promoting the Christian Gospel through verbal persuasion and by providing a reading room, library and social facilities for meetings and fellowship. Outdoor and indoor missions were enthusiastically sponsored and, following a successful campaign run by Mr. Lane in 1895, it was decided to move into the sphere of residential accommodation as a further means of Christian witness to the young men of the town.

Realising the new venture needed a lady's touch, the committee appointed Miss Stanley of Chipping Campden as honorary lady superintendent. The opening of the new premises at 7 Cambray was celebrated by a house warming party, at which the President, Mr. Ley Wood, described the difficulty the Association had in finding a house suitable for the work they proposed to carry on. They had almost decided after three months search to erect a new building when they heard of the very suitable quarters in Cambray, where the members could enjoy all the advantages of a club, while the religious side of the work would not be neglected. Three years later, a new HQ was opened almost opposite at 31 Cambray but the residential side remained at Number 7.

Although the local Association briefly closed down in 1911 it reopened in 1913 and in 1919 hit the big time when it acquired three adjacent properties on the Promenade, numbers 16, 17 and 18, later renumbered 51, 53 and 55. Opened in 1921 by

Field Marshal Sir William Robertson amongst great pomp and ceremony, it was clear that someone had invested a large sum of capital for the project although there must also have been a mortgage because in 1936 the Association was forced to approach the National YMCA Council for a loan of £3,000. It was turned down, however, so number 51 was quickly sold to Pearl Assurance. The back was retained, however, because the timber framed gymnasium, known as the Royal Well Hut, occupied the rear of all three addresses.

The residential accommodation was by today's standards somewhat spartan but at the time was better than most and attracted a big intake each year, many of whom stayed a long time. Permanent residents were classified as staying three months or more, who paid between 25s and 27s 6d per week for a shared room (approximately £1.25 to £1.37 in today's currency), while single rooms retailed at 30 shilling per week (£1.50). This included room, full board, boot cleaning and baths! Boot cleaning? Yes! At the time it was regarded as a perfectly normal hotel service with clean shoes being a pre-requisite of all respectable young men. A smart appearance meant everything.

During the Second World War everything changed when the premises were overrun by servicemen with overflows at Bayshill Unitarian Church and Royal Well Chapel. A full account of the Royal Well and other canteens may be found in Chapter 7. Most of the wartime residents were temporary of course but many expressed gratitude for the treatment they received during their short stay.

After hostilities ceased in 1945 the country had to rebuild socially, industrially and domestically, and many young men came into Cheltenham from all over the country. One of the major employment companies was Smith's Industries at Bishops Cleeve and a sizeable number of their apprentices were accommodated at the Promenade during the early 1950s. They evidently took a full part in the Association's activities and much successful Christian witness was in evidence, with some of them staying up to three years.

In 1956 the Association moved to its current location in Vittoria Walk after which the Promenade premises were acquired by Cheltenham Borough Council. Originally a boarding house belonging to Cheltenham Ladies' College, Farnley Lodge dated from the 1820s and was surplus to requirements because the roads were by then deemed too dangerous for the girls to cross to and from lessons in Bayshill Road. The spacious accommodation was quickly transformed from austere dormitories into mainly double rooms with adjacent communal bathroom facilities, later known as the South Wing which was contained largely within the ornate Italianate tower.

During the early-1960s, however, the government embarked on an ambitious expansion programme for higher education, and teacher training in particular. In 1965 this prompted the committee to erect a new accommodation block mainly for students. Called the North Wing it created a substantial number of study bedrooms. Throughout the 1960s the friendship and camaraderie amongst the residents was very strong, about two thirds of whom were students, the rest mainly apprentices. They engaged in many joint activities and often wiled away the evening in the coffee bar.

As times changed, however, so did the accommodation and residents. Provision for students gradually gave way to working with the local Housing Department and substantial grants enabled the Association to offer accommodation in the North Wing to homeless young men, whilst retaining the South Wing partially for bed and breakfast for tourists and backpackers. During the late-1990s the top floor of the North Wing was altered to self-contained flatlets and other rooms were provided with cooking facilities. Inevitably, this had a knock-on effect on the café which shrank in size and trade. The current management structure includes an Assistant Chief Executive in charge of housing, assisted by a number of junior support workers.

It was suggested around the turn of the 21st Century that the South Wing be named after former Secretary, Wilf Pearson, the North Wing after former President, Alex Evans, and the West Wing office block after the YMCA's founder, George Williams. No final decision was reached, however.

Badminton – Another popular YMCA activity for all age groups down many decades.

Basketball – This was an activity spawned by the YMCA at the start of the 20th Century and has been played at Cheltenham ever since. In the late-

1930s it benefited from the talents of four resident American missionaries. Post-war John Llewellyn and Graham "Flash" Gordon ran it for many years with Martin Outram latterly in charge. "Central" YMCA, as they were then called, were founder members of the Cheltenham & District Basketball League in 1960 and won both the Senior and Junior Leagues in the inaugural season. It was the major sport at the YMCA and in 1965 Cheltenham became the British National Junior YMCA champions at Crystal Palace by beating Nottingham and Wales YMCAs, also winning Division 2 of the local league with the all-American Cheltenham YMCA Comets coming runners-up in the senior competition. The club still runs two teams with players aged 15-60 enjoying themselves every Friday night.

Bible Study – As one might expect, this has always played a key part in the YMCA and has been held on various days at various times. In 2005 the preferred spot was on Wednesday mornings.

Billiards and Snooker – Billiards, a 19th Century game invented by the British Army in India was played with two white balls and a red one, and was extremely popular. World championships were big affairs but the game is hardly heard of today, partly because with the advent of colour television in the early-1970s the profile of snooker was raised overnight to national level and virtually extinguished its rival. Using more balls and infinitely more complex it has remained quite popular but, paradoxically, has declined in associations such as YMCAs where the large open rooms required have since been put to other uses, including the three snooker table areas originally located in the basement of Vittoria Walk. Nevertheless, before television became a national pastime and reduced much of the population to couch potatoes, there was quite a following and as the 1938 Annual Report put it: "Two teams took part with considerable success in the Cheltenham League and exhibition games were given by the well-known professional Mr. Claude Faulkner and by the ladies' world champion, Miss Joyce Garner". The final demise of snooker and billiards came in 1964 when the three tables were sold and the room converted into a television lounge.

Boxing – Now exclusively the preserve of specialist clubs, this sport was once very popular in boys clubs, especially in inner urban areas. It certainly took place under the auspices of the YMCA when it was in the Promenade before the war, and also at Pilley Lane post-war.

Boys' Club - – (see Satellite Youth Work) Baker Street YMCA ran as a major offshoot from 1940 to 1967 and three other boys club work took place during the 1960s at St. Thomas' Mission Church (the former Royal Well Hut), on the Alma Road estate in Up Hatherley; at Pilley Lane Baptist Church; and at Vittoria Walk which was then referred to as the Central YMCA.

Camera Club – This has been in existence, on and off, for many decades.

Charity Shop – The Cheltenham YMCA Charity Shop was established during the early-1990s by Paul Sargison, son of former Secretary, Bill Sargison, and brother of subsequent Assistant Chief Executive, Angela Gilbert. Temporarily situated in the Regent Arcade and then the Lower High Street, under the direction of Sheila Green (after whose death two rooms were named in her honour at Vittoria Walk) it grew steadily and by 2005 was the biggest of the YMCA's 82 nationwide collection of shops. Ann Pierce took over the management in 1997 shortly after it moved along the pedestrianised Strand to 63 High Street and, assisted by a dedicated band of 30 volunteers, many of whom were retired, oversaw a massive upturn in trade. Previous assistant manager, Julie Lawson, and her successor Anne Ragsdale, were also key players among the hard-working labour force serving a shop which stood proudly for the stated aims of its parent body, a Christian organisation welcoming people of all faiths to help raise money for the YMCA locally, nationally and abroad with Y Care International..

The shop deservedly won many awards and by 2000 had achieved the honour of the highest national sales and profit. Although other shops have since closed the gap Cheltenham still stands at the top of the list. In 2004 the Queen, the YMCA Patron, sent a letter of thanks and congratulations from Buckingham Palace. In 2003 the annual turnover exceeded £100,000, an enormous sum and a worthy tribute to all those involved. All donated goods were sorted for suitability and those accepted were steam cleaned, ironed and pressed. With an average selling price of £3.50 it was small wonder that hun-

▲ ▶ *In 1965 Cheltenham became National YMCA Junior Basketball Champions, defeating Nottingham YMCA and the combined Welsh YMCAs at Crystal Palace. They also hosted and won the South West League Championship, beating Brislington Squirrels and Plympton Grammar School. Standing left to right (above): Glynn Williams, Graham Gordon, Brian Read, John Shaw, Mike Harding, Gordon Cummings (coach); sitting: John Llewellyn, Brian Hopkins, Malcolm Smith and John Woodley. The picture on the right shows the team in civvies when drainpipe trousers were all the rage. Coach Gordon Cummings is in the centre and YMCA Secretary Des Willcox at the rear.*

dreds of people visited the shop every day of the week from Monday to Saturday in search of a bargain. A stockroom of high quality merchandise saw regular changes of shop window displays, with any surplus goods not sold within two weeks passed on to other local charity shops. Not even expensive retail outlets could compare with that kind of turnover of stock!

Cheery Circle – A social club run by Mrs. E. Mason with bring and buy sales, bingo, chats etc.

Chess – Teams once played in a local league but the game now has a much lower profile with computers destroying much of the former attractions of the game because even the best players in the world now struggle to beat an automaton! Sad!

Children's Work – Apart from the normal club activities in recent years there has been a thriving children's work based both at the YMCA and in supportive churches such as St. Philip and St. James in Up Hatherley. A special Children's Activity Worker, Francis Barton, was appointed in 2003 who developed the work apace with regular weekly events, holiday play schemes and, in 2005, an after school club at Hesters Way Junior School.

Cricket – There were three pre-war men's teams but, in conjunction with the national decline in all day cricket, and owing to high maintenance work and costs, these were eventually reduced to one and finally disappeared altogether during the early-1980s. Post-war matches were played at the Burrows Field, Leckhampton, the same venue as the Junior football until the turn of the 21st Century. Recent junior cricket coaching came under the watchful eye of the Hon. Treasurer, Peter Nock and in 1989 the Under 15 team won the Cheltenham and District Knockout Cup, no mean achievement, defeating both Cheltenham and Gloucester on the way. Sadly, this section died out in the early-1990s.

Crusaders – The Crusaders Union began as a boys' organisation just after the turn of the 20th Century and later added a Girls section which was represented in Cheltenham by a group which met on Sunday afternoons in Vittoria Walk from the late-1950s until the mid-1970s. The leaders were Miss Margaret Rice and Mrs. Marjorie Bennett. Essentially a Bible Class Crusaders is, like the YMCA, interdenominational, and thousands of young people, the author included, found a personal relationship with Christ at one of the many camps and house parties which Crusaders ran all across the country and abroad.

Hope Rudge took over from Margaret Rice in 1968 and the class grew to about 50 girls. Sue Leigh (later Mummery) and Viv Seller (later Hughes) were both assistants. In time, boys began hovering around the buildings whenever the girl were present which was finally solved by a move to Berkhampstead School and the class going mixed!

Cycling – Like many others clubs, this was popular when an enthusiastic person ran it but when almost everyone could afford four wheels and the roads became dangerous for anyone on two wheels, then trips into the surrounding countryside became less of an attraction.

Dancing – This has taken various forms from traditional ballroom dancing right through to discos. The latter was usually more attractive to teenagers but during the early-1970s had to be curtailed through violence caused by outside third parties.

Drama – The Cheltymca Drama Society was a big club pre-war and raised a great deal of money by putting on three plays a year but post-war television put a stop to activities of this kind.

Fencing – Once quite popular but stringent safety rules have since marginalised such sports.

Film Programmes – Private 16mm film clubs were once all the rage during the winter months.

Fitness – The supervisor in 2005 was Ali Hill who ran a variety of activities.

50+ – The Sports Development Co-ordinator for this active group in 2005 was Rose Harris.

Football (Senior Men) – When the YMCA was established in the mid-19th Century there was no such game as Association Football, nor was there anything called Rugby Football. The two gradually emerged as different parts of the country adopted similar codes which had hitherto been largely localised. One variation involved kicking and heading the ball while the other was concerned more with running at your opponents while holding the ball. In time, the former became known as Association Football (later named Soccer), mainly because it was formed by a largely Northern Association which paid professionals to play. Meanwhile the latter became known as Rugby Football, partly because of the actions of William Webb Ellis of Rugby School who allegedly picked up the ball and ran with it. This is far from the truth, however, because original football was more akin to rugby than soccer but a professional form of Rugby in the North of England became known as Rugby League and, until near the end of the 20th Century, had nothing to do with the amateur sport of Rugby Union.

We know that Association Football – henceforth known as just "Football" – was a popular sport at Cheltenham YMCA by the turn of the 20th Century and it seems likely that, in common with most towns of commensurate size, it had been in place for some considerable time before that. The first actual reference we have is in 1891 when the Athletics Club was formed, when it was commented that Football and Cricket Clubs already existed. The YMCA fielded teams at adult level right through to the 1990s by which time the sport had expanded to such an enormous number of local teams, including many public house sides, that there was no longer a demand for a men's team.

Parallel to the decline of the men's teams, however, was a significant rise in boys' teams covered in the next section.

▲ *Cheltenham YMCA won a remarkable treble in 1970-71. As champions of Cheltenham League Division 3 they then beat Ebley 2-1 after a 1-1 draw to win the County Intermediate Cup, then St. Mark's 3-2, also after a 1-1 draw, to win the Junior Charities Cup. A celebration dinner was held at the Carlton Hotel at which the guest of honour was Tony Book, captain of the all-conquering Manchester City team which contained former Cheltenham YMCA player Mike Summerbee. Standing from left: Nigel Barker, Steve Chandler, Doug Weldon, Pete Lowndes, John Cannon, Chris Kisiel (captain with trophy), Bob England, Bill Stephens, Rick Yeates; front from left: Tim Yeates, Chris Ballinger, George Vogel, Neil Jubb, Dave Houghton, plus two unknown boys.*

Back to the beginning! Cheltenham YMCA was one of seven founder members of the Cheltenham Association Football League in season 1899-1900, the others being St. Paul's United, Cheltenham Town, Christ Church, Cavendish, Roseleigh and Charlton Rangers. There were no champions during the inaugural year, indeed there was no trophy, but St. Paul's dominated for the next few seasons.

The first season was not without controversy. Although YMCA lost 10-0 to Roseleigh, they did better than Cheltenham Town who failed to raise a team. The game had not been postponed, however, and so Roseleigh kicked-off and duly scored after which the referee abandoned the match!

YMCA did not field another league team for two years – coming 7th out of 9 teams in 1902-3 – but in 1903 and 1904 also had a team in the newly formed Division 2. Then followed a barren spell, part of which was a break during the First World War, until a team was entered in the Youth (Junior) League formed in 1923, although no champions were again listed. This situation lasted for another four seasons during which a team was run twice in Division 4 and once in Division 1, the discrepancy presumably being explained by the strength of players available at the YMCA at the time. Although paperwork was minimal compared to today, there was an unwritten rule that only bona fide registered members of clubs were allowed to play, although there was some difficulty with registrations at various clubs. One can be quite certain, however, that only YMCA members would have been considered for the YMCA teams. "Ringers" were unheard of.

A period of friendlies then took place until a team was entered in Division 3 in 1934 which became Division 2 the following season. To this was added a team in Division 4 in 1936 which ran until 1938 when war intervened. Surprisingly, a wartime competition did take place in Cheltenham, initially at adult and youth level and then under what was known as the Works and Services League. The relatively young Baker Street YMCA team played in Division 2 of the latter during season 1944-5.

Post-war a team was entered in Division 4 which progressed to Division 3, and from 1948 until 1956 two teams featured with the first team playing in Division 1 from 1950 through to 1955. During this period the Baker Street Youth team also won several trophies (see Chapter 8).

Later success was patchy and after Paul Sargison, son of the Secretary Bill Sargison, who had come through the junior ranks, hung up his boots during the late-1990s then Cheltenham YMCA men's team finally came to an end. This was not entirely surprising, however, because by then there were a large number of teams playing at every level from Sunday morning pub teams through to Saturday afternoon County League standard. Added to this literally dozens of children's teams, things had come a long way since just seven adult teams lined up for the start of the 1899-1900 season!

Just for the record Cheltenham YMCA were Champions of Division 2 in 1938-9 and in 1949-50. They also won the Senior Division Charities Trophy (Dimmer Cup) in 1951-2 and the Junior Division Charities Trophy (Midwinter Cup) in 1946-7. Baker Street YMCA won the Youth Division in 1950-1, 1955-6, 1956-7 and 1957-8. They also won the County Youth Shield in 1951-2, 1955-6 and 1957-8.

Football (Junior) – This was started by YMCA Secretary Bill Sargison in the late-1970s. There were few if any organised junior leagues in England until the late-1960s, prior to which all schoolboy football was confined to school teams or playing friendlies in the local park. The Cheltenham Junior League was formed in 1972 and YMCA joined a few years later. A separate Cheltenham Minor League later came into being but the two were amalgamated towards the end of the 20th Century to become the Cheltenham Youth League, running teams from Under 9 through to Under 16. By this time the Football Association had abolished 11-a-side games below the age of 11 in favour of shorter 7-a-side matches with hockey-sized goals. This created many new teams but also, paradoxically, fewer matches because the increased number of pitches required proved impossible to find with the Under 9 and Under 10 leagues playing alternately once a fortnight instead of every week.

Bill Sargison ran several teams but when he moved on to become the South West Area Regional Secretary of YMCA England he was succeeded by board member Jerry Evans, later to become Chief Executive at Gloucester YMCA in 1990 before returning to Cheltenham YMCA in a paid capacity as Assistant Chief Executive (Housing) in March 2005. Although centrally situated, Cheltenham YMCA tended to draw its junior teams from areas of the town where friends congregated. Later this centred on the Leckhampton area where Carys Jones, the wife of Jerry Evans' successor in 1990, Ken Jones, was a primary school teacher. Ken was succeeded by a number of short term secretaries before the post was jointly taken on by the then junior football club chairman and board member, Peter Worsley.

Jerry was an enthusiastic leader and arranged two reciprocal footballing exchanges with Gottingen, Cheltenham's twin town in Germany where the boys visited what was then the East German border. One player broke his leg within five minutes of kick off but was pleased to discover that Gottingen was a major medical centre so he was well looked after!

Prior to the late-1980s teams only began at Under 9 level but the age limit was brought down when it became obvious that YMCA boys were being targeted by other clubs who ran friendly teams as young as Under 6! This proved an instant success and Friday night sessions in the gym – travelling across outdoors to Sandford Park during the summer – attracted up to 50 boys of junior school age. Inevitably, more junior teams were established with regular fixtures for boys as young as six!

This created problems with the changing rooms, however, which were filled to capacity, especially on Friday evenings, Saturday mornings and Sunday afternoons, much to the dismay of adult members changing in there at the same time! The board was therefore asked by Chief Executive, Adrian Sharpe,

Fencing has always been a minority sport but it found favour for quite a time at Cheltenham YMCA as this picture from the late-1950s shows.

if they would build a football changing room outside the main building opposite the south wing, thus avoiding mud being trampled inside. The idea was great in principle but, unfortunately, owing to Council restrictions and regulations linked to listed buildings, the initially projected size was reduced so much that only one team could be comfortably accommodated. This, together with stringent and burgeoning child protection guidelines, and the removal of the home pitch at Sandford Park, resulted in a white elephant which was little used by the intended occupants.

Another aspect was the shift in recruitment areas. As new clubs were founded so the traditional YMCA areas became taken over, specifically Leckhampton by Leckhampton Rovers, and Up Hatherley by Southside Tigers. Charlton Rovers already covered Charlton Kings with Cleeve Colts accounting for Bishops Cleeve which left only Hesters Way and Whaddon as largely untapped resources which had staggered along with a profusion of short-lived clubs at different age levels. Inevitably, and with several adult personal school connections, this now became the YMCA's territory resulting in most home matches being transferred from the Burrows Playing Field in Leckhampton to the larger King George V Playing Fields near Coronation Square. Sadly, the changing room camaraderie had by now disappeared for almost every club in the league. Gone were games of British Bulldog to end weekly training (when even parents joined in), plus communal singing and water fights in the showers, to be replaced by guidelines recommending banning the publication of children's names in local newspaper photographs and prohibiting parents from taking pictures of their own children during matches.

Nevertheless, considerable success took place in terms of silverware but far more important was the weekly provision of football and friendship extended to hundreds of local boys, many of whom look back with pride on their association with Cheltenham YMCA. Running such a large club, however, was not without its problems and, like all public associations and schools, it reflected rather than created the society to which it belonged. Finance was an ongoing headache, especially the provision of kit for the increased number of teams which was solved mainly by private sponsorship especially from Kraft Foods although, the biggest donor came in the early-1990s.

Mike Naylor was boss of locally based Endsleigh Insurance and a football fanatic who sponsored Burnley FC, several other teams and also a local Cheltenham men's league. At one point he even sponsored the Football League itself! He graciously agreed to an overture from Cheltenham YMCA in the form of Secretary, Ken Jones and Club Chairman, Peter Worsley, and generously provided a complete new strip for all the teams plus the considerable cost of trophies at the annual presentation evening at which Worsley had suggested all team members should receive a small award rather than just the lucky few. At each age group four additional awards were made; Most Improved Player; Clubman; Sportsman; and Players' Player, to which were added two special trophies donated in memory of David Nock and Darren Staton, two club members who died tragically young. Including a replica, each was awarded to an older boy who had proved outstanding by leadership and example, both on and off the field.

SOME AMUSING HEADINGS FROM THE 1970s — CAN YOU IDENTIFY THEM ALL?

- HANDS OFF MY FEATHERS!
- FOILED AGAIN!
- ON THE MAT
- 74 CHELTENHAM RETROSPECT YMCA 75
- JUNIOR WORK
- THE PLAY GROUP
- NOTES MUSICAL
- IT IS THE YMCA NETBALL TEAM!
- BOARD PEOPLE
- SYMCA SCENE
- GOAL LINES
- HOSTEL 73
- BEYOND THE SCHEME
- YMCA LIAISON WORK BRITISH COUNCIL
- NIGHT ON A BARE MOUNTAIN!!
- WAIST AWAY!

▲ Ann Pierce turned the Cheltenham YMCA Charity Shop into the best in the country. Assisted by a dedicated team of volunteers she set the standard which all other charity shops followed.

▲ Long-serving and popular Rose Harris dealt with all ages from kindergarten to the over-50s.

▲ Dave Tizzard did much excellent work with children and then married receptionist Shirley Morton.

▲ Adrian Sharpe originally originally joined Cheltenham YMCA in August 1981 as a Project Supervisor on the Youth Opportunities Programme. In December 1990 he became the first designated Chief Executive.

▲ One of the last events of the Women's Auxiliary around 1960. This once active group gave valuable back-up service for many years.

▼ A sponsored bikini-clad car wash set up to raise much needed funds in 1972.

▲ Adrian Sharpe (left) with Assistant Chief Executive (Programme) Jim Jenkinson who left to become Chief Executive of a new Rotherham YMCA in Yorkshire, then Regional Development Officer for the YMCA Central Region.

The relationship with Endsleigh worked brilliantly until Naylor was tragically killed in a car crash in France when everything changed overnight. Endsleigh initially agreed to continue sponsoring just Burnley and Cheltenham YMCA but this was withdrawn after a couple more years when they explored new pastures. The author did, however, benefit by two free tickets to watch his home team, Bury FC, lose to Chesterfield in the 3rd Division play-offs at Wembley in 1995!

Subsequent sponsorship was at a more modest level but grateful thanks is publicly expressed to all the many companies and individuals who donated cash and kit down the years. The boys did their best to justify the sponsor's names emblazoned on their shirts and track suit tops. In 2002-3 no fewer than six teams won honours, of which five reached a cup or plate final. Recent long-serving managers included Les Babbage and Kevin Taylor both of whom, after following their own sons right through to Under 16 level, promptly returned to the youngest age group and started all over again! Jeff Carbin and Les Babbage succeeded Peter Worsley as Secretary in 2004.

Records for the early years of the junior leagues are incomplete but among other awards, not including regular 6-a-side triumphs which took place across the county and all points between Worcester and Birmingham, Cheltenham YMCA won the following awards:

Cheltenham Youth Football League
U9 League Champions 2002-03
U9 Sportsmanship Winners 1999-2000
U10 Cup Winners 1998-99
U12 League & Cup Double Winners 2002-03
U14 League Champions 2001-02

Cheltenham Minor Football League
U12 League Champions 1987-88
U13 League Champions 1988-89
U14 League Champions 1984-85
U14 League & Cup Double Winners 1986-87, 1989-90
U15 Cup Winners 1990-91
U16 League & Cup Double Winners 1996-97

Cheltenham Junior Football League
U10 League & Cup Double Winners 1985-86;
League Cup Winners 1993-94

Gloucester League U16 Winners 1991-92

Gloucestershire County Cup
U16 Gloucestershire North Winners
& overall County Champions, defeating
Brislington Juniors 2-0 in the Cup Final
at Bristol 1991-92
U16 Gloucestershire North Winners
& losing Cup Finalists 1996-97
(also reached several semi-finals)

▲ The 1970-71 Annual Football Dinner at the Carlton Hotel. Celebrating a unique treble are from left: R.E. Yates (Secretary), Mrs. Yates, Lionel Fitz (President), Mrs. Mavis Fitz, Roger Hunt (YMCA Secretary), Mrs Hunt, Tony Book (Captain of Manchester City and Guest of Honour), S. Hastie (Chairman), Mrs. Hastie, Chris Kisiel (Team Captain). Book was linked to Bath YMCA before he became a professional.

Football (Ladies) – Started by Jerry Evans in the late-1980s, mainly in conjunction with St. Paul's and St. Mary's College, it blossomed briefly when a Scottish international suddenly appeared on the scene when the YMCA became effectively the Cheltenham team, playing matches all over south west England as far away as Truro in Cornwall. When the international moved away, however, and Jerry left for Gloucester YMCA in 1990, then the team linked up with Cheltenham Town.

Meanwhile, under new Football Association guidelines, a handful of girls played for the YMCA Junior Football Club at primary school level, transferring to ladies' teams when they reached secondary school age.

Full Members Group – Once an important private debating group this club as a distinct entity ceased some years ago when the number of associate and full members began to decline.

Gymnastics – There was once a time when gymnastics was seen not just as an individual activity but as a joint event always shared with others. Right from early times Cheltenham YMCA took fitness very seriously and the 1938 Annual Report indicates the importance attached to young men's gymnastic displays. Special instructors were employed as full-time staff and outdoor displays were well attended. Individual skills were not neglected, however, and competitions were keenly contested.

This interest and enthusiastic support continued until well after the war and Saturday, February 23rd, 1963, was a big day for what was described as "The Central YMCA, Cheltenham" which hosted the first ever British Junior Men's Gymnastic Championships. Organised by SWAGA (South West Area Gymnastic Association) in co-operation with the British Amateur Gymnastic Association, it proved a great success. Commencing at 1.30pm, with finals at 6.30pm, competitors performed routines on the following equipment: vaulting horse, floor exercises, pommel horse, horizontal bar, trampoline, parallel bars and rings. The prizes were presented by the Mayor, Councillor A.E. Trigg, the overall winner being M. Booth of Huddersfield who was pictured in the Echo receiving his trophy from Cheltenham YMCA President, Alderman Arthur Dye.

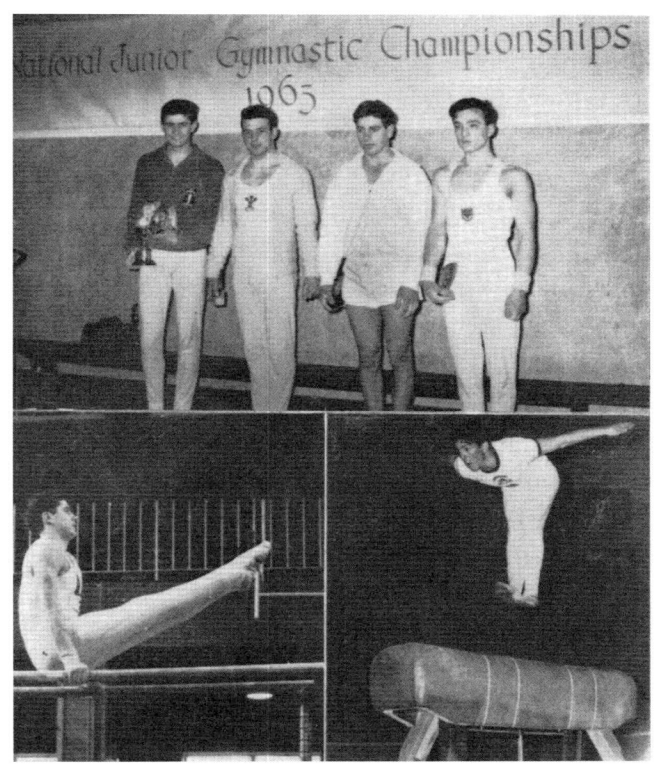

▲ *An extract from "The Gymnast" magazine in 1963 when the National Junior Championships were held in the sports hall at Cheltenham YMCA on Saturday, February 23rd. The reporter heaped much praise on both the event and the organisers.*

The post-event report in the national Gymnast Magazine began as follows: "Cheltenham. What thoughts are conjured up by that name? Britain's foremost watering spa? Doddering old gentry partaking the waters for their last fling before passing on? Well I hope not, for nothing could be further from the truth, at least not for us who were at the Cheltenham YMCA on Saturday, 23rd February." The report went on to praise the organisers and everyone who took part, including several from clubs which they had not previously heard of. Other YMCAs were well represented and there were two pictures of competitors from Swansea, YMCA one of whom, Picton Jones, was the overall runner-up.

In the last three decades, however, gymnastics has been reinvented and, once mainly the preserve of young adults, is now an extremely popular activity with young children. Latterly, under the dedicated leadership of Jenny Hall who began as a volunteer in 1993, the club has gone from strength to strength and has a queue of eager potential new members. By 1997 classes operated four nights a week with extra volunteer coaches being drafted in to assist. In 2000 Jenny Hall and Rosemary Harris organised a parent toddler kindernastics section and, with 80 gymnasts on role for the main section, a waiting list was opened the following year. By 2005 several more volunteer coaches had been trained and the membership increased to 130.

Gymnast of the year for 2003 was Sam Coe who went on to higher honours winning a gold medal at the National Development Tumbling Preliminaries in March 2004, a bronze at the British Finals in May, and the gold at the South west Championships in July. In March 2005 he again took the gold in the March Preliminaries followed by a silver in British National Finals. As a tribute to the encouragement he received at the YMCA he returned to coach twice a week.

Holidays – Over the years these have taken many forms, especially camping both locally and further afield. As the 20th Century progressed so young people expanded their horizons and in 2002 a group even attended a YMCA convention in Prague in the Czech Republic.

Judo – Largely a post-war sport this was run successfully for many years by Alan Davies who was succeeded by Syd Parker, with Paul Harness latterly in charge. Lack of space after the move to Vittoria Walk forced an early temporary exile to Pittville Circus but it returned to the fold after the sports hall was completed.

Karate – On the death of Manfred Polster his mantle was taken on by Andy Sanders who led the British team in Brazil in 2005.

Kendo – This Oriental sword-based martial art began in 1972, when enthusiastic club leader John Richards switched from Bristol to his home town. John always appreciated the help and encouragement of the YMCA management and staff in the early stages and tried to repay the compliment by involving himself in the programme and activities committee and with promotional events. His first of seven appearances for the Great Britain team was at the 3rd World Kendo Championship in Milton Keynes in 1976, notably defeating the Belgian team captain before being eliminated by a Canadian. His contributions towards promoting the activity in Great Britain included being national secretary, grading officer and editor of Kendo News, and chairing the organising committee which brought the Sir Frank Bowden team Takai to Shu Do Kan at Cheltenham on four occasions. After moving to Switzerland he was succeeded by his son John Edwin, and Philip Belcher.

Lectures and Talks – Much more emphasis was given in times past to what learned folk had to say and this club was genuinely popular, although sometimes rather esoteric in nature. During the last war it was taken very seriously indeed.

Listening Post – This Christian Counselling Service was founded in 1991 and the Director, David Walker (a former Senior Probation Officer and Methodist Local Preacher) was delighted to find an initial base at Gloucester YMCA. The early days were a real step of faith but the great variety of problems encountered quickly confirmed the need for it. A county-wide demand led to an expansion into Cheltenham YMCA in 1994, with a further 20 trained counsellors from many local churches. Stroud opened in 1996, and Tewkesbury in 2001. A most exciting venture, more than 200 Christians in Gloucestershire undertook a two year training course with Sheila Appleton taking over as Director in 2001. Listening Post had supportive links with 70 different churches and became one of the best examples locally of working together in partnership to meet real community needs, confirmed in recent years by the increased number of referrals from the medical profession.

Motor Club – This was formed amongst the residents and their friends in 1964 and lasted until about 1970. Several rallies were organised, some overnight, and also a self-styled gymkhana which included playing hockey with the sticks brandished out of an open window! Apparently many of the cars were new, paid for by wealthy parents whose student sons were studying locally! The special Moonraker night-time rally was started by Chairman, Percy Gardner. Litigation was a long way ahead but marshals had to ensure their own cars were marked so as not to upset the local police.

Music Calling – The Cheltenham YMCA classical recorded music group was formed in 1956 and met in the lecture room once a fortnight on a Monday, the alternate week being taken by the Cheltenham Recorded Music Society. Sadly, Music Calling just failed to make its half century and the final meeting was held in April 2005.

▲ *A fine action shot of an informal volleyball match which residents used to enjoy on Sunday mornings.*

The origins of Music Calling within the YMCA movement dates back to 1942 when Leslie Ling, a wartime YMCA Secretary took advantage of the facilities provided by the fine American YMCA building in Jerusalem to create a centre for the performance of classical music. Ostensibly for the British Forces it was also open to members of the local population. One of the greater effects was to lessen local racial tensions because, like sporting occasions, all those attending were united by an interest in the same thing.

After nearly 50 years of successful operations in Cheltenham, however, with the increase in the number of local concerts and the availability of recorded music in the shops, there was no longer a need for such a group. Barry Lloyd was the mainstay for many years.

Netball – A team was run for many years at Vittoria Walk during which time the rules changed. Originally, as in basketball, it was possible to throw the ball from one end of the court to the other but zoning, as in ice hockey, outlawed this practice and made it a more skillful game. During the late-1960's and early 1970's friendly matches were played against local youth clubs using basketball nets in the sports hall, prior to participation in the inaugural Gloucestershire Netball League, often fielding two teams. Members supplied junior and senior county players, umpires and committee members to Gloucestershire Netball Association down the years, and also supported the Gloucestershire Youth Association by organising, playing and umpiring at National tournaments.

Cheltenham also organised two National YMCA Tournaments during the 1980s, playing at Bournside School with teams coming from as far afield as North Shields and Essex sleeping on the sports hall floor for the weekend. Young YMCA players represented England and Scotland at BUSA tournaments whilst at University. Wendy Yeates took the YMCA into the Gloucestershire League with Marilyn Hopkins and Vicki Wood latterly in charge, although the team moved to bigger training facilities at Bentham in 2004.

Overseas Work Fund – This was the forerunner of Y Care International which was founded by Terry Waite as a Refugee and International Development Agency during the early-1980s. Much money has been raised over the years, especially via sponsored events.

Popular Music Group – The 1950s and 1960s saw an upsurge in what was termed Pop Music and all self-respecting youth clubs ran at least one session a week, usually but not always, at weekends.

Saturday Night – This was one of many Christian youth clubs run down the year and over the Millennium period was run by Graham Philpott.

Snooker – see under Billiards & Snooker

Squash – Two squash courts were built after the gymnasium was extended into a sports hall and have remained popular ever since. Latterly under the leadership of Savaskis (Sam) Costa, various teams have competed in the local league.

Swimming & Lifesaving – Before the swimming pool was opened in Tommy Taylor's Lane and long before schools such as Dean Close, Cheltenham College, Cheltenham Ladies' College and St. Edward's opened their doors to the public, Cheltenham YMCA enjoyed exclusive evening use of the pool which currently lies underneath the floor of the Playhouse Theatre, then known as the Montpellier Baths.

Table Tennis – Cheltenham and Baker Street YMCAs totally dominated the Cheltenham scene, between 1927 and 1971, when they won Division 1 no fewer than 25 times, the names of Peter Cruwys, Bob Griffin and Ian Harrison being synonymous with success. In 1960 Cheltenham hosted the national finals of the YMCA table tennis competition when Wimbledon defeated Doncaster, and 1971 saw the visit of England table tennis coach, Bryan Merrett, on the occasion of Cheltenham hosting the Midland Area finals. During this time there were often as many eight tables set up for evening sessions in the main sports hall.

Trampolining – A sport within a sport. An invaluable gymnastics event which also had its own dedicated following.

Lawn Tennis – This club played at Montpellier when grass courts were available, since superseded by almost universal hard courts, the YMCA itself once having such a court behind the Promenade.

Training Agency – This is covered fully in Chapter 11 and was a series of government schemes taken up by Cheltenham YMCA under the initial leadership of Bill Sargison.

Volleyball – A game invented by the YMCA during the early-20th Century, it has apparently always been a fringe activity in whatever gymnasium was being used at the time. It was during the 1970s, however, when the sport came into its own both locally and nationally.

Whist – Largely an offshoot of the Women's Auxiliary, whist drives tended to be for older people.

Women's Auxiliary – This fine body did much for Cheltenham YMCA down the years and attention is drawn to the wartime chapter in which their sterling work in the YMCA canteens is reported in some detail. Their existence as a separate body largely disappeared with the integration of men and women in mixed activities during the 1960s.

Yoga – Bryan Mitchell first began taking yoga classes in 1976 and during the next 30 years used several different venues throughout the building. There are several different systems of yoga, some very gentle rising to vigorous, the purely physical YMCA version being described by Bryan as "strong" but stopping short of vigorous. Catering for people who wanted to work hard at a series of dynamic stretching asanas (postures) rather than those looking for something more gentle and relaxing, the age range was quite staggering. Rising from late-teens the oldest member in 2005 was 79, a lady who was more than capable of adopting the more advanced asanas, including an unsupported headstand! Always popular, the classes were held on Tuesday and Thursday evenings, and Wednesday mornings.

Youth for Christ – This international movement was started in the USA by evangelist Billy Graham as a means of helping young people who committed their lives to Christ but could not find a suitable church. It began over here during the early-1950s and spread rapidly across the country. The Cheltenham branch had its HQ at the YMCA for a number of years before moving to new premises in Priory Road at the turn of the 21st Century.

Satellite Youth Work – Apart from the ongoing work at Baker Street YMCA, which began in 1940 and lasted until January 1967, there was also considerable effort expended elsewhere. When the Royal Well Hut was taken down and rebuilt as the St. Thomas Mission Church on the Alma Road estate in Up Hatherley during 1956, a good deal of YMCA support went with it and remained there until it was eventually demolished. In conjunction with Ruth Campbell, the Borough Youth Officer, other work also took place at Pilley Lane Baptist Church. Secretary, Bill Sargison, was closely linked to St. Philip and St. James, Up Hatherley, which later benefited from Assistant Chief Executive (Programme) Angela Gilbert and children's worker, Francis Barton giving valuable holiday time assistance from 2004.

The 1960-1 Handbook listed the four clubs in detail. What was known as the Central YMCA Boys Department was for 12-15 year-olds and met on Mondays and Wednesdays from 6-7.30pm. Membership was 5 shillings per annum which entitled them to Boy membership and when they reached 15 they were invited to become Associate Members. Boys and parents were invited to call in and meet the leaders.

St. Thomas's was described as a mixed youth club for young people aged 14-20 who lived on the Alma Estate in Up Hatherley. Meetings took place in the ex-Royal Well Hut situated on the corner of Thirlmere and Windermere Road, which trebled as St. Thomas' mission (a daughter church of St. Marks), a scout hut, and a YMCA youth club. Admission to the latter cost sixpence a time but with the added bonus that members could also take part in Central YMCA activities.

There was an appeal for adult leaders, hardly surprising when the total membership was estimated at about 120 of which 90 usually turned up! One successful leader was a railwayman called Glyn Evans who responded well to the needs of the area and who proved a hard act to follow when he moved away to become a YMCA secretary in Hornsey, North London. As there was a waiting list, potential new members were invited to make early enquiries and on certain occasions overspill accommodation was provided at the Lakeside Bungalow which was part of the old Lakeside Junior School before it moved in the mid-1960s to its present location on Hatherley Road. Across from the road from St. Thomas', it was located to the right of the parade of shops and was used in the evening as a library. Now demolished it became Lakeside Infant School but lasted longer than St. Thomas' itself which was closed in the mid-1960s after the congregation dwindled away, the YMCA work closing in 1964. The scouts later moved to a new home developed from a former prefab next to the Bass House.

Pilley Boys Club was open on Monday and Friday evenings at Pilley Lane Baptist Church, specifically for those who lived in Pilley and Leckhampton. A full programme was run in accordance with YMCA principles and included table tennis, boxing, physical training, snooker and cricket. The subscription was also sixpence with Monday catering for boys aged 10-16 from 7-9pm and Fridays for boys aged 13-18 from 7-9.30pm. It closed in 1963.

Baker Street YMCA is the subject of a separate chapter.

▲ Ian Harrison (left) was the England No. 1 table tennis player, partnered here at the YMCA in 1960 by Kevin Edwards. The sport was once very popular and the local Association ran a number of teams with matches and training taking place in the Lesser Hall, the annexe to the Sports Hall.

CHAPTER 13
A PRESIDENT LOOKS BACK
Memoirs of Rev. Lionel Fitz

Lionel Fitz was elected President of Cheltenham YMCA in 2003 following the death of the former President, Alex Evans MBE, in December 2002. This chapter is based on a section of his unpublished autobiography but, in accordance with the rest of the narrative, has been translated into the third person.

He first joined Cheltenham YMCA as a member of the Junior Department in 1938 but, after enjoying all the facilities described elsewhere in the book and like so many other young men, was overtaken by world events. He remembered the youth leader, A.J. Moxon, a former Derbyshire 2nd XI county cricketer being ambidextrous and instead of playing the usual tennis backhand shots, simply switched his racket to the more convenient arm! Serve and volley was not yet the staple diet of men's tennis!

In early 1942 Lionel, a member of the 125 (Cheltenham) Squadron of the ATC, attended an RAF selection board in Oxford and after three days was recommended for Aircrew Training and placed on deferred service. Billeted near Lords Cricket ground in North London he got little sleep at night owing to anti-aircraft fire. Posted to St. Andrew's in Scotland he later attended Cranwell and trained as an Air Wireless Operator. He graduated as an Air Navigator W/T at No. 33 Air Navigation School Hamilton, Ontario in Canada in October 1944. Returning to England he was posted to Braunstone in Leicestershire then to the Operations Training Unit at Moreton-in-Marsh as an Airfield Controller. Disappointed that it was too late to be posted to a squadron for the war in Europe he was demobbed in January 1947 at Blackpool.

One weekend when he was home on leave he went to Whaddon Road to watch Cheltenham Town play soccer. Thoughts of the "Robins" ever playing in the Football League were just a distant dream at the time although Cheltenham was one of the bigger towns without a fully professional side. Walking down the road he stopped to watch a game on Whaddon Rec. and discovered one of the teams was Cheltenham YMCA. After the game was over he talked to some of the lads who asked if he would play for them. He agreed but left it until after he was demobbed when he went down to the YM in the Promenade and signed on, playing regularly in the 1st X1 for a team which won the 3rd division of the Cheltenham League. They also won the Junior Charities Cup beating Rotol Apprentices at the Burrows Field, Leckhampton, on which occasion he was marked by Peter Rushworth who went on to play for the "Robins" and Leicester City.

In 1947 the YMCA Secretary was a relatively older man, Charles Belcher, who died in 1966, aged 81. He had nobly held the fort during the war years, particularly organising the Forces work when there were few other activities. Immediately post-war the YMCA was a tightly knit community because the Senior Club had been restarted with a nucleus of older boys from Baker Street YMCA. There was a canteen on the ground floor and members used to sit by the window watching the world go by in the Promenade. In the basement were three billiards and snooker tables where many improved their skills before playing in the Cheltenham League. At the back of the premises was a large wooden building known as the Royal Well Hut, where members practised gymnastics, football, table tennis and basketball. There was also a small hostel for about 18 residents.

The best room in the premises, however, was occupied by a group of women attached to the YMCA whose leader was Mollie Bose. They were much older than the new intake of members and did not mix. They must not, however, be confused with the Women's Auxiliary who did so much stalwart wartime work.

Each evening there was an epilogue in the basement usually taken by Charles Belcher or his assistant, Mr. Moxon. Following one such epilogue Charles approached Lionel about Full Membership which was open only to committed Christians. They were eager to have a younger man on the

Executive Committee and so Lionel was duly elected at the 1947 AGM. At his first appearance he discovered the committee consisted of chairman Councillor Arthur Dye (Headmaster of Naunton Park School, Councillor H.T. Bush, Dr. Morley (the Borough Health Officer), George Hitchman (owner of a tailor's shop), Vic Dymock (a local builder) plus humble little Lionel. The meetings were conducted in a very business like manner and no one was ever in any doubt that Mr Dye was in charge. It was also made plain to Lionel that he was the members' representative.

Like many others of his generation, Lionel went to the YM most evenings when there was often football training in the hut after a three or four mile run. Other times they would play table tennis, snooker or just mess about. On Saturday evenings most members met up for a drink in the Fleece Hotel (on the corner of Henrietta Street and the High Street) before moving on to the Town Hall dance. After the Fleece Hotel was demolished together with the other buildings in the block – including the old Grammar School – they went instead to the George Hotel which was situated at what is now the entrance to the Beechwood Arcade.

When Belcher retired as Secretary he was replaced by Fred Daldry, a much younger man who had recently been demobbed from the Navy. From a YMCA family he had already helped out at Cheltenham as a young man. As a member of the Plymouth Brethren he was very much against smoking and drinking but was a very good basketball player and instructed any members who were keen to improve. Belcher had been a keen and active member of Cheltenham Rotary and when he retired instead of a personal present he asked the Rotary to provide furnishings for the YMCA chapel which are still in use today.

The Football section was very active and Lionel had what he described as "…. the privilege of being the chairman of the committee with Ken Stone as secretary. It was decided to raise money for the section's funds by running periodic dances in the hut. Bill Wheeler and a group of the lads made a portable stage with an illuminated canopy and engaged the band run by the Tilley twins, Peter and Paul, from the St. Paul's area. In later years they enlarged the band considerably and were the main attraction at the Town Hall. Vic Pearce had access to the Printing Dept at the UCAL (United Chemists Association Ltd.) and printed some impressive tickets. Right from the start the dances were very popular but needed a great deal of stewarding to keep out undesirables. Held once a month they were also highly profitable and built up a sizeable bank balance."

Rev. Lionel Fitz spent 60 years on the board of Cheltenham YMCA. After taking early retirement he was ordained to the Anglican ministry at St. Matthew's Church.

On the playing fields the football club was no less successful. In 1947/8 they won promotion from Division 3 and also the Junior Charities' Shield. In 1949/50 they were League Champions again and promoted to Division 1. In addition, there was now another side in Division 3. The most successful season was 1951/2 when they were runners up in Division 1, quarter-finalists in the County Amateur Cup and winners of the Senior Charities Cup. There were also some very good inter-YMCA matches. On one occasion they travelled to Bristol to play Totterdown YMCA and also had an excellent day out on the south coast when they took two teams to play Bournemouth YMCA.

In 1952 the basketball team played an American Services side before a huge crowd in an exhibition match at the Town Hall. Arranged by the Sports Council, the YMCA team wore a very smart American style strip specially for the occasion.

In an athletics match for the Inter-Association Regional Sports, Cheltenham YMCA were well ahead on points before the final event, the 4 x 100 yards relay. In fact they only needed to finish to pick up the trophy. Unfortunately the first runner dropped the baton and, as anchor man, Lionel was left fuming, an emotion which only dimmed slightly over half a century!

YMCA membership was growing rapidly and there was difficulty in accommodating the numbers wanting to take part in all the activities. The Executive Committee therefore engaged local architects Barnard & Partners, to draw up plans for a permanent gymnasium on the site of the hut. The architect responsible was Barry Lloyd who was soon to become inextricably linked with the YMCA. After the plans were prepared and an estimated cost received the Committee launched an appeal for funds. At the time Ken Williams was the Regional Appeals Secretary with whom several preliminary meetings were held, after which a special Cheltenham Appeals Committee was set up involving several local businessmen and Mr. D. Wainwright, manager of Barclays Bank on the corner of Rodney Road and the High Street. Things went well and it was arranged for Princess Elizabeth, who was coming to open Princess Elizabeth Way, to receive the "purses" on behalf of the YMCA during a function at the Town Hall. It was a great occasion, attended by both Lionel and his mother.

The Table Tennis section was very successful, winning everything in the local leagues. At Peter Cruyws' suggestion two famous English internationals came along to run a series of coaching sessions, Victor Barna and Johnny Leach doing a splendid job. Bob Griffin and Stan Griffin later became internationals themselves and together with Peter Cruyws, gained their county caps.

Fred Daldry was very keen to promote the "C" in "YMCA" and instructed members as to the Aims and Purposes of the Association, with a Bible Study and discussion group one evening a week. At that time there were also several apprentices from Smith's Industries living in the hostel who were active members of Cambray Baptist Church. Enthusiasm for their faith resulted in many lively discussions and much spiritual fruit. They came under the general guidance of Mr. Moxon who was a Diocesan Reader at St. Peter's Church and, as there was a rather Liberal Evangelical (the phrase did exist in those days) rector at St. Matthew's, Lionel even found himself being challenged by the need to make a personal commitment.

Fred Daldry also organised a monthly Sunday tea table conference to which he invited some of the YMCA national leaders to speak, followed by questions and tea. These were well attended and informative, getting everyone away from a parochial view of the YMCA and into the realisation it was not just a national but an international movement.

One day Lionel received a phone call asking him to attend a very important committee meeting at lunch time. When the members arrived they were informed by Arthur Dye that he had dreamt the previous night that they had bought Farnley Lodge and so that morning had put in an offer on their behalf! Previously a Ladies' College boarding house in Vittoria Walk it had been empty for some time because the College Council had decided it was too dangerous for girls to cross the Promenade to and from lessons. Everyone trooped round to inspect the building which was very old fashioned with huge dormitories upstairs and kitchens in the basement. It was much bigger than the Promenade premises, however, and in addition had a fair amount of ground for extensions. There and then the whole committee endorsed the chairman's decision to purchase it at the asking price of £12,500, a vast sum of money 50 years ago.

Lionel was fairly confident the three town councillors on the executive committee knew what they were doing, however, and that the Town Council would be interested in buying the Promenade premises. Mr Lawson, of Lawson & Lawson, was therefore instructed to put it on the market. Meanwhile, the offer to the Ladies' College Council was accepted but the initial offers received for the Promenade were not at all encouraging. The Town Council insisted the District Valuer had put a figure of approximately £12,500 on the buildings which the committee thought very under-priced. The National YMCA was therefore consulted and recommended the use of their London Agents. After lengthy negotiations the Town Council increased their offer to £27,500, more than twice their original figure. This was duly accepted!

Around this time Fred Daldry was offered the post of Secretary at Kingston-on-Thames YMCA. He had done a tremendous job in taking Cheltenham forward from an almost total loss of membership during the war back into an active and

▲ *The wartime Air Training Corps 125 Squadron, probably taken in 1941 at their headquarters at the old Pate's Girls Grammar School situated in North Place. This was almost certainly the last photo of this particular group because shortly afterwards it split into two different squadrons. Lionel Fitz is in the third row from the front, sixth from the right (excluding the two bandsmen on the end).*

vibrant growing association. He departed to the Home Counties with everyone's blessing.

The move to Vittoria Walk coincided with the appointment of Ken Williams as Fred's successor. He was not, however, very interested in sport and physical activities because although he had been the Appeals Officer, he had no experience of running a local YMCA. The initial move proved difficult in terms of establishing organised activities and the new building also lacked the intimate and friendly atmosphere of the Promenade. Most of the footballers who had played together during the successful years were now that bit older and had either a wife or girl friend in tow. Most drifted away and the soccer teams no longer held their own. Soon there was only one team which was rapidly demoted down the leagues until the YMCA finally pulled the metaphorical plug and withdrew altogether. It was later successfully resurrected, however.

The cricket team was still doing fairly well and a successful application was made to the Lords' Taverners for a grant for a pitch, plus netting and matting. This was laid out in the grounds and Tom Graveney, who later retired around the corner in Suffolk Parade, came along to open it. He batted against the YM bowlers and also bowled to the batsmen although, according the local newspaper, nobody got him out. It was a very enjoyable event.

1955 had been the 100th Anniversary of the founding of Cheltenham YMCA and it was decided to erect a purpose-built recreation hall and hostel block, plans which were transferred to Vittoria Walk after the move in 1956, so once again Cheltenham YMCA found itself fundraising. The British Council made a grant of about £20,000 on condition that a number of YMCA rooms were reserved for the use of overseas students. Indeed, there was now quite a strong international flavour with several overseas visitors.

The building contract was awarded to Vic Dymock's company who made an excellent job of it. Before the contract was completed, however, Ken Williams left to take up a Regional appointment and later became National Secretary of the YMCA in Wales. His successor was Wilf Pearson who was another Methodist lay preacher. The new extensions were formally opened by Charles Irving the supportive local MP and the ceremony was also attended by the mayor and several other dignitaries.

Lionel had by now become quite involved with the movement at both Regional and National level and attended regular meetings. The Regional Secretary was Mr. Wickens who always wore striped trousers and a black jacket and the gatherings were held at the Central YMCA in Colston Street, Bristol where the General Secretary was Len Gunn. Bristol was a big association rather like a Gentlemen's Club. The lounge had large leather sofas, the restaurant was available to non-members and it had its own concert hall. It also boasted a sports complex on the outskirts of the city. Lionel attended the first post-war National Assembly at

Bristol and subsequent Assemblies over the years at Manchester, London and Warwick. Later, he was elected a member of the SW Regional Council and also Chairman of the North Gloucestershire & Herefordshire YMCAs. Wickens' successor as regional secretary was Morley Manaton who was keen on networking and outreach.

Sadly, the senior officers of Cheltenham YMCA died over a comparatively short period of time. First to go was the President, Alderman P.T. Smith then, at quite a young age Alderman H. T. Bush, and finally the long serving chairman, Alderman Arthur Dye who had been made a Freeman of the Borough in 1965. He was also awarded the Gold Order of the Red Triangle for services to the YMCA movement and had been nominated for an OBE shortly before his death which was therefore awarded posthumously. The new chairman was Percy Gardner who owned a bakery and several retail shops. Also a staunch Methodist he was a great benefactor of Mersey Road Church in Whaddon.

With the new facilities the membership grew and so did the number of residents. In 1955 Lionel had been elected to the Committee of Baker St. YMCA Boys' Club and after the death of Alderman Bush, was appointed by the Executive Committee as the new Chairman. This branch of Cheltenham YMCA had been set up in 1940 to take over the Junior work of the Association when the premises in the Promenade were being set aside for work with the Armed Forces. Over the years it had been very successful particularly at football. It carried all before it in the Youth Leagues and several players went on to play professionally. Three initially went to Swindon Town under manager Bert Head with Mike Summerbee later transferring to a very successful Manchester City team under Joe Mercer and Malcolm Allison. Micky Holder also played for Swindon Town.

Vic Dymock ran Baker Street YMCA Boys Club for many years and as a deacon of Gas Green Baptist Church founded a company of the Boys' Brigade there. Part of the YMCA premises were set aside each week for BB band practice and other activities, including a Bible Class on Sunday mornings. Lionel remained chairman of Baker Street until its permanent transfer to Gas Green Church as a Youth and Community Centre in 1967.

Baker Street was also affiliated to the Gloucestershire Association of Boys' Clubs and was selected for a visit by the Duke of Gloucester. As the chairman Lionel escorted him around the premises and introduced him to other dignitaries. One of the highlights every year was the Annual Dinner when Vic Dymock did an extremely good job making sure the lads were dressed in their Sunday best and on their best behaviour. Several boys gave reports and a well known person was always invited as guest of honour to present the trophies and prizes.

Vic resigned shortly after Lionel took over as chairman to devote more time to the Boys' Brigade and so a new young leader named Clarke was appointed from the National Council's recommended list. It was not a success, however. The Boys' Club and the Boys Brigade had been closely linked under Dymock's dynamic leadership and it became clear he felt the building should be linked to the youth work of the Church. When Clarke handed in his notice Lionel therefore recommended to the Executive Committee that the Youth and Junior work of the association be transferred back to Vittoria Walk under the direction of the General Secretary. This was unanimously agreed.

After the death of the "big three" Vic Dymock was left as the sole trustee of the association and it was decided that David Wainwright (the treasurer), Barry Lloyd and Lionel should take their place. The Executive Committee, chaired by Percy Gardner and at the instigation of Wilf Pearson, became known as the Board of Management. The demand on the sports hall was now so great that it was felt a smaller hall was needed for activities such as Judo. In order to raise the money it was decided to sell off the piece of land fronting Oriel Road. This, however, meant the loss of the Cricket pitch and a grassed area which was replaced with an office block with car parking facilities underneath.

When David Wainwright retired as manager of Barclays Bank in the High Street he also resigned from the Board of the YMCA at which point Lionel was elected as Hon. Treasurer and also Chairman of the Finance Committee.

When Wilf Pearson resigned to become General Secretary of Liverpool YMCA the board appointed as his successor, Des Willcox previously Secretary at Bath YMCA. He and his wife Pearl quickly settled into the job and, being younger than Wilf and interested in sports and young people, advanced the work still further. A coffee bar was created for the members to meet and chat and Roger Hunt was made assistant secretary. Roger's wife, a qualified doctor, took a position within a local practice.

Further improvements were made to the buildings, altering dormitories into single and double rooms and erecting an office for the Secretary on the side. For this work an overdraft was taken out.

When the Cheltenham Shopfitting Cricket Club folded because of lack of interest, Lionel switched his cricketing prowess to the YMCA who already had a very good team, with his batting talents enhancing it still further! Home matches were played at the Burrows, a corporation ground at Leckhampton which later became a regular home for the junior football teams. The club also enjoyed some excellent matches against Northampton YMCA played on the former Northampton racecourse.

On several occasions Des Willcox, Roger Hunt, Lionel and his son Timothy journeyed up to the Midlands to watch Wolverhampton Wanderers, then a strong force in the old First Division of the Football League. When Des left to become General Secretary of Plymouth YMCA, Roger was appointed as his successor. Des and Percy Gardner had got on very well together, both Methodists with Des playing the organ at the Mersey Road church where Percy was a pillar of strength.

Shortly after Des left, Percy became President. In his place as chairman was elected Alex Evans who was Head of Food Technology at the North Gloucestershire Technical College. Alex was also a Methodist friend of Percy's.

After Roger left to join the staff of the YMCA National Council, Lionel received a phone call from Des Willcox to say that he knew of a good candidate for the vacant Cheltenham position. Trusting Des' judgment Lionel immediately asked him to apply and so it was that Bill Sargison was appointed, whose father had been Provost of a West Indies cathedral. Bill had a great deal of YMCA experience having been on the staff at Bristol under Len Gunn and, at the time of his application to Cheltenham, was at Birmingham YMCA under Will Steele. It proved to be an excellent choice.

Together with his wife Miriam, and their two young children, Angela and Paul, Bill was soon fully involved. He was particularly interested in sport and several new innovations were put in place during his time, including squash courts, fitness equipment, and a sauna. His energy and enthusiasm were also accompanied by a new vision for the local Association.

The hostel now had an occupancy of nearly 90 beds which was the main source of income so it was decided to appoint an assistant secretary whose main task was to keep the hostel full. Richard Gooch an ex-Harrow public schoolboy was appointed and proved very good at making contacts in the town with businesses and the local Information Bureau.

Alex Evans MBE was Chairman and then President of Cheltenham YMCA until his death in December 2002.

The sports and fitness activities were also expanding and it was decided to appoint a secretary for the Programme. Richard Pascall, a County Rugby player, who introduced equipment for body building which many of his friends joined to use.

When Percy Gardner died Alex Evans became President and Lionel was elected chairman. He also became chairman of the personnel committee with the new Treasurer being an assistant manager from the Bank. With Bill Sargison's drive, plus his two competent assistants, the place was really buzzing. There were also some interesting Board meetings, especially after Bill set up what can only be described as a "think tank" into which he processed his ideas and visions.

A big expansion and new initiative was now brought on-stream. The Government introduced a scheme for training out-of-work youngsters called the Youth Opportunities Project and Bill felt it was a golden opportunity to make use of the YMCA premises during the daytime, thus increasing income. "From little acorns oak trees grow."

After a while the Government expanded the project which was renamed the Youth Training Scheme. Numbers continued to grow and extra staff were engaged. The syllabus was also expanded to involve training in practical skills, such as bricklaying, motor mechanics, typing etc. Rapid growth continued apace and new space was acquired from St. Paul's Church. Then the board purchased 4 Wolseley Terrace and 33 Rodney Road. The income was considerable but the capital expended on salaries, tools, typewriters, computers, desks and other office equipment and furniture was enormous.

Recruiting and engaging specialist staff and instructors in effect turned this branch of the YMCA into a small College, under an excellent principal called Linda Burley. After a while it was realised that 33 Rodney Road was too far away from Vittoria Walk and with re-adjustments was no longer required. By now the YMCA Training Scheme had its own administrative staff and kept separate accounts. The Association reserves began to grow and everything seemed very healthy.

It therefore came as quite a blow when Bill Sargison left to become the South West Regional Secretary of the National YMCA. His contribution had transformed Cheltenham which was now amongst the biggest YMCA Associations.

He was a hard act to follow and his successor was Phil Willerton who had worked at Wimbledon YMCA. Although he stayed only a relatively short time he made a valuable contribution on funding for the housing department. Not everyone agreed this was a good idea, however, because there were often strict definitive strings attached. Sensing all was not well, Lionel resigned from the board but was re-elected twelve months later, by which time Barry Lloyd had become chairman, a capacity in which he ably served for the next decade. In between there had been a successful application for a sizeable grant but it had been secured with very severe restrictions imposed on the Association.

Following Willerton's departure to Watford YMCA, an internal appointment was made. Adrian Sharpe (who had since married Linda Burley) had been an instructor on the Training Scheme which was about to be wound up. He applied for the post and although he had no previous experience of YMCAs was felt to be a safe pair of hands. So it proved and he was particularly good on building and maintenance aspects of the work.

The Board now introduced a new sub-committee to consider how the Christian aspect of the Association could be given greater prominence and Lionel was asked to chair it. The Board had only previously engaged staff on an ad hoc basis so in August 1996 it was decided to assess other needs and recommend a new staff structure. Adrian as Chief Executive, was invited to officially appoint an Assistant Chief Executive (Programme) and Assistant Chief Executive (Housing). Into these posts came respectively Jim Jenkinson (who was already in position), and Cathy Turner who had previously been at Norwich YMCA.

In 1991 Lionel was invited by the SW Trust Fund to be a representative for the north of the region, set up to receive profits from a board game they had marketed called "Cheltenham Challenge" (see colour picture on page 187) and also the profits from the YMCA Charity Shops. The Trustees met twice a year to approve the investments and to consider applications for grants from Associations and individuals, with Bill Sargison and Lionel usually travelling together to meetings. There were three representatives from the north and three from the south (Devon & Cornwall). Bill Ayres from Bath was the Chairman and Des Willcox the Secretary. In due course the Trustees invited Lionel to become chairman of the Charities Shops committee which meet twice a year in Cheltenham to receive details of the opening and closing and management of shops in the Trust areas, and to approve the accounts.

During Adrian's time as Chief Executive considerable alterations, additions and improvements were made to both the exterior and interior of Vittoria Walk, often undertaken with considerable financial assistance from Housing Corporation grants. Not the least of these was the removal of the old entrance and a skilful exterior reconstruction coupled with wholesale internal rearrangements. In addition the board purchased Balcanton House in Tryes Road, Leckhampton for a secondary housing project as move-on accommodation for students. With the winding up of the Training Scheme it was decided to keep the building in Wolseley Terrace and let it out for income. A decision was also taken by the Board to appoint investment managers to handle the Association's funds, including Stocks and Shares.

In the year 2000 the Board became a company limited by guarantee with the existing becoming its first directors. Don and Dorothy Staight, previously connected with Wimbledon YMCA, had been active participants for some time and when Barry Lloyd stepped down, Don was elected as the first chairman of the new Board of Directors.

At the end of December 2001 Adrian Sharpe retired, the first retirement in office since Charles Belcher left around 1950. After a thorough two day selection procedure David Wallace, an experienced Chief Executive from West Kent YMCA (Sevenoaks, Tonbridge and Tunbridge Wells) was appointed. Angela Gilbert (nee Sargison) was appointed as the Assistant Chief Executive (Programme) in succession to Kate Grant who had succeeded Jim Jenkinson. A highly capable person, Jim had been appointed on the strength of his personal links as a member with Cheltenham YMCA and was soon on the move to establish a new YMCA at Rotherham in South Yorkshire. Once this was completed he was promoted to Regional Development Officer for the Central Region. Also with the appointment of David Wallace came two other posts, viz. a Personal Assistant and an Accounts Clerk.

The patriotic Welsh President, Alex Evans, whose favourite phrase in committee, in a lilting Welsh accent, was "Through you. Mr. Chairman", received an MBE for services to education, specifically in catering.

In 2004 Don Staight completed five years as the first Chairman of the new Board of Directors and was succeeded in office by fellow director and former Junior Football Secretary and Chairman, Peter Worsley.

▲ During the war many of the YMCA junior members joined either the Air Training Corps, or the Sea or Army cadets. The latter are seen returning from a camp at Bridport in 1942, leaving Lansdown Station via the old railway yard opposite Libertus Road. The Cheltenham YMCA members include from left: John Wynn, Gil Chivers, Alex Devore (all with bugles), unknown corporal, Dick Smith, Cecil Causon, Vic Cleevely and Ken Woodland (all with drums). The dog was a stray adopted in Dorset and brought back as a mascot.

CHAPTER 14
A VISION FOR THE FUTURE
by David Wallace,
Chief Executive of Cheltenham YMCA

The world has changed beyond all recognition since the early days of 1855 but George Williams' vision for the Movement is just as inspiring and relevant today.

1855 was a very special year for another reason. Not only did the early pioneers of Cheltenham YMCA meet in the Old Town Hall in Regent Street to share a life-changing idea for the young men of the town but in Paris the inaugural meeting of the World Alliance of YMCAs also took place. It was here where YMCA leaders agreed the basis on which YMCAs in different parts of the world would come together. This statement, referred to as the "Paris Basis", has been a continuing source of inspiration not only for the YMCA but also for other ecumenical bodies. It states: "The Young Men's Christian Association seeks to unite those who, regarding Jesus Christ as their God and Saviour according to the Holy Scriptures, desire to be His disciples in their faith and in their life, and to associate their efforts for the extension of His Kingdom."

It expresses that Christ is at the centre of the Movement, which is conceived as a world-wide fellowship uniting Christians of all confessions. It is also consistent with an open membership policy committed to the principle of equality regardless of sex, marital status, race, colour, nationality, religion, ethnic origin, disability, age or sexual orientation. This basis was adopted by the founders of Cheltenham YMCA who were both evangelical and ecumenical in their approach, qualities which have been consistent throughout the past 150 years, with leaders expressing their Christian faith by channelling their energies through a rock solid commitment to supporting all young people, particularly in times of need.

The strength of the voluntary sector has always been one of flexibility allowing them to respond quickly in times of crisis and to meet the needs of the moment. The local YMCA in Cheltenham is just such an organisation which has met a wide range of needs and challenges down through each and every decade. This is still reflected today, where our vision is to provide young people with a place to which they belong, a voice that is listened to and opportunities throughout life's journey to realise their God-given potential.

The world facing today's young people is a complex tapestry of massive pressures including the widespread disintegration of the nuclear family unit; easy access to the temptations of alcohol, drugs, smoking, and substance misuse; health issues including stress, sexual promiscuity and obesity; increased subversion through politics and religious factions; the fear of terrorism; the influences of music, television, computers, advertising, and the written word; an increase in violence and street crime involving knives and guns; an increase in easy credit leading to greater personal debt; and a steady and marked decline in life skills and Christian values afforded by schools and parents. This is a world where materialism rules the roost and people's rights have taken over from their responsibilities — even in Cheltenham!

Life has changed for the YMCA too and the challenges are immense. Housed in a heavily extended building dating back to 1828, present day expectations, together with ever changing legislation and standards have meant that the YMCA in Vittoria Walk has had to take stock of its future on the present site. A recent feasibility study was therefore commissioned by the Board of Directors to explore the options open to them.

This is a climate where demand far exceeds provision for suitable accommodation with support services, and where children's work is being delivered from community based locations at Up Hatherley and Hesters Way. Fundraising has been seriously affected by the Lottery; members and cus-

David Wallace, is marred to Susan with three children, Euan, Fiona and Paula. A graduate entrant, qualified youth and community worker, and experienced senior YMCA staff member, he has served the movement for 27 years, with stints at Romford YMCA as an Assistant Secretary/Youth Worker (1978-1984), Aberporth YMCA as General Manager (1984-1988), and West Kent YMCA as Chief Executive (1988-2001). He then joined Cheltenham YMCA as Chief Executive in 2001. Areas of expertise include corporate management, youth and community work, and building development projects. Credited with setting up Aberporth YMCA in Wales and also West Kent YMCA (possibly the first modern area-based YMCA in the UK incorporating Sevenoaks, Tonbridge and Tunbridge Wells), David is an evangelical Christian who has served as a magistrate, held the post of Hon. Secretary of the Association of Professional Staff for the British Isles, and attended international YMCA events in Sweden, Switzerland and the USA. He recently cycled from Lands End to John O'Groats in eight days in aid of Y Care.

tomers demand the highest quality state of the art facilities; traditional programme trends have altered with increased accountability and quality standards; and there has been a constant financial viability issue coupled with a decline in volunteers.

Exciting times indeed at Cheltenham YMCA where each generation has a responsibility to continue the work of the previous one. Looking ahead, a typical five-year plan would include increased supported and move-on accommodation (both on and offsite) with a complete range of support services; on-going upgrading of present facilities at Vittoria Walk; a radical review of our current programme; the development of children's work to additional satellite sites; the expeditious development of our youth work programme; increased partnership working with external agencies and neighbouring YMCAs; an increase in volunteering at all levels of the organisation; an increase in personal development opportunities incorporating the international dimension; and of course achieving financial stability.

Cheltenham YMCA has a long history of helping young people find acceptance, community and activity. It is part of a national Christian movement which is the largest voluntary sector provider of safe, supported accommodation in England for single men and women between the ages of 16 and 35 — every night almost 7,500 young people stay at a YMCA — and also part of the largest provider of health and fitness services that promote physical activity and healthy living. The YMCA is a movement that pioneered ecumenism, games and sports, and relevant social action around the world.

150 years of service to young people and the wider Cheltenham community is a great achievement — certainly one to celebrate — but the work is not complete and continues with the same verve and motivation as our forefathers.

Roll on the 21st Century!

CHAPTER 15
PICTORIAL SUPPLEMENT
A BLACK AND WHITE MISCELLANY

▲ *Where it all began in 1855. The Old Town Hall stood on the site of what is now the Regent Street entrance to the Regent Arcade and probably began life as a riding school. It was then used by Salem Baptist Church, an offshoot of which became Cambray Baptist Church. During the early years of the 20th Century it again became a riding school (seen here in 1910) before being used for storage by Cavendish House.*

▲ *Baker Street YMCA football teams and supporters taken during the season 1945-6 and showing great strength and solidarity. Gil Chivers and Bernie Cresswell identified all but one of the people and commented on how many were still married more than 50 years later! Back row left to right: Ivor Newland, Arthur Milan, John Tovey, Trevor Dymock, Stan Bettridge, ? Midwinter, Len Hopson, Joe Vallender, Clive Jefferies, unidentified; middle row: Vic Dymock, Dennis Evans, Neal Cooper, Joe Patrick, ? Smith, Brian Townshend, Ken Barnett, Ernie Clark, Trevor Wren, John Midwinter, Roy Evans, Bob Griffin, Les Godwin (who later became Mayor of Cheltenham), Mr. Newland; front row: Dennis Wellon, Gil Chivers, Bert Carter, Dennis Benbow, Ted Miles, Ken Jakeway, Bill Newland, Ken Russell, Stan Newland; on ground: John Edmunds, Geoff Stanford.*

◀ Gil Chivers scores the second goal for Cheltenham YMCA in the Junior Charities Cup Final (Midwinter Cup) at Leckhampton Primary School ground, season 1946-7. On the touch-line are some Italian POWs (prisoners of war). YMCA won the match 3-2.

▼ Baker Street YMCA football team 1946. From left: Vic Dymock (Leader), Charles Belcher (YMCA Secretary), Gil Chivers, Stan Newland, Fred Ballinger, Bill Newland, Ernie Clarke, John Edmunds, Doug Eardley, Bob Griffin, Dave Hall, Peter Cruwys, Derek Rowley, Ted Miles.

▶ Goal mouth action at Cheltenham Town's ground in the Senior Charities Cup Final, Easter Monday 1952. The Moreton Town goalkeeper (on ground) saves from Cheltenham YMCA's Vic Pearce with Gil Chivers in the far background. YMCA won 3-1. The spectators are under the old covered section opposite the main stand called the Chicken Run which was damaged by gales in 1987. It was redeveloped and later replaced by a stand after Cheltenham gained entry to the Football League in 1999 (see pages 189 and 190).

▶ Cheltenham YMCA cricket team circa 1950, taken on a day they played Northampton YMCA. Back row left to right: Vic Cleevely, Bernie Cresswell, Dave May, Bob Griffin, Charlie Nash, Jack Pearce; front row: Ray Jones, Gil Chivers, Stan Newland, John Fennell and "Doc" Davies.

◀ Cheltenham YMCA in 1951 at Horton Road, Gloucester. Opposite the old hospital, this ground was eventually used by Gloucester City football club but was built on after the Tigers moved to a purpose-built stadium at Meadow Park during the late-1980s. Back row from left to right: Arnold Wills, Bernie Cresswell, Stan Owen, Gerry Norman, Lionel Fitz: front row; Doug Kirkland, Dennis Sullivan, Joe Dymond, Derek Cook, Frank Godwin and Barry Salter.

▶ After the war the Royal Well Hut received a new floor to replace the one destroyed by the boots of the Service troops. It was also given an external facelift including — just in case anyone was in any doubt — its own name in large letters either side of the Red Triangle logo. This picture is of a mixed outing during the late-1940s, unusual in the fact that most activities of this kind in the country at large were still segregated, as was virtually all secondary education.

▶ The Baker Street Boys' Brigade was almost synonymous with the YMCA and most of the band were dual members. They are seen here in about 1951, marching down Clarence Parade away from the junction with Clarence Street in the background. The band made quite a spectacle, was always well turned out for the period and won many awards.

◀ There were three snooker tables on the ground floor of the Promenade premises but they were always known as billiard tables until the multi-ball multi-coloured game took over in popularity after the war. From left to right: Bill Newland, Doug Kirkland, Les O'Brien (with cue) and Mick Patrick. Sadly, the latter was killed during the Korean War soon after this picture was taken in the early-1950s.

▶ A happy band of pilgrims! This photo was taken on the steps of the main entrance outside 55 Promenade on the occasion of the annual May morning breakfast in 1951. YMCA Secretary, Fred Daldry, is back right while Lionel Fitz, later Chairman and President, is front left. The bicycles to the right were stored in the basement and were used mainly for residents to get to work. Kate's Cafe and Kitchen was one of many eating places nearby.

▲ A YMCA South Western Region Camp photo taken somewhere in Somerset or Devon, during August 1948. There was a massive post-war boom in camps of this kind, particularly for teenage boys who commonly slept between six and ten to a bell tent, often Army surplus. A marquee similar to this was used for meals and evening devotions led by the camp chaplain. For most of the lads it would have been their only holiday of the year and there are about six Cheltenham members in this picture. Anyone enjoying a family holiday as well would have been considered quite wealthy.

Tented camps prevailed into the 1970s for many Christian youth groups but went out of fashion when greater affluence, more creature comforts and a television dependent culture put paid to simple outdoor activities and pleasures of this kind. An effective compromise for many families was the post-war development of Butlin's holiday camp chalets but these eventually succumbed to the rise of cheap package holidays abroad. Modern camping is a far cry from these days of no hot or running water, when a dip in the sea was the nearest most people came to a proper wash!

◀ Judo has been a popular YMCA activity for many years and this picture dates back to the 1950s. The man with the bare torso on the right of the throw is Ron Collett who was also a Methodist lay preacher and enjoyed playing the chapel organ at both the Promenade and after the move to Vittoria Walk. A highly disciplined sport, Judo, like some other martial arts, has a graded hierarchy of ability and difficulty denoted by the award of different colours of belt.

▲ Although it was more commonly known as Baker Street Boys Club, Baker Street YMCA catered mainly for older teenagers and was a well-known and an important part of the Cheltenham social and sporting scene. This picture of an annual dinner with female guests was taken around 1947. The camaraderie was such that many of the "boys" kept in touch with each other throughout their adult lives and almost 60 years later many of these couples, who eventually married, were celebrating their golden wedding. They epitomised the YMCA movement at its very best and several went on to play a significant part in the post-war development of Cheltenham.

◀ The vital role of vice presidents in the history of Cheltenham YMCA should never be underestimated because without them the work would probably have floundered on more than one occasion. Many local dignitaries were more than happy to actively support the work and two of the more famous were Alfred Martyn (right) and George Dowty (left) who was later knighted. Martyn succeeded his father in the family business of H.H. Martyn, skilled craftsmen extraordinaire and, after recognising the potential of his younger protege, later put up the capital on which was built the Dowty Aerospace company. Both men served the YMCA well and were more than generous with both their time and money.

PREMISES OCCUPIED BY CHELTENHAM YMCA

▲ *Cheltenham YMCA was founded on November 23rd 1855 in the Old Town Hall which was situated near the entrance to the southern end of the Regent Arcade (see pages 10 and 166).*

▲ *The first rented premises were in St. Mary's Churchyard. Unfortunately, no record exists of exactly where but it must have been near St. Mary's Parish Church above.*

▲ Within a year of its inauguration the YMCA moved to Regent Mansion, 64 Regent Street, now incorporated into Cavendish House.

◀ In 1863 the Association moved to Bedford Buildings located on Clarence Street by Well Walk. This equates to the present day site of Cheltenham Museum next to the Library.

▼ From 1864 to 1866 the YMCA was located at 156 High Street, a building situated close to the old Grammar School and nearest to the camera in this picture of the shopping block which replaced the area (see page 17).

▲ In 1866 the YMCA moved to Promenade House on Clarence Parade, also known as Clarence Parade Hall, formerly home to the *Gloucestershire Echo* newspaper.

▲ In 1870 the Association moved again, this time to 2 Cambray (now renamed Cambray Place), the first of several premises occupied in close proximity.

▶ In 1876 the YMCA was once more on the move, just round the corner to 396 High Street, later renumbered 124 and now home to the Abbey Bank. It is difficult to be precise as to why the tenancies were so relatively short but finance and space probably had something to do with it.

▼ 1879 saw another move, this time to 7 Clarence Street, which was renumbered 11 in the 1930s. It is now home to the Bristol and West Building Society. It is significant that all the rented premises were near the centre of town but even so there were still occasional suggestions that they should be even more central.

▲ Basketball was invented by the YMCA in 1891 but this clever logo dates from almost a century later.

▲ 1881 saw another move, this time to 6 North Street over a shop owned by Mr. Pilley, part of a site now occupied by Boots. Compare this photograph with the one on page 23 where the YMCA sign is still visible several years after the premises were vacated.

◀ 1895 saw the Association back in Cambray, this time at number 7, a building which was soon converted into Cheltenham YMCA's first boarding house and retained as a separate entity for several years into the 20th Century, although vacated before the First World War. There was, however, fun and games with some of the early residents as described in Chapter 3.

▲ In 1897 temporary non-residential accommodation was found at 323 High Street (renumbered 278 during the 1950s), now the central section of the Furnishing Studio.

▲ 1898 saw the biggest step of faith yet. Renting was finally abandoned and 31 Cambray purchased outright. 7 Cambray was retained as a boarding house just opposite but the new financial millstone proved a headache until an extraordinary sequence of events occurred, fully described in Chapter 3. Compare the picture above with those on pages 20 and 21.

▲ In another major leap of faith, immediately post-First World War, Cheltenham YMCA bought numbers 16, 17 and 18 on the Promenade (later renumbered 51, 53 and 55). Situated just to the right of centre where the first floor recesses begin, they were officially opened via a grand ceremonial occasion in 1921 and served as YMCA HQ until 1956.

▲ In time the Promenade premises became too small. Situated at the rear was a timber-framed building known as the Royal Well Hut (see pages 62, 63, 75, 81 and 168) which served as a gymnasium and also housed the junior department. Plans to redevelop this were well advanced during the mid-1950s until a huge and unexpected rise in the rateable value caused a rapid rethink and a move to Vittoria Walk in 1956. Compare the present-day Council Chamber above with the YMCA plans for the same spot on page 114.

▲ This is what the former Baker Street Boys' Club looks like today. Situated at the rear of Gas Green Baptist Church it was a hive of YMCA activity from 1940-1967 fully described in Chapter 8.

▶ There were close ties between Baker Street YMCA and Gas Green Church, firmly cemented by long-time leader Vic Dymock who was awarded the MBE at Buckingham Palace for services to the community on November 30th, 1980.

▲ *This picture of Cheltenham YMCA's current premises in Vittoria Walk was taken around 1990. An Ionic column entrance once fronted the pavement (see page 119) while the elegant looking Italianate tower on the right was added to the original 19th Century building in about 1928.*

▲ *The North Wing, also visible on the left of the top picture, was opened in 1965 specifically to cater for the government initiative in increasing the number of trainee teachers, in Cheltenham's case at St. Paul's College.*

▲ *Compare the picture opposite with Vittoria Walk here in 2005. During the mid-1990s the front of the building was restored to its original late-Regency style and won a local civic award. The main entrance is now below street level, underneath the raised white door behind the bush. A YMCA minibus is visible on the right.*

▲ *The Cheltenham YMCA Charity Shop has held top spot nationally for many years. Under the initial leadership of Paul Sargison and Sheila Green, and later Ann Pierce assisted by a dedicated band of YMCA volunteers, it has set a very high standard for other local charity shops to follow (see page 142).*

▲ ▶ *Two properties were acquired to help during the time that Cheltenham YMCA was expanded as a Training Centre during the 1980s and 1990s.*

Above is 4 Wolseley Terrace which was retained after the training scheme came to an end and is now rented out to the Isbourne Foundation.

Right is 33 Rodney Road which was later sold and is now home to a variety of small companies.

◀ *Balcontan House on Tryes Road was acquired as move-on accommodation for students vacating Vittoria Walk. However, as St. Paul's and St. Mary became the University of Gloucestershire so times changed and the property was sold in 2004.*

A COLOUR MISCELLANY

THREE YMCA PRESIDENTS WHO WERE ALSO MAYORS OF CHELTENHAM

▲ Percy Tyler Smith, affectionately known as "PT", was President of Cheltenham YMCA from 1936 until his death in 1957. He was Mayor of Cheltenham from 1949-1951.

▲ Horace Trinley Bush, Mayor of Cheltenham from 1946-1949, wrote the YMCA Centenary booklet. He succeeded Smith as President but died relatively young soon afterwards.

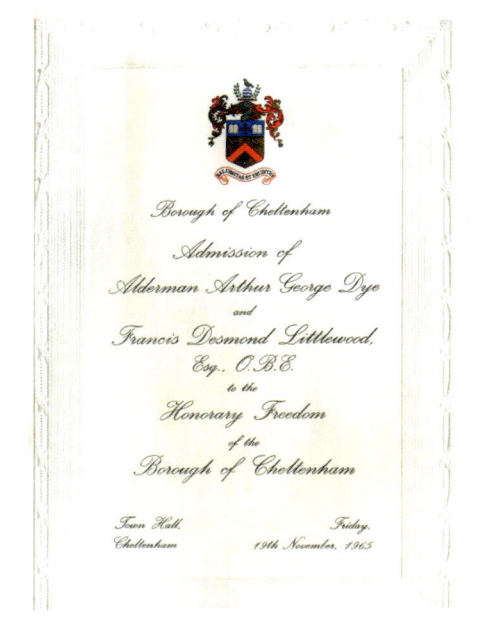

▲ Arthur Dye, former headmaster of Naunton Park School, was a dynamic YMCA Chairman who succeeded Bush as President and pioneered the move to Vittoria Walk in 1956. He was Mayor of Cheltenham from 1959-1961 and in 1965 was awarded the Freedom of the Borough along with former Town Clerk, Frank Littlewood (see page 83). He died on Boxing Day 1971, shortly after being awarded the OBE. A local primary school is named after him.

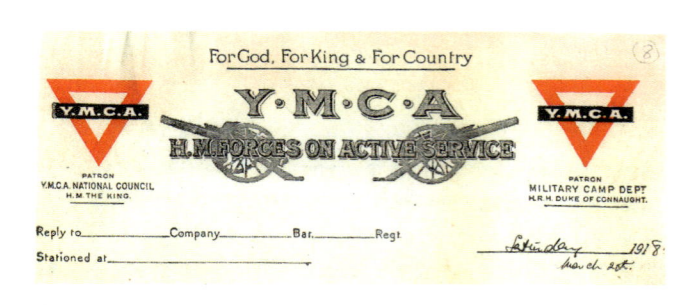

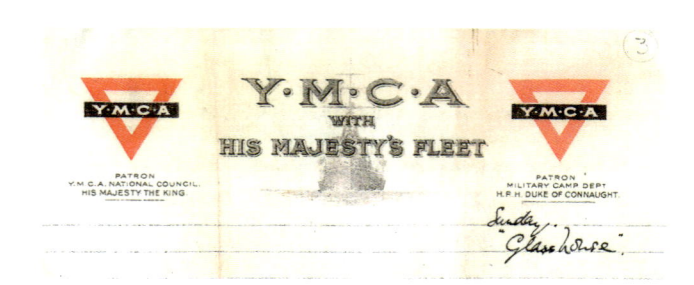

◀ During the First World War — or Great War as it was known at the time — the YMCA became a very important international relief organisation respected by everyone. Even King George V commented on its suitability for rebuilding the country after hostilities ceased in 1918.

During the war itself a system of YMCA huts was established right across Europe (see Chapter 4) and headed YMCA notepaper was made available to anyone in the Armed Forces or Ancillary Services. These three rare examples show the recently introduced red triangle logo which was established as the national symbol, representing Body, Mind and Spirit.

When Cheltenham YMCA moved into the Promenade in 1921, it was opened by Field Marshal Sir William Robertson. The only man ever to rise from Private to the top rank, he had much to say about how the YMCA was a force for good and should be encouraged by everyone in the land (see Chapter 5).

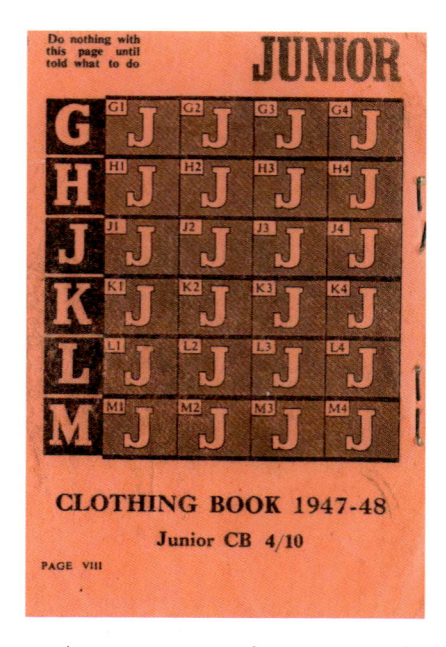

▲ Anyone over retirement age in 2005 will remember the ration books which ruled the lives of the nation until the early 1950s.

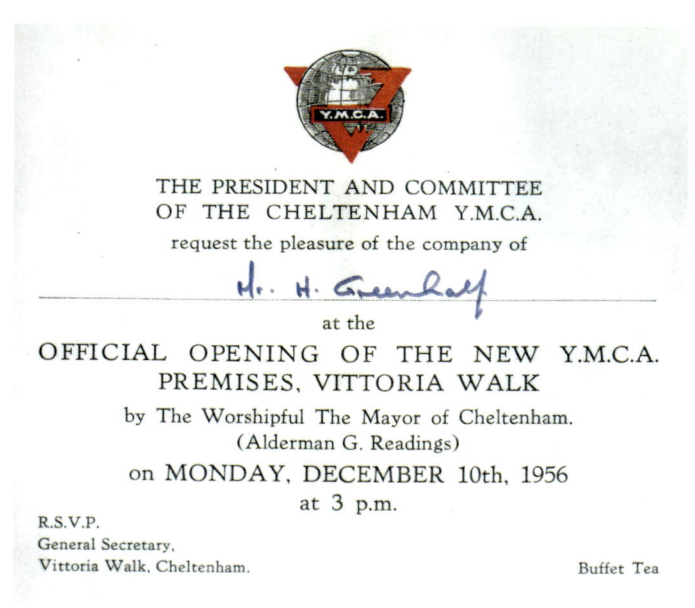

▲ An amazing sequence of events caused Cheltenham YMCA to move from the Promenade to Vittoria Walk in 1956. A full account of this truly remarkable story may be found in Chapters 10 and 11.

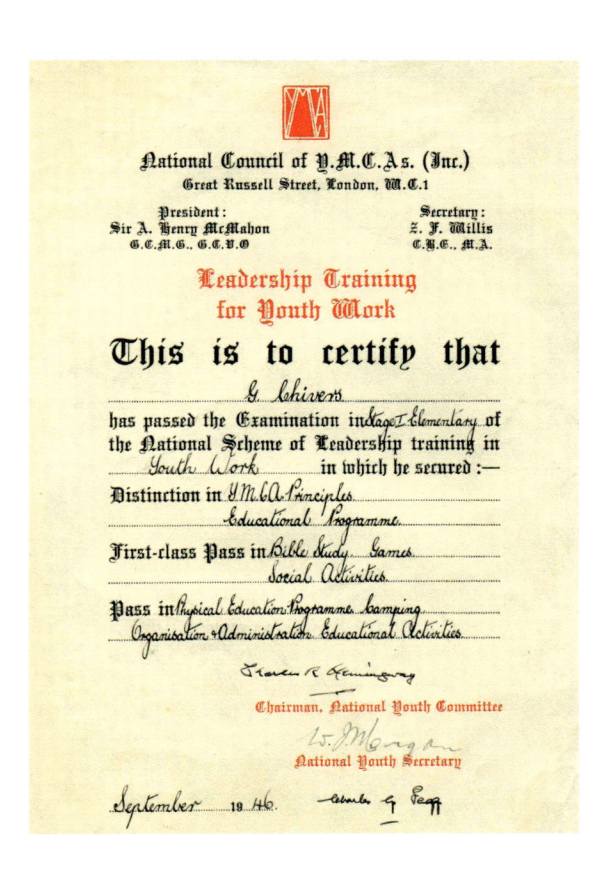

▲ ▼ The YMCA was decades ahead of recent government initiatives to provide training and certificates across a broad spectrum. YMCA Leadership Training in Christian youth work certainly dates from at least the 1930s and was far more rigorous than one might expect today. The certificates above left and below show just how seriously the YMCA took its responsibilities in education, sport and pastoral care.

The certificate above right is typical of many awarded during the 1980s and 1990s when Cheltenham YMCA was an important Training Centre for many young people.

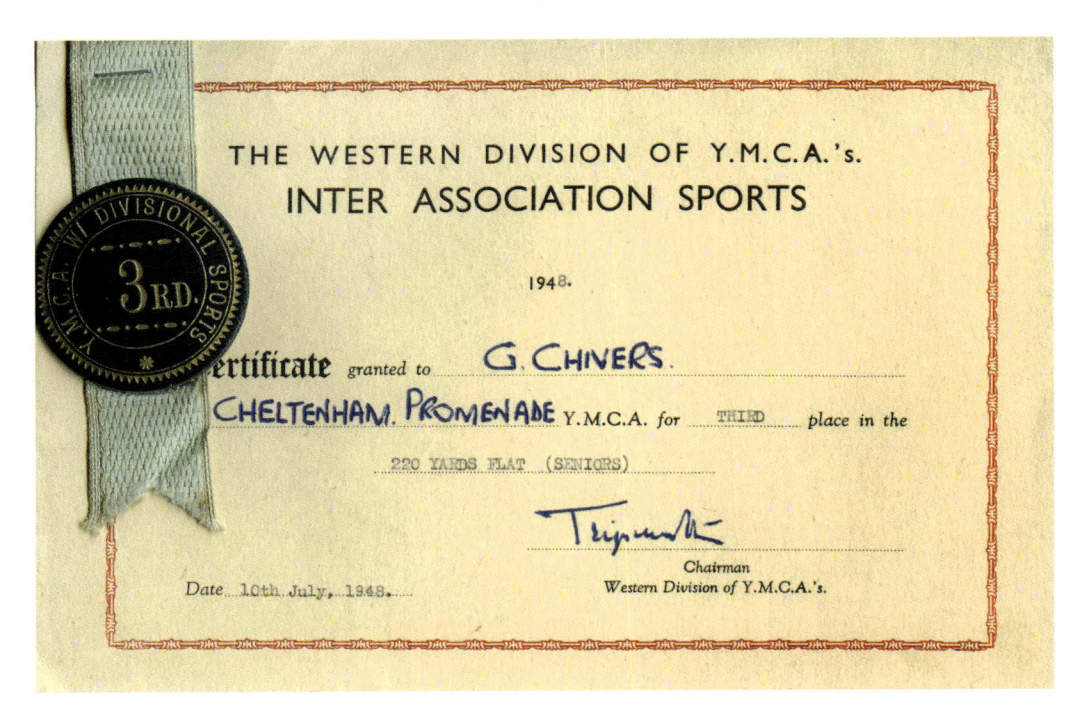

◀ Three key figures in the recent history of Cheltenham YMCA. Left to right — Peter Nock, a long serving and outstanding Treasurer, Jim Jenkinson, an Assistant Chief Executive who later went on to establish Rotherham YMCA before becoming Regional Development Officer for the YMCA Central Region, and Don Staight who was Chairman from 1999-2004.

▶ Rose Harris, back row in cerise, with a Senior Club outing to Lydney House.

▲ The YMCA men's basketball team contains some long serving players (see page 143). Left to right: Martin Outram, John Llewellyn, Graham "Flash" Gordon, Alan Norbury, Ed Bishop, Dave Whiting, James Bruton and Richard Rawcliffe.

▶ Under the leadership of Jenny Hall (below) and a dedicated band of volunteers, gymnastics has proved very popular in recent years.

▲ ▶ Probably the most famous sportsman to emerge from Cheltenham YMCA was footballer Mike Summerbee, above right and second from the front row on this picture of Manchester City with the FA Cup, League Championship, and Charity Shield in 1969. He played 8 times for England and is seen right scoring with a diving header against Burnley.

© Ian Penney/Breedon Books

A more recent product was Simon Danielli who played junior football for the YMCA but made his name with the oval ball and became a rugby union international for Scotland.

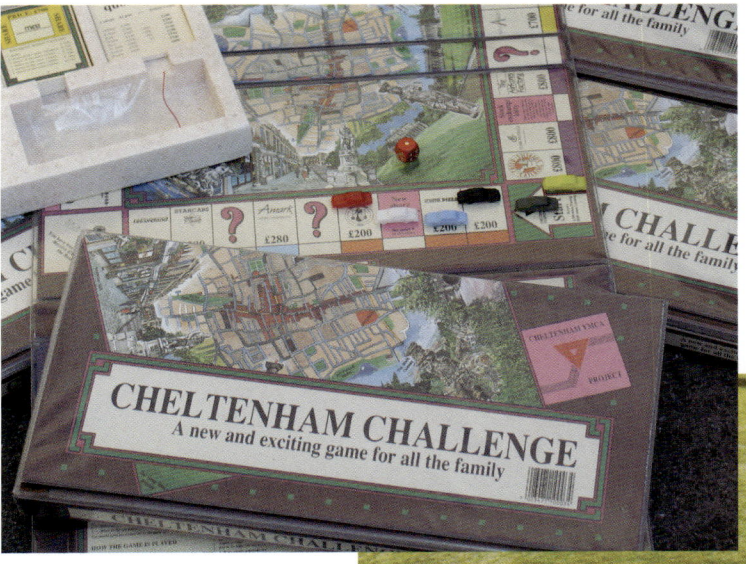

◀ During the 1980s, a clever idea for fund raising saw a YMCA board game based on Monopoly adapted for different towns around the country. Local companies sponsored different squares with. Cheltenham's nearest rival adopting the "Gloucester Game".

▶ In 1969 this impressive floral display was mounted by Cheltenham Parks in Montpellier Gardens to celebrate the 125th anniversary of the national YMCA movement.

187

▲ This publicity shot was taken on behalf of Endsleigh Insurance during the early-1990s. The power behind the throne was Mike Naylor whose personal generosity to football — he even sponsored the Football League — came to a sad end when he was killed in a car crash. His company nevertheless continued to support Cheltenham YMCA for some years afterwards.

▲ The most successful Cheltenham YMCA team of all time. From Under 10 upwards they never finished outside the top two and in their final year, 1991-2, won the Under 16 Gloucestershire County Cup when they beat Brislington Juniors 2-0 at Bristol, having first defeated Fairford in the Northern Section play-off. The manager throughout was Ken Jones, back left.

▲ The Cheltenham YMCA Under 16 team, season 1997-8, pictured just before completing a cup and league double at Cheltenham Town's Whaddon Road ground before it was redeveloped after promotion to the Football League at the end of season 1998-9. This side also reached the Gloucestershire County Cup Final played at Forest Green and were within five minutes of beating Bitton Boys from Bristol before conceding a late equaliser in a 2-2 draw, eventually losing a very close replay 2-1. The manager throughout was Alan Derrett (back left) assisted by Danny Mitchinson (back right).

▲ Not many sides go from bottom to top in one season but the Under 14 team in 2001-2 did exactly that. Under the new dynamic management of Chris Davis (back right) ably assisted by referee Andy Richards (back left), the team was totally transformed. Instead of going for more glory locally they then opted for a move from Cheltenham to the more competitive Gloucester League where they did extremely well during the following two seasons, reaching the cup final on each occasion.

▲ The 2002-3 Under 12 Cup Final was one of the most exciting in recent years. Twice coming back from a two goal deficit, Cheltenham YMCA's Scott Geary (on the left of the players in red and white) turns away after scoring the winner in the closing stages. The 5-4 victory against old rivals Cleeve Colts secured a deserved double (see below).

▲ The victorious Under 12 double-winning squad of 2002-3, in front of the main stand at Cheltenham Town. The semi-final against Cirencester Town was won with a golden goal in the last minute of extra time and the league effectively secured against the same team with a last minute winner. The outstanding team manager was Les Babbage (back centre), assisted by Glen Sutherland (far right), and Lawrence Gorry (second right).

© Rachel Spence

▲ This unusual picture dates from May 2005 and shows the majority of players and managers from Cheltenham YMCA's many different teams. It was taken in secret in the YMCA sports hall and then presented to long-serving Junior Football Club Chairman and Secretary, Peter Worsley, at the Annual Presentation Evening, when he retired from football to take up his post as the Chairman of Board of Directors. The job of getting a large number of boys together in secret on a Saturday morning was a major logistical exercise! Well done everyone concerned!

▲ Rev. Lionel Fitz first became involved with Cheltenham YMCA in 1938 (see Chapter 13). Following retirement he was ordained to the staff of St. Matthew's Church. A former Chairman of the Board he was elected President on the death of Alex Evans in 2002.

▲ Barry Lloyd gave more than 50 years devoted service to the YMCA. After designing the extension to the Promenade he played a key role in developing Vittoria Walk (see Chapters 10 and 11). Following many valued years as Chairman, he became a Vice President.

▶ The author of this book was Peter Worsley, a retired deputy headmaster who first became involved with Cheltenham YMCA as a football parent in 1986. He soon became a referee and assistant manager, then both Chairman and Secretary of the junior football section.

Invited to join the Board in the early 1990s he became Chairman in 2004. It was his suggestion which led to the book being commissioned but without realising how much research would be involved nor how deep the history of Cheltenham YMCA would prove to be. It is hoped the end result justified the twelve months hard labour which went into it!

After teaching, Peter joined the staff of "This England", an international patriotic organisation publishing several magazines, where he worked for many years as an Assistant Editor. He has written four other books: "British Dance Bands" (Volumes One and Two); "London Lights, A History of West End Musicals"; and "Cheltenham College Junior School 2000, A Social and Pictorial History 1841-1999" (an unpublished manuscript held in the Cheltenham College Archives, accession numbers 3764 and 3765).

▲ The Cheltenham YMCA Board of Directors photographed in September 2005. Back row left to right; Hugh Harries, David Shoesmith, Dorothy Staight, Ben Reed, Mike Hunt: front row left to right; Don Staight (Vice Chairman), Peter Worsley (Chairman), Rev. Lionel Fitz (President), Barry Lloyd (Vice President), and Peter Nock (Treasurer). Inset left; Steve Jordan; right Simon Measures.

▲ A happy photo showing some Cheltenham YMCA staff, also in September 2005. Back row from left; Dave Whiting (Basketball), Callum Ferguson (Housing Support), Pat Kirycos (Reception), John Wilcock (Admin Support), Katherine Parker (Reception), Mike Gyde (Reception): middle row from left; Francis Barton (Children's Worker), Jenny Pollard (Centre Administrator), Vince Wood (Housing Support), Angela Gilbert (Assistant Chief Executive, Programme): front row from left; Jerry Evans (Assistant Chief Executive, Housing), Miriam Hall (Reception), Kathy Burrows (Gymnastics), Emma Jones (Gymnastics), and Loic Wall (Reception).

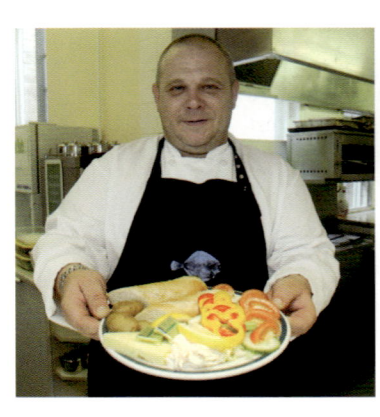

© Antony Thompson

194

INDEX

After considerable deliberation it was decided this index would deal only with people mentioned in the book. An initial attempt was made to include all connected places and organisations but it became too unwieldy and would have taken up valuable space earmarked for pictures. References to churches, schools, Christian organisations etc. have therefore been omitted. This is not in any way to play down valued links and contributions from groups such as Cheltenham Borough Council, Cheltenham College, Dean Close School, Cheltenham Ladies' College, The Famous outfitters, many church ministers, advertisers and a long list of sponsors. They were just too numerous to list, especially as some were mentioned several times!

References to the different YMCA locations can be found on page 7 with sub-divisions and satellite work such as the Royal Well Hut, Wartime Canteens, Baker Street YMCA, St. Thomas' Mission Church, Pilley Lane Youth Club etc. described in the ongoing text.

Thousands of people have been associated with Cheltenham YMCA since its inception 150 years ago and to those who felt they deserved a mention but have been unintentionally omitted, we apologise.

Name	Pages	Name	Pages	Name	Pages
Adam, Ronald F	86	Barton, Francis	143, 155, 193	Box, JS	62
Adams, Anthony	99, 100	Bassett-Green, WH	112	Boyce, CW	26
Adams, Mr.	45	Batten, S	32	Boyd, WA	29
Adlard, Mrs. FW	84, 92	Beak, Daniel	30, 32, 43	Brant, Miss	96
Agg-Gardner, James	48, 49	Beale, Dorothea	56	Bray, AJ	69
Ainger, Arthur	110	Beard, HG	32	Brazener, Bert	40
Aldred, Mr.	84, 92	Beauchamp, Earl	44	Bready, J Wesley	9, 11
Allen, Ken	113	Beaufort, Duchess of	96	Britten-Austin, P	96
Allen, Mr.	45	Beaufort, Duke of	104, 105, 112, 128, 130	Brooks, C	57
Allison, Malcolm	160			Broom, Arthur	29, 39, 40, 43
Amory, Viscount	130, 131	Becher, Mrs.	44	Broom, HW	22, 31, 35
Anderson, Miss	92	Beckinsale, Albert	32, 33	Brown, Frank	40
Andrews, R	57	Beckinsale, Douglas	98	Brown, Morton	9, 11, 16
Appleton, Sheila	152	Beetham, Miss	35	Brown, Ronald	62, 66, 70
Arbuthnot, Evelyn Mary	35	Beetham, Mr.	32	Browne, John	9, 11, 13
Argyll-Saxby, CF	45	Belcher, Charles	71, 88, 108, 156, 157, 163, 167	Bruton, James	186
Askwith, WM	125			Buckland, JW	16, 44
Aston, J	17	Belcher, Philip	152	Budd, Maj.-Gen.	32
Avers, Morris	40	Bell, Canon	34	Burley, Linda	132, 138, 162
Avery, A Holland	113	Bell, Dave	106	Burroughes, H	112
Avery, HM	65	Bell, W Moody	31	Burrows, Brian	111
Ayres, Bill	162	Benbow, Dennis	166	Burrows, Kathy	193
Babbage, Les	150, 190	Bendall, AJ	32	Burton, RE	65
Baden-Powell, Gen.	26, 29, 34	Bennett, Marjorie	144	Bush, HT	16, 31, 37, 55, 62, 64, 65, 98, 99, 108, 112, 113, 116, 118, 123, 126, 157, 160, 183
Baden-Powell, Lady	27	Bentnall, AL	78		
Baggs, WH	112	Bettridge, AJ	65, 90, 112, 114		
Bagnall, Miss	92	Bettridge, Stan	166	Butler, Mr.	45
Bagnall, Mrs. WH	92	Biggs, CW	114, 115	Cambray, WT	58, 65
Bailey, Trevor	126	Birt, Arthur	112, 113	Campbell, Ruth	129, 155
Baker, Mrs. JE	110	Bishop, Ed	186	Candole, HS de	21, 36
Baker, Mrs. WA	60, 71, 90, 96, 97, 110, 113, 115	Black, Jim	125	Cannon, John	145
		Blake, T Jex	32	Carbin, Jeff	150
Baldwin, Arthur	40	Bliss, E	69	Carpenter, J	19
Baldwin, Reg	101	Bloodworth, Mr.	45	Carter, Bert	166
Ballinger, Chris	145	Bolton, P	54	Carteret, C de	36
Ballinger, Fred	167	Book, Tony	130, 145, 150	Causon, Cecil	163
Barker, Nigel	145	Boorne, Ernest	22	Chamberlain, Brian	132
Barna, Victor	158	Booth, M	151	Chamberlain, Neville	74
Barnett, HO	57, 62	Boothroyd, GW	54	Champion, Len	110
Barnett, Ken	166	Bose, Miss Mollie	94, 156	Chandler, James	27
Barter, H	100	Bowden, Frank	152	Chandler, Steve	145
Bartholomew, JS	32	Bowles, William	40	Channon, WC	32

Chaplain, W	100	Davies, Alan	152	Fennell, John	168
Charlton, WJ	43	Davies, "Doc"	168	Ferguson, Callum	193
Chivers, Gil	110, 163, 185, 166, 167, 168	Davies, SC	66	Ferrieres, Baron de	15, 17, 21, 33, 98
		David, Chris	189	Finck, Herman	74
Churchill, Winston	88	Davis, Jeff	102	Fisher, G	27
Clare, EG	34	Dawes, Leo	48	Fisher, KJ	65
Clark, Ernie	166, 167	Dawson, Philip	132	Fitz, Lionel	74, 88, 108, 110, 112, 115, 117, 126, 135, 150, 156, 168, 169, 192, 193
Clarke, Mr.	160	Dawson, W	90		
Clarke, Stanley	49	Dawson, WA	18		
Clarkson, Herbert	98	Dennis, HA	29	Fitz, Mavis	150
Clauss, Paul R	57, 62	Dent, May	130	Fitz, Timothy	161
Cleevely, Vic	163, 168	Derrett, Alan	189	Flecker, James Elroy	30, 34
Clissold, Gilbert John	39, 40	Devereux, Joseph	39, 40	Flecker, William	25, 29, 34, 44
Close, Francis	11, 13	Devore, Alex	163	Fletcher, Mrs. LB	60
Cobb, Mary	129	Dimmer, George	48	Forrester, Bruce	132
Coe, Sam	152	Downton, Mr.	15	Foster, HW	16, 17
Cole, AN	26, 35, 37, 40, 41, 42, 43	Dowty, George	64, 65, 68, 90, 112, 171	Fowler, Claude	113
Cole, Arthur	62	Doxey, H	69	Fowler, Mrs. WJ	60
Cole, Jack	35	Duthie, JH	99, 100	Fowler, T	17
Cole, Percy	35, 41	Dye, Arthur	55, 58, 64, 65, 74, 82, 96, 108, 109, 112, 113, 114, 115, 116, 117, 118, 125, 126, 128, 130, 131, 137, 138, 151, 157, 158, 160, 167 183	Frost, Bob	110
Cole, Reg	35, 40, 42			Fyffe, Mrs. V	84, 92
Collett, Ron	170			Gardner, Miss	23
Colwell, E	43			Gardner, Percy	131, 137, 152, 160, 161
Compton, GB	99	Dyer, Frank	129	Garner, Joyce	66, 142
Consterdine, R	62	Dyer, Mr.	48	Gayford, J	131
Cook, Charlie	40	Dymock, Colin	107	Geary, Scott	190
Cook, Derek	168	Dymock, Hazel	107	Gerrard, Mrs.	68
Cook, Dr.	15	Dymock, Tony	107	Gibbins, Bill	99
Cook, H	68, 69, 94	Dymock, Trevor	166	Gibson, ECS	48
Cooke, CT	9	Dymock, Vic	88, 99, 100, 104, 106, 107, 108, 109, 112, 113, 115, 125, 126, 157, 159, 160, 166, 179	Gilbert, Angela	142, 155, 161, 193
Cooke, TG	55			Gilbert, Ken	126
Cooper, JC	17, 33, 115			Giles, Arthur	40
Cooper, Neal	166	Dymond, Joe	113, 168	Gill, HW	40
Costa, Savaskis	154	Eardley, Doug	167	Glass, J	21, 36
Courtney, Mrs.	84, 92	Edinburgh, Duke of	129	Godwin, Frank	168
Cousins, HA	112	Edmunds, John	166, 167	Godwin, Les	166
Cox, AP	29	Edwards, Horace	32	Godwin, Percy	40
Cox, TA	21	Edwards, Kevin	155	Gooch, Henry	90, 94
Creese, William	13, 14, 19, 20, 22, 36, 52	Edwards, Norman	55, 57	Gooch, Major	84, 92
		Edwards, Rowland	23	Gooch, Richard	132, 161
Cresswell, Bernie	166, 168	Edwin, John	152	Goodliffe, JB	90, 112, 113
Cross, Ken	110	Ellis, William Webb	144	Gordon, Graham	142, 143, 186
Crosweller, WW	90	Emmett, George	125	Gordon, JHC	47, 48
Cruwys, Peter	113, 154, 158, 167	England, Bob	145	Gorry, Lawrence	190
Cruwys, Tom	74	Esdaile, EJ	15	Gosling, Percy	40
Cryer, Arnold	126	Evans, A Weaver	29	Gough, Miss P	92
Cummings, A	34	Evans, Alex	141, 156, 161, 163, 192	Goulder, JL	115
Cummings, AW	65	Evans, Charles	9, 11, 15	Graham, Billy	127, 129, 154
Cummings, Gordon (i)	27, 29, 40	Evans, Dennis	166	Grant, Kate	163
Cummings, Gordon (ii)	143	Evans, Edward E	35	Granville, H	50
Daft, A	69	Evans, Glyn	155	Graveney, Tom	125, 126, 132, 159
Daldry, Fred (i)	71	Evans, Jerry	146, 151, 193	Green, Sheila	119, 142, 181
Daldry, Fred (ii)	71, 109, 110, 157, 158, 169	Evans, Mrs.	60	Griffin, Bob	154, 158, 166, 167, 168
		Evans, Roy	166	Griffin, Ernest	40
Daniell, Mr.	21	Evetts, John	112, 116, 125, 128, 131	Griffin, Stan	158
Danielli, Simon	187	Farr, Ron	112, 113	Griffiths, C	57
Davey, JEF "Pop"	57, 58, 61, 62, 65, 68, 88, 90, 94, 98, 100	Faulkner, Claude	66, 142	Grimwade, HC	65
		Fawcett, F L'Estrange	26	Guinness, Grattan	34

196

Gunn, Len	159, 161	Hoseason, Mrs.	92	Kitchener, Lord	41
Gyde, Mike	193	Houghton, Dave	145	Kite, Mrs.	48, 50
Hall, Dave	110, 167	Houghton, LAC	85, 94	Knight, Alan	113
Hall, Jenny	151, 152, 186	Houlton, S	18, 21, 22	Knight, Francis	50
Hall, Miriam	193	Hounslow, Joseph (Jack)	39, 40	Knight, Norman	128
Hammond, Wally	63	Howell, John	65, 84, 90, 96	Knowles, Major	89
Hampson, Tony	133, 137, 139	Huddlestone, RB	9, 11	Laffan, RS de Courcy	25
Handcock, WF	15	Humphreys, RR	9, 10	Laird, Miss HM	96, 100
Hannaford, Paul	138	Hunt, Julie	133	Lane, WR	19, 36, 37, 140
Hanson, EC	112	Hunt, Mike	123, 124, 125, 135, 193	Lang, J	16
Harding, Mike	143	Hunt, Elaine	150, 161	Lang, Rev.	19
Hardy, HH	46, 48, 49	Hunt, Roger	130, 133, 150, 161	Lawson, Julie	142
Harewood, Earl of	104	Hunt, William	40	Lawson, Mr.	158
Harness, Paul	152	Hutchinson, Constance Helen	35	Le Besque, Penny	132
Harper, Derek	125, 137	Hutton, William	26, 33	Leach, Johnny	158
Harries, Hugh	193	Hyett, Richard	106	Leak, HA	27
Harris, Alick (Alec)	40	Ireland, de Courcy	102	Leavey, DE	99
Harris, F	57	Jacobs, Harold	40	Lee, WT	39
Harris, Rosemary	134, 144, 149, 152, 186	Jaffray, Mrs.	92	Leigh, Sue	144
		Jakeway, Ken	166	Lewis, Brian	113
Harrison, Ian	127, 154, 155	James, HA	18, 19, 24, 25	Lewis, David	65
Harrison, Mr.	16	James, Irene	60, 65, 71, 75, 76, 78, 79, 83, 86, 93, 94, 95, 97	Lewis, Maj.-Gen.	20, 21, 22
Hartley, Bill	136			Lewis, Teddy	40
Harwood, Charles	40	Jefferies, Clive	166	Lewis, WG	15
Hastie, Mrs.	150	Jefferies, E	26, 29	Ley Wood, T, see Wood RL	
Hastie, S	150	Jeffery, Miss	60	Ling, Leslie	153
Haviland, B	112	Jellie, Harvey	29	Lipson, Daniel	43, 64, 65, 83, 90, 92, 112
Haw Haw, Lord	88	Jenkinson, Jim	149, 162, 163, 186		
Hawkins, Bob	113	Jennings, Miss M	68	Littlewood, Frank	83, 183
Hayman, Mrs. PB	92	Jones, Carys	146	Llewellyn, John	142, 143, 186
Hayward, J	57	Jones, Emma	193	Lloyd, Barry	112, 113, 114, 119, 120, 129, 153, 158, 160, 163, 193
Hayward, W Curling	65	Jones, Ken	146, 147, 188		
Head, Bert	160	Jones, Melville	19	Long, W Turner	27, 47
Heawood, GL	65, 100	Jones, Picton	151	Longhurst, TJ	19
Henderson, EB	116	Jones, Ray	168	Lott, Felicity	71
Henn, WF	62, 66	Jones, Winston	113	Lott, John	71
Hennell, Col.	11	Jordan, Steve	193	Lowndes, Pete	145
Herring, R	57	Jubb, Neil	145	Lulham, Mrs.	76, 97
Heykens, Johnny	74	Kay, Roger	21	Mace, AH	62
Hicks, L	57	Kearsey, EM	39	MacPherson, T	31
Hicks-Beach, WW	118	Keech, Harold	40	Maidment, William	40
Higgins, Miss	60, 71, 96	Keen, Edward	40	Manaton, W Morley	112, 131, 160
Higgs, King	48	Keen, RC	39	Mann, AW	112
Hill, Ali	144	Kelland, WJD	39	Mann, H	65
Hill, Mr.	45	Kelson, GT	62	Margrett, Charles Henry	48
Hitchman, George	50, 55, 57, 63, 65, 98, 99, 100, 108, 157	Kennedy, Judge	62, 66	Marshall, J	34
		Ketelbey, Albert	74	Marshall, LJ	69
Hitchman, TB	50	Ketley, W	17	Marsham, Mrs. S	86
Hitler, Adolf	88	Kilminster, Mr.	33	Martyn, Alfred W	64, 65, 88, 90, 171
Holder, Micky	160	King George V	26, 31, 38, 43, 45, 104	Martyn, HH	64, 74, 90
Holtham, Doug	101	King George VI	26	Masters, C	36
Hooper, A	65	King, FW	39	Matheson, Mrs.	92
Hopkins, Brian	143	Kingsale, Lord	47, 48, 49	Matthews, S	57
Hopkins, Ken	110	Kinnaird, Lord	26	May, Dave	168
Hopkins, Marilyn	153	Kirkham, Mr.	18	McClellan, Mrs.	85, 92
Hopson, Len	166	Kirkland, Doug	168, 169	McDowall, Mr.	92
Horlick, James	30, 50	Kirycos, Pat	193	McDowall, Mrs. RFC	90
Horsley, Mr.	32	Kisiel, Chris	145, 150	McKenzie, Gen.	34

McKenzie, John	129	
McTevendale, W	85, 92	
Mead, Harry	40	
Measures, Simon	193	
Mercer, Joe	160	
Merrett, Brian	131, 154	
Midwinter, John	166	
Midwinter, ?	166	
Milan, Arthur	166	
Miles, Ted	166, 167	
Millard, S	19	
Miller, Basil	66, 71, 94	
Miller, Jenny	132	
Mills, Dennis	34	
Minal, Peter	129	
Mitchell, Bryan	154	
Mitchinson, Danny	189	
Moody, DL	25	
Moore, Bobby	104	
More, J	17	
Morgan, Wynter	48	
Morley, DE	58, 65, 108, 112, 157	
Morris, D	62	
Morris, David	131	
Morris, SC	57, 62	
Morton, Shirley	149	
Moss, Mr.	45	
Moss, V	69	
Moxley, AG	112, 114	
Moxon, AJ	50, 51, 55, 57, 58, 61, 62, 63, 65, 68, 72, 88, 90, 94, 98, 100, 108, 156, 158	
Moyle, T Cave	44	
Nash, Charlie	168	
Naylor, Arthur	57, 58, 71, 72, 73, 88, 90, 99, 108	
Naylor, John	58, 65, 71, 188	
Naylor, Mike	147, 150	
Neale, H	19	
Neale, Les	113	
Neat, Mrs. CG	60	
Neller, M	9	
Newland, Bill	110, 166, 167, 168	
Newland, Ivor	110, 166	
Newland, Mr.	166	
Newland, Mrs.	102	
Newland, Stan	166, 167, 168	
Newton, John	15	
Nicholson, Mrs. W	92	
Nock, Peter	144, 186, 193	
Nock, David	147	
Noot, H Evan	21	
Norbury, Alan	186	
Norman, Gerry	168	
Notcutt, Mr.	16	
Nunn, Mrs. A	60	
O'Brien, Denis	103	
O'Brien, Les	169	
Oliver, WH	113
Osborne, Mrs. NG	90, 96
Outram, Martin	142, 186
Owen, JA	19
Owen, Stan	112, 113, 168
Page, James	17
Page, RE	65
Paice, Miss	76
Papworth, JB	119
Parker, Katherine	193
Parker, Syd	152
Pascall, Richard	132, 161
Patrick, Joe	166
Patrick, Mick	169
Payne, Mr.	45
Pearce, GP	19, 32
Pearce, Jack	168
Pearce, Vic	110, 157, 167
Pearson, Col.	48
Pearson, Wilf	119, 125, 128, 130, 141, 159, 160
Pennell, DW	19
Peters, Charles	124
Peters, Mrs.	124
Philips, JB	127
Phillips, HA Beynon	21, 22, 23
Phillips, Joe	113
Phillips, L	57
Phillipson, ECW	112, 113
Philpott, Graham	154
Pierce, Ann	142, 149, 181
Pilley, Mr.	18, 23, 33, 176
Pite, Arthur	71
Pite, Edward	71
Pite, Mrs. AG	68
Player, John	30
Playle, John	22, 26
Pollard, Jenny	193
Polster, Manfred	152
Powell, Baden,	see Baden Powell
Power, Miss W	62
Prince Christian	52
Princess Helena Victoria	20, 38, 52, 57, 83, 86, 97, 113
Princess Margaret	131
Princess Royal	20, 104, 105, 112
Pritchard, HE	43
Pruen, ST	19, 26, 28, 29, 30, 31, 34, 35, 36, 44, 45, 46, 47, 50, 53, 56
Pugh, Cecil	39
Purnell, Alfred	43
Pyke, WF	27
Queen Elizabeth II	107, 109, 142, 158
Queen Mary	20, 82, 83, 84, 86, 91, 104, 113
Queen Victoria	8, 25, 36, 38, 52
Ragsdale, Anne	142
Rainbow, J	57
Rawcliffe, Richard	186
Rayner, Sidney	29
Raynham, Hamish	132
Read, Brian	143
Readings, George	64, 65, 112, 117, 125
Reed, Ben	193
Reid, J McClymont	30
Remfry, M	65
Rice, Miss Margaret	144
Richards, Andy	189
Richards, John	152
Richardson, Don	113
Rickerby, John	40, 41, 54
Rickerby, TE	19, 21, 26, 28, 29, 30, 31, 32, 34, 35, 36, 38, 40, 41, 45, 46, 47, 48, 50, 53, 54, 55, 56, 127
Riley, A	99
Roberts, Earl	48
Roberts, Peter	126, 128
Robertson, William	48, 49, 141, 184
Rogers, Col.	21
Rogers, Ernest	47
Romsey, Earl of	125
Roper, H	98
Rosebery, Lord	8
Rous, Stanley	66
Rowbotham, C	19
Rowley, Derek	167
Roxby, EL	18, 21, 23, 36
Rudge, Hope	144
Rushworth, Peter	156
Russell, Ken	166
Russell, Lord John	15, 16
Russell, Mike	125
Sacker, Graham	39, 40
Salter, Barry	168
Sanders, Andy	152
Sankey, ID	33
Sargison, Bill	132, 133, 139, 142, 146, 154, 155, 161, 162
Sargison, Miriam	132, 161
Sargison, Paul	142, 146, 161, 181
Satchell, Mr.	45
Sawyer, J	21
Shoolbred, Dr.	119
Scott, Terry	113
Scougall, J	9, 11
Seacome, Robert Owen	32, 48
Seller, Viv	144
Sewall, Mrs.	92
Sexty, Mr.	32
Shaftesbury, Lord	10
Sharpe, Adrian	132, 134, 135, 138, 149, 162, 163
Shaw, John	143
Shelley, Mr.	45
Shennan, KGW	126, 128
Sheriff, RC	62, 66, 67

Shirer, F	19, 36	Thompson, HH	53	Whittaker, E	112
Shoesmith, David	193	Thomson, Keith	132	Whitwell, H	21
Simpson, Miss CA	84	Thorence, Miss	95	Wickens, EE	84, 159
Skillicorne, William Nash	30	Tilley, Peter	157	Wigley, Charles John	39, 40, 43
Slade, Mr.	34, 36	Tilley, Paul	157	Wilberforce, William	9
Smith, Arthur	40	Titheradge, Dion	66, 67	Wilcock, John	185, 193
Smith, Dick	163	Tizzard, Dave	133, 149	Wilcox, Mrs.	60
Smith, Ernest	40	Tovey, John	166	Willcox, Des	124, 128, 130, 137, 143, 161, 162
Smith, H Alwyn	112	Townshend, Brian	166		
Smith, Hind	21	Treeby, Mr.	16	Willcox, Pearl	124, 128, 161
Smith, James	9, 11, 14	Trigg, AE	151	Willerton, Phil	133, 134, 162
Smith, JW	62, 69	Trye, JH	60, 62, 66, 67, 68, 80	Williams, C	33
Smith, K	69	Trye, Elizabeth	60, 62, 65, 67, 68, 71, 73, 75, 76, 79, 80, 82, 86, 92, 93, 95, 97	Williams, George (I)	8, 13, 14, 19, 20, 21, 22, 26, 34, 36, 53, 68, 141
Smith, Malcolm	143				
Smith, PT (Percy)	58, 62, 65, 67, 73, 82, 83, 84, 90, 99, 112, 113, 114, 115, 118, 123, 160, 183	Trye senior, Mrs	86, 89	Williams, George (ii)	40
		Trye, RE	32	Williams, Glyn	143
		Tucker, NS	65	Williams, Ken	112, 114, 115, 116, 124, 125, 158, 159
Smith, R	69	Turnbull, Dr.	31		
Smith, Will	40	Turley, Sgt.	43	Williams, Whyla	71
Smith, ?	166	Turner, Cathy	162	Willis, Frank	96, 110, 113
Snowdon, Lord	123, 131	Turner, William	29, 30, 31, 32, 42, 44, 45, 46, 48, 50	Willis, Richard	43
Spurgeon, Charles H	29			Wills, Arnold	113, 128, 168
Staight, Don	163, 186, 193	Twissells, LH	50	Wilmote, Henry	17
Staight, Dorothy	163, 193	Vale, W	34	Wilson, HA	48, 50
Stanford, Geoff	110, 166	Vallender, Joe	166	Winterbotham, Clara	48, 49
Stanley, Miss	36, 140	Verney, SJ	84, 92	Wisdom, Norman	88, 89
Starmer-Smith, H	99	Virgo, JJ	58	Wood, Robert Ley	19, 20, 21, 34, 35, 36, 53, 140
Staton, Darren	147	Vogel, George	145		
Steele, Will	161	Vollans, AS	69	Wood, Vicki	153
Stephens, Bill	145	Voyce, AT	66	Wood, Vince	193
Stevens, Mr.	45	Wainwright, DI	112, 113, 158, 160	Woodland, Ken	163
Stewart, RB	84	Waite, Phyllis	80, 83, 86, 87, 97	Woodley, John	143
Stone, Joe	110	Waite, T Wilfred	65, 80, 82, 83, 86, 99	Woodward, Eric	62
Stone, Ken	110	Waite, Terry	4, 154	Worsley, Peter	146, 147, 163, 192, 193
Stuart, Aimee	62, 66	Waldteufel, Emile	74	Wragge, Philip	119
Stuart, Philip	62, 66	Walker, David	152	Wray, Martin	128, 137
Stucke, H	16	Walker, Phyllis	129	Wren, Trevor	166
Sullivan, A	57	Walker, S	9, 11, 32	Wynn, F	48
Sullivan, Dennis	168	Walker, WP	39	Wynn, GH	18, 21, 22, 36, 45
Summerbee, George	104	Wall, Loic	193	Wynn, John	163
Summerbee, John	104	Wallace, David (i)	57, 66, 67, 100	Yapp, Arthur	48, 49
Summerbee, Mike	104, 107, 145, 160, 187	Wallace, David (ii)	138, 163, 165	Yates, J	100
		Ward, EL	58, 65	Yates, Mrs.	150
Sutherland, Glen	190	Ward, Mrs. EL	87	Yates, RE	150
Swainson, Mrs.	84	Waterfield, Reginald	25, 44	Yeaman, ID	53
Swainson, RH	102	Web, ELL	90	Yeap, David	130
Symons, John Christian	14	Webb, Arnold	38	Yeates, Rick	145
Tarleton, TH	9, 10, 11	Webley, Mrs.	113	Yeates, Tim	145
Tarr, Mrs.	60	Webster, Mrs. JE	60, 65, 71, 95, 96, 97	Yeates, Wendy	153
Taylor, Bert	29	Weldon, Doug	145	Yeend, Mr.	45
Taylor, Kevin	150	Wellington, Duke of	48	Young, Chris	130
Taylor, PP	65	Wellon, Dennis	166	Young, Leslie	29
Thody, Mrs. WH	60	Wentworth, Cyril	40	Zebedee, Ernest	41, 50
Thomas, Anthony	99	Wesley, Charles	9		
Thomas, F Treherne	38	Wesley, John	9		
Thomas, Mrs FT	38	White, Albert	40		
Thomas, Peter	113	White, W	27		
Thomas, Sid	40	Whiting, Dave	186, 193		

BIBLIOGRAPHY

100 Years, 1844-1944, The Story of the YMCA – YMCA 1944
100 Years Young! Cheltenham YMCA Centenary Booklet – H.T. Bush, YMCA 1955
Around Cheltenham, Francis Frith's Photographic Memories – John Bainbridge, Frith 2000
Book of Cheltenham, The – Roger Beacham
Cambray Baptist Church, 150 Years – Sylvie Pierce, 1993
Cheltenham Betrayed – Timothy Mowl, Redcliffe 1995
Cheltenham Chronicle and Gloucestershire Graphic – various newspaper cuttings
Cheltenham College, The First Hundred Years – M.C. Morgan, Cheltonian Society 1968
Cheltenham College Junior School 2000, A Social History 1841-1999 – Peter Worsley, unpublished but held in the Cheltenham College Archives, accession numbers 3764 & 3765
Cheltenham Examiner – various newspaper cuttings
Cheltenham At War in Old Photographs – Peter Gill, Alan Sutton Publishing 1994
Cheltenham in the 1950s – Peter Gill, Sutton Publishing 1996
Cheltenham Looker-On – various newspaper cuttings
Cheltenham YMCA – Annual Reports & General Archives
George Williams and the YMCA – Clyde Binfield, Heinemann 1973
George Williams in Context – Clyde Binfield, Sheffield Academic Press 1994
Gloucestershire Echo – various newspaper cuttings
Gymnast Magazine, The, Vol. 3 No. 4 1963 – British Amateur Gymnastic Association
Held in Honour - Cheltenham and the Second World War – Graham Sacker, Promenade Publications 2000
History of Cheltenham YMCA 1956-1996, Historical and Comparative Aspects of Sport (written student assignment) – Paula Hannaford
Leaving All That Was Dear, Cheltenham and the Great War – Joseph Devereux & Graham Sacker, Promenade Publications 1997
Memories of Cheltenham – Wynn Marine Ltd., True North Books 2000
Our Work for the Troops – Cheltenham YMCA 1941-2
Souvenir Tribute to the Royal Well Military Canteen, A – Cheltenham YMCA, Sept. 1939-May 1946